MEXICAN
ARCHÆOLOGY

PLATE I

MEXICO

HUMAN SKULL, INCRUSTED WITH MOSAIC, REPRESENTING TEZCATLIPOCA

MEXICAN ARCHÆOLOGY

AN INTRODUCTION TO THE ARCHÆ-
OLOGY OF THE MEXICAN AND MAYAN
CIVILIZATIONS OF PRE-SPANISH AMERICA.
BY THOMAS A. JOYCE, M.A. WITH MANY
ILLUSTRATIONS AND A MAP

NEW YORK: G. P. PUTNAM'S SONS
LONDON: PHILIP LEE WARNER
MDCCCCXIV

PREFACE

THE object of this small book is to summarize shortly the extent of our knowledge concerning the life and culture of the Mexican and Maya peoples of pre-Spanish America. It has no pretence whatever to finality ; indeed, the time is not within sight when a complete elucidation of all the problems connected with this most fascinating area can be put forward. At the same time it is useful to pause occasionally and summarize results, if only because attention is thereby drawn to the more serious gaps in the data available, and it becomes easier to direct the course of future investigations. An ulterior motive lies in the hope that a little stimulus may be given to American studies in this country, which have languished sadly during the past few years. This fact is all the more to be regretted since Englishmen, such as Dr. A. P. Maudslay, have done so much in the past to unveil the mysteries of ancient American civilization, and the collection at the British Museum, though small, is rich in the finest collection in the world of Mexican mosaics. At present, as far as the Old World is concerned, the torch has passed to Germany, the labours of whose investigators, in particular of Dr. Seler, have done so much to place the study of American antiquities upon a thoroughly scientific footing. No part of the world, perhaps, has formed the subject of so many wild theories as ancient

Mexico, and few present so many fascinating riddles to
the expert. It has therefore been impossible in the
present work to keep clear of controversial ground, but
I have tried as far as possible to take a sane view of each
problem, and to indicate in some measure the evidence
for each conclusion. Many of the suggested solutions
are purely tentative, and must doubtless be modified in
the light of subsequent investigations. This remark
applies especially to the scheme of dating which forms
an appendix. I am quite prepared to be accused of
rashness in presenting it, and I admit that it is purely
provisional. But I think it may have its use as a frame-
work for history, and it will at least serve the purpose of
exciting criticism. Subsequent to its preparation a
monograph on " Maya Art," by Dr. Spinden, has made
its appearance under the auspices of the Peabody
Museum in America, in which the author provides a
somewhat similar scheme. His table differs somewhat
from mine, but I think that the reasons for my dating,
which I give in the last chapter, render mine the more
satisfactory, and I have therefore made no alteration.
His full treatment of Maya art has however led me to
curtail my remarks on that subject, since much of what
I had written appears on his pages ; and I have rather
given emphasis to those points of difference which exist
between us.

My original intention was to include in the present
book a sketch of the archæology of Nicaragua, Costa
Rica and Panama, but the material proved too great,
and I have thought it better to deal thoroughly with
the related cultures of the Mexicans and Maya rather
than to give an incomplete or over-compressed picture
of the archæology of a wider area. Even as it is I fear

that certain chapters may have suffered from over-condensation, more especially that on the Mexican gods. However Mexican religion is in itself rather an intricate subject, and requires studying in considerable detail if a proper view of the life and culture of the people is to be obtained. Religion amongst the Mexicans was the mainspring of all private and public life, and few of the archæological remains cannot be brought into direct relation with it. Yet even Mexican religion is not as complicated as it appears at first sight; it is in reality the language, with its fondness for long compound names, which renders it so difficult a study to the amateur in the initial stages. I had also intended to add a bibliographical note, similar to that with which I concluded my volume on South America. But in view of the existence of an admirable bibliography in Dr. Walter Lehmann's little monograph, "Methods and Results in Mexican Research," I judged it unnecessary.

I find it difficult to express to the full my thanks to the many friends whose encouragement and assistance are really responsible for such success as this book may achieve. Without the work of Dr. Maudslay and Dr. Seler its production would have been impossible, and I owe them both much gratitude for the great generosity which has led them both to place their illustrations at my disposal. Professor Holmes, of the Bureau of American Ethnology, has shown me similar kindness in permitting me to reproduce five of the charming illustrations in his admirable monograph, "Archæological Studies among the Ruined Cities of Mexico," published by the Field Columbian Museum (now the Field Museum of Natural History) of Chicago.

I am also deeply indebted to Sir Hercules Read, to Colonel Ward and to Mr. Cooper Clark for much advice and the use of valuable photographs, and also to the Trustees of the British Museum and the Director of the Peabody Museum for the loan of certain illustrations. To Dr. Wallis Budge I owe much for his kind encouragement ; it is in fact to him that the inception of the present work is due. I must also express my gratitude to my wife for many hours spent in the preparation of line-drawings, and to my colleague, Mr. H. J. Braunholtz, of the British Museum, for assistance in the laborious task of proof reading. Finally I should like to thank my publishers for the consideration which they have always extended to me, as well as for their enterprise in producing a series of archæological works which will, I trust, do much to stimulate interest in the efforts of the present to unveil the past.

T. A. JOYCE.

London,
January, 1914

CONTENTS

xi

ILLUSTRATIONS

PLATE IN COLOURS

xii

PLATE IN LINE

ILLUSTRATIONS IN THE TEXT

ILLUSTRATIONS

Mexican Archæology

INTRODUCTION

ANCIENT Mexico, the Aztec city of Tenochtitlan, built upon an island situated in a great highland lake, the scene of the almost incredible exploits of Cortés, has long been familiar as a name to the western world, chiefly owing to the wonderful account compiled by Prescott. The story of the fall of Aztec civilization before the Spanish invaders has deservedly won a great hold upon popular imagination, for every page is redolent of romance, and indeed few, if any, writers of fiction have conceived a tale so full of incident, or have brought their heroes to victory in the face of greater odds. Moreover, the existence of Aztec civilization, an organized empire with cities built of stone and rich in gold and gems, burst upon the Old World as a thing almost beyond belief.

The purpose of the present work is to afford some connected account of this pre-Spanish culture, and to correlate the accounts of eyewitnesses and early visitors with the material remains which the investigations of later times have revealed. But in order to obtain a proper view of Mexican culture it is necessary to transcend the limits of Mexico itself. In the country to the south and east, in Guatemala and northern Honduras, are the remains of ruined buildings which are, both architecturally and artistically, superior to those of Mexico proper, and

B

which had been deserted before the coming of the Spaniards. These were the work of the Maya, a people whose name is far less familiar to the general public than that of the Aztec, but who, as I hope to show, evolved a culture of their own when the Aztec were yet primitive nomadic hunters, and who furnished the latter people with the materials for that civilization which so astonished the followers of Cortés.

The actual area with which this book deals is, roughly, that portion of Mexico which lies between the tropic of Cancer and the northern strip of Honduras. It is divided naturally into two portions, a northern and western, and a southern and eastern, by the depression which cuts across the isthmus of Tehuantepec. The natural division corresponds very conveniently with the archæological ; to the north and west lies the seat of Mexican culture, to the south and east, of the Mayan ; but it must be remembered that the Maya-speaking people extended at the conquest practically throughout Vera Cruz, though they had by that time fallen under Aztec influence. I propose therefore to divide this book into two corresponding sections, dealing first with the " Mexican " area, and later with the " Mayan." Both from the chronological and cultural points of view the Mayan area should come first, but, as will appear later, we are dependent to so great an extent upon our knowledge of Mexican civilization for our interpretation of Mayan archæology, that it will be more convenient to give the Mexican priority.

The main geographical features of the Maya country are given at the commencement of the section dealing with its archæology. The region immediately under consideration is shaped rather like an inverted pear, and consists in the main of a plateau bordered by two converging chains of lofty mountains, which are skirted exteriorly by a strip of low-lying coast. The uniformity of the plateau is broken in many places by steep ravines, or *barrancas*, formed by the slow action of rivers, and by occasional highland lakes, such as Chapala, Pazcuaro and Mexico. Much of the ground is volcanic, and the names of the volcanoes Popocatepetl and Iztacciuatl in Mexico province, and of Orizaba on the Puebla-Vera Cruz border, are familiar to everyone. The Mexican valley forms the apex of the triangular plateau, and the natural route thence to the south lies *via* Tehuacan and Teotitlan del Camino, a fact which should be kept in mind in studying the tribal migrations. The height of the mountain-chains and their proximity to the coast explain the fact that there are but few important rivers in Mexico ; most of the streams on the plateau drain into land-locked basins, and practically the only rivers which pierce the mountain barrier are the Panuco on the east, and the Lerma and Rio de las Balsas on the west. Climate and vegetation are dependent upon elevation ; the coast is tropical, but the elevation is so abrupt that the traveller passes with remarkable rapidity from palms, bananas, coconuts and rubber, according to locality, to slopes clad with fir and oak and plains of wheat and maize. In the same way, table-lands rise in successive terraces from Tehuantepec through Oaxaca and Puebla to Mexico which has an elevation of nearly 7500 feet above the sea-level, and enjoys a more temperate climate than New York or Chicago fourteen to sixteen hundred miles further north. The country is conveniently divided into three zones, according to its elevation ; the so-called " tierra caliente " (hot country) runs from the sea-level to 3000 feet, the " tierra templada " (temperate country) from 3000 to 6000 feet, and the " tierra fria " (cold country) thence to the 9000 foot level. The most important vegetable product from the economic point of view was maize, which constituted the chief food of the natives. The varieties and development of the maize-plant as we know it imply centuries of settled life and patient cultivation, and it is an interesting fact that for years the identity of the wild plant from which it was produced remained a mystery. Other plants of economic importance were cacao, vanilla, tobacco and cotton, grown in the hot regions, and the agave or Mexican aloe which flourishes also in the higher country. The fauna includes jaguar (" tiger "), puma (" lion "), ocelot, deer, peccary, alligator, rattle-snake, turkey, humming-bird and the quetzal, the beautiful plumes of the latter being one of the most highly-prized articles of adornment. The distribution of these animals is not however constant throughout the whole area, but many of them are confined to the warmer countries. Little more need be said, for the purposes of this book, of the physical nature of the country, save that the rain-fall is not excessive, being heaviest upon the Atlantic slope; and that, while the land appears to be rising gradually on the Pacific side, much has been lost to the Atlantic on the east. With these few words of introduction an attempt will now be made to describe the inhabitants of the country and the culture which they built up before they came in contact with the Old World at the beginning of the sixteenth century.[1]

[1] A word of explanation should be said concerning the Mexican language. Like other American tongues its structure is such that long compound words and names are built up of significant elements, many of them being thus equivalent to a whole sentence. The practice is not unknown in this country, for is not " Obadiah Bind-their-kings-in-chains-and-their-nobles-in-links-of-iron" familiar to every reader of Macaulay? At the same time it adds considerable difficulty to the study of Mexican archæology. As regards pronunciation, the chief points to be noted are as follows : X is always pronounced as SH and J as H ; C is always hard except before E and I ; CH is sounded as the CH in CHILD ; Z as in ZEBRA.

In Maya we find a happy tendency to monosyllables. X again is pronounced as SH ; but C is always hard.

CHAPTER I—MEXICO : TRIBAL HISTORY

AT the time of the conquest by the Spaniards of the province of Mexico, the dominant people was the Aztec population of Tenochtitlan (Mexico city), inhabiting a town built on an island in the lake of Tezcoco, or rather that portion of it known as the lake of Mexico. The Aztec were confessedly immigrants, who had wandered south less than five hundred years before the conquest ; by their superiority as fighting-men they had won the hegemony over the kindred tribes which they found settled in the valley of Mexico, and had extended their power to both oceans and as far at least as the isthmus of Tehuantepec. Both they and their immediate predecessors spoke the same language, called Nahua (strictly, *Nahuatl*), and they appear to be a branch of the great Shoshonean family which reaches as far north as the state of Montana. Beyond this, their ethnography and language would seem to connect them rather with the coastal tribes of the far north-west than with those to the east of the Rockies, but on this point little can be said at present. Immediately to the north and north-west of the settled peoples of the valley, the steppe country was inhabited by tribes who lived mainly by hunting, called Chichimec and Otomi, the former being almost purely nomadic, the latter to some extent settled. The Chichimec spoke for the most part a language which was essentially Nahua, but the name itself possessed for the Mexicans rather a cultural than a linguistic significance, and meant little more than " nomadic hunters." The Otomi tongue was different, and extended down

5

to the valley of Toluca, through the people known as
Mazaua to the Matlatzinca. South of the last, among
the Tlalhuica around Cuernavaca, Nahua again prevailed. In the hilly volcanic country around lakes Pazcuaro and Chapala, a third speech was found, the
Tarascan, of which the exact affinities are still doubtful. The Rio de las Balsas appears to be about the
southern limit of the Tarascan tongue, but its northern
is less certain; it extends into Jalisco, and may at one
time have reached up into Zacatecas where remains in
Tarascan style have been discovered (at La Quemada).
Roughly south of the Rio de las Balsas and a line drawn
thence to Teotitlan is the Mixtec-Zapotec group of
tongues; the Mixtec extending from Acatlan to Toto-
tepec, and the Zapotec to the east, from the Nahua-
speaking Teotitlan to Tehuantepec, the Mazatec occupying the northern portion of this strip. The
Mixtec-Zapotec language bears many structural analogies to the Otomi group mentioned above. Along the
east coast, from the Panuco valley southward, were
two peoples, speaking dialects of yet another language,
the Maya tongue. In the north were the Huaxtec,
primitive Maya, extending as far south as Tuxpan,
where they were in touch with the linguistically related Totonac. To the north they stretched beyond
the Panuco, but the remains of this region are practically unknown. There is evidence too that they
once extended far further west than they did at the
conquest, but the expansion of the Nahua had penned
them up in the narrow strip of coast, and an Aztec
fortress was established as far east as Meztitlan to keep
the border. The Totonac, inhabiting Vera Cruz to
the south, had suffered similarly from Mexican en-
croachment, and the river Nautla formed a strip of
Aztec territory which almost severed their country in
two. At the time of the conquest their principal
centres were Papantla and Zacapoaxtla. East of them,

in Coatzacoalcos and Tabasco, were the peoples known to the Mexicans as Olmec, Xicalanca and Nonoualca, who, according to legend, were once settled in the neighbourhood of Tlaxcala, but were driven thence by the historical Tlaxcalans when they immigrated into the country.

The early history of these tribes is very difficult to elucidate from the tangled mass of migration myths, often contradictory, which have survived. What may be termed the historical period starts only with the election of the first Aztec king, some years after the settlement of the tribe at Tenochtitlan, and this takes us back only to about 1376, or not much more than a century before the Spanish conquest. The Aztec, when they arrived, found a number of Nahua-speaking " Chichimec " in occupation of the valley, and these "Chichimec" had themselves found the remains of a culture far above their own, to which they gave the name of Toltec. Now the "Toltec question" has been hotly debated from early times ; to the Mexicans the Toltec were the people of a golden age, and their state was the prototype of peaceful civilization. Some writers have gone so far as to deny them actual existence at all, regarding them as a purely mythical people to whom the Mexicans conveniently attributed the invention of all useful arts of which they could not readily explain the evolution otherwise. Others have exalted their culture to a pitch far above, one might almost say, the human, and have credited them with a knowledge transcending that of latter-day civilization. I do not propose to plunge into the welter of controversial theories, but to regard the matter from a strictly practical point of view, which seems to me to be as follows. The Aztec and their immediate fore-runners the " Chichimec " were merely nomadic hunters when they settled in the valley, and their knowledge of arts and crafts, which need a settled life for development, had not advanced beyond a very primitive stage. They found the remains of a people who had for years been living as settled agriculturists, and ruined cities which their untutored minds regarded as something bordering on the marvellous. The agricultural population whom they subdued, more cultured but less warlike than they, told them stories of a powerful empire, stories which no doubt lost nothing in the telling. To this empire they gave the name of Toltec, from the city of Tulan (or Tollan) which was its reputed centre. Modern research has proved conclusively the existence, at those very localities especially associated with the Toltec, of pre-Aztec ruins, and of a relatively high culture which prevailed throughout the valley (and beyond) for a period considerably longer than that which elapsed between the Aztec immigration and the Spanish conquest. As a mere matter of evidence I cannot see that any name can be given to this pre-Aztec culture other than that of Toltec, and, further, that it is possible to deny at least a foundation in fact to the myths connected with this people. However, even so, the difficulties connected with the question are not entirely solved ; Sahagun states definitely that the Toltec spoke Nahua, and relates a migration myth which brings them into contact with the Nahua peoples before their settlement in Tulan. Another legend makes the founder of their state a Chichimec, one Mixcoamazatzin, whose name bears a strong resemblance to that of the Chichimec hunting-god, Mixcoatl, compounded with the native word for the miraculous deer, mazatl, with which he was associated. Further, excavation has proved that before the "Toltec" culture, another of lower grade existed in the valley. This culture, at present the earliest of which traces can be found, strongly resembles that of the Tarascan, and it rather merges into that of the Toltec, while the latter is separated from that of the later Nahua by a definite line of demarcation. As far as the evidence goes at present, it is fair to draw the conclusion that the first settled agriculturists in the Mexican valley were of the same stock as the agricultural people around lake Pazcuaro ; that upon them descended a Nahua tribe from the north, coming in sufficient strength to impose their language, who built up a culture which surprised the subsequent immigrants of similar race when, at a considerably later period, they followed in their footsteps. The tendency of rude hunting tribes to rapid development when they adopt settled life has not yet been fully recognized. There is no finer training for the human faculties than the pursuit of hunting ; it hardens the body, sharpens the observation, and engenders a perpetual readiness to meet sudden emergencies. Agriculture on the other hand, while promoting the development of the useful arts to a certain pitch, is apt to result in stagnation. Students of African ethnography are well aware that nearly all the great kingdoms which have bloomed from time to time in Central Africa have had their origin in the descent of a nomadic tribe upon an agricultural, the former becoming sedentary and developing the arts which they received from the latter far beyond their previous limits. This point however is rather by way of illustration, for it does not wholly suffice to account for the Toltec civilization, though it helps to explain the rapidity with which the Aztec assimilated and developed the remains of it. The Toltec culture bears a definite relation to remains which occur at many sites in Oaxaca and Yucatan, these again are closely connected with the magnificent remains of the early Maya of Chiapas, Guatemala and Honduras. The exact relationship existing between the Maya and the Toltec can only be discussed after the archæology of the former has been considered, but it may be stated in anticipation that, as far as we can say at present, the finest Maya remains appear to antedate those of the Toltec, and therefore that the development of Toltec culture is in part due to Mayan inspiration filtered, I believe, through the early inhabitants of the Zapotec country.

The consideration of what may be called the mythical period of Mexican history is rendered all the more difficult by the fact that all the legends have been collected among later immigrants who wished as far as possible to trace some connection between themselves and the earlier settlers. Toltec descent, if it could be established, raised a family at once to a patrician status, and most of the immigrant tribes sought their rulers among the descendants of a Toltec house. There is therefore the danger of fictitious genealogies, such as exist among so many Sudanese tribes desirous of proving "Arab" descent; but apart from this we are confronted at the outset with a difficulty which is not easy of solution. Sahagun states that the first inhabitants, the Toltec, the other Nahua, the Olmec and the Michoacans, arrived at the Panuco valley and worked down the east coast before turning inland. Ixtlilxochitl represents the Toltec as coasting down lower California and Jalisco. Of the two writers Sahagun is by far the more trustworthy, but at the same time it is difficult to see what Ixtlilxochitl had to gain by deliberately transferring the scene of the migration from one coast to the other. The story of Sahagun is, in brief, as follows. The migrants penetrated as far as Guatemala, and then settled for a time at a place called Tamoanchan, mention of which occurs in nearly all migration legends. Here the wise men who led them departed, taking the god under whose guidance they travelled and the picture-writings which contained their lore, and sailing eastward over the sea. The rest remained behind, under the governance of certain lesser sages, of whom the chief were Oxomoco and Cipactonal, " awaiting the dawn for the administration of society." The Olmec also split from the main stem at this point. From here the others went to

Xomiltepec, and then to Teotihuacan, a site remarkable
for extensive pre-Aztec ruins, where they elected rulers,
and then to Coatepec, where the Otomi branched off.
Later the tribes who still remained associated foregathered at Chicomoztoc, another locality mentioned
in nearly all the myths, where they established cave-
temples. Hence the Toltec departed to Tulanzinco,
and subsequently to Tulan ; after they had separated, the Tarascans also split off, finding their way
to Michoacan. Later still the Nahua, including the
Tepanec (founders of Azcapotzalco), the Acolhua (of
Tezcoco), and the eventual populations of Chalco,
Uexotzinco and Tlaxcala respectively. The Aztec
alone remained wandering in the northern steppes until
they too eventually reached the valley of Mexico. It is
hardly worth while entering into the details of Toltec
history as recorded subsequent to their settlement ; the
" Annals of Quauhtitlan," a native tradition of considerable age and value, gives a list of five kings ; Torquemada and Ixtlilxochitl furnish an entirely different
list, the latter mentioning one king in addition to those
quoted by Torquemada. All that need be said is that the
Toltec were ruled by priest-kings, representatives of
their god Quetzalcoatl, who, according to one legend,
was their first ruler, and that the downfall of their power
was heralded by the separation of the temporal and religious authority. The cause of that downfall seems to
have been the gradual incursion of later Nahua immigrants ; signs of degeneration are not wanting in the
legends connected with the later reigns, in particular
the introduction of human sacrifice. At the fall of the
kingdom, a great emigration took place in the direction
of the east, to Tabasco and beyond, and, so the story
tells, *via* Tehuacan and Teotitlan to Soconusco. Many
of the Toltec however remained behind, especially in
Colhuacan, Cholula and Uexotzinco. The arrival of the
Tlaxcalans, which probably occurred about this time,

drove the Olmec further east in the path of the Toltec, with whom they claimed to be one and the same people. No doubt however the Tlaxcalans absorbed a large percentage of Toltec blood, a fact which intensified their friendship for the people of Uexotzinco and their ineradicable hostility to the Aztec. From a careful consideration of many points of evidence, I am inclined to think that the date given by the " Annals of Quauhtitlan " for the destruction of Tulan, viz. 1064, is not far wrong ; how long the state had lasted is more difficult to say, but that it must have flourished for an extended period is obvious from the fact that the remains characteristic of the Toltec culture at Azcapotzalco form a stratum over three metres thick.

Certain of the manuscripts give the ancient home of the Aztec as Aztlan, and picture it as an island in the centre of a lake, with a city called Colhuacan on the opposite shore. From here the Aztec started in the year dated 1. *tecpatl* (" one stone knife," i.e. 1168 A.D.), and at Colhuacan received their god, Uitzilopochtli, and joined themselves to eight other related tribes. Five of these ultimately formed the population of the following cities, chiefly in the Valley of Mexico, Uexotzinco, Chalco, Xochimilco, Cuitlauac, Malinalco (see the map of the Mexican Valley, Fig. 1); the others being the Chichimec, Tepanec (founders of Azcapotzalco) and Matlatzinca. Later they arrived at Tamoanchan, the " House of descent," a word probably meaning little more than the " place where the tribes separated," for here the eight tribes left them to continue their journey alone. Hence they went to Chicomoztoc, and Cuextecatl Ichocayan, the " place where the Huaxtec weep," where they are represented as having made prisoners from among this nation. After wandering in the steppes they came to Tulan, and then to Chapultepec ; and, after having been reduced for some time to slavery in Colhuacan, settled finally in Tenochtitlan.

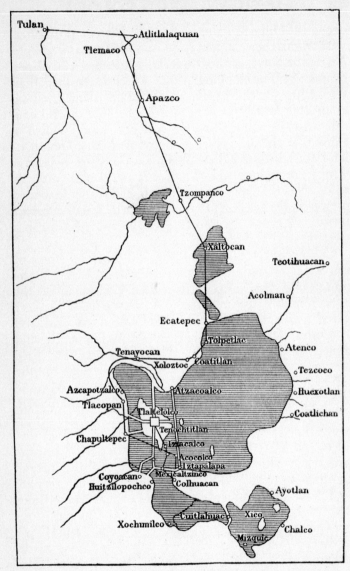

FIG. 1.—Map of the Valley of Mexico. The black line shows the traditional route of the Aztec.

It is difficult to estimate the amount of authenticity which may be attributed to this legend ; the description of the ancient home seems to reproduce the geographical position of Tenochtitlan, situated on an island opposite a mainland town called Colhuacan, in a rather suspicious manner. Still it seems to have been a habit of the Nahua tribes to select such situations for their cities, in proof of which one need only mention such towns as Zumpango, Xaltocan, Cuitlauac, Xochimilco and Acocolco, a previous residence of the Aztec. Fig. 2 illustrates the portion of the Boturini codex which pictures the start from Aztlan to Colhuacan, the footsteps indicating the route, and the eight figures to the right accompanied by glyphs, representing the eight tribes mentioned above, reading from bottom to top. The situation of Aztlan, if the place is not entirely mythical, has given rise to a good deal of controversy ; some have identified Colhuacan with Culiacan on the coast of Sinaloa, while Seler suggests that it was in fact the historical city of that name, Aztlan being the island of Acocolco whence the Mexicans were deported as slaves to Colhuacan, a historical fact. The term Colhuan was in historical times restricted to the inhabitants of this city, with whom the population of Xochimilco and Malinalco were closely connected. Chicomoztoc figures as a halting-place in practically all legends dealing with the Nahua immigration, and in some it is regarded as the starting-point. Besides the tribes above mentioned, the following are also represented as having made some stay there : the Huaxtec, Olmec, Xicalanca, Totonac, Michoacans, Tlalhuica, Acolhua (Tezcocans), Tlaxcalans, the inhabitants of Teotitlan and Tehuacan, and the Mixtec. Beyond this we shall see later that this place seems to be connected with the early history of certain Maya tribes whose migration legends have been preserved. Indeed it seems bound up with the mythical history of all the tribes of Mexico and the

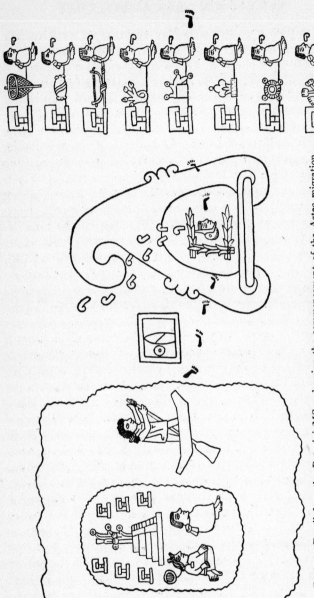

FIG. 2.—Detail from the Boturini MS., showing the commencement of the Aztec migration. From left to right: Aztlan on an island; the Aztec crossing the water; the date 1. *tecpatl*; the city Colhuacan; eight other tribes, reading downwards, the Matlatzinca, Tepanec, Chichimec, Malinalca, Cuitlauaca, Xochimilca, Chalca, and Uexotzinca.   (*After Seler*)

greater part of Central America, with one striking exception, the Zapotec, and as such must belong to an earlier movement of tribes than the actual Aztec migration from Aztlan. The Nahua-speaking tribes, including the Toltec, and the Michoacans, called themselves Chichimec, a term which, as mentioned above, possesses rather a cultural than a racial significance, and means wandering hunters. In fact the Aztec are shown in manuscripts as skin-clad archers on their migration, fighting with the inhabitants of the valley, who are represented as dressed in textiles and armed with the macquauitl, or wooden sword edged with obsidian. The first inroad of Chichimec after the destruction of Tulan (though no doubt that destruction was caused, at any rate in part, by the pressure of nomadic tribes from the north), is said to have taken place under the leadership of a chief called Xolotl, coming from a country named Amaquemacan *via* Chicomoztoc and Tulan. Xolotl established his court at Tenayocan, and proceeded to extend his power over the other cities round the lake, incorporating such of the Toltec as remained in his empire. Shortly after, another influx of Chichimec took place, under three chiefs, Acolhuatzin, whose immediate followers called themselves Tepanec, Chiconquauhtli, leading a band of Otomi, and Tzontecomatl, chief of the Acolhua (in the narrower sense). These chiefs allied themselves with Xolotl, and the first two were given his two daughters in marriage, receiving at the same time the towns of Azcapotzalco and Xaltocan respectively as residences. Tzontecomatl married a woman from Chalco and established himself at Coatlichan. Colhuacan at this time was ruled by Pochotl, a descendant of the last Toltec king, and Xolotl seems to have exercised a loose suzerainty over all. The invaders rapidly adopted the remains of civilization which they found in the valley, and applied themselves to agriculture ; the old name of Chichimec was dropped, and

that of Acolhua, in the wider sense, was adopted.
From this point historical tradition has been so well
reduced to order by Clavigero, whose work, translated
into English, is still easily accessible, that I do not propose to give more than a mere summary of events. A
list of the various "kings," together with approximate
dates which I suggest after a careful comparison of
many sources, is given in Appendix III. The principal point to be noted is the transfer of the political
centre from Tenayocan to Tezcoco, which took place
in the reign of Xolotl's third successor, Quinatzin,
who removed his "court" thither ; from this point
dates what may be termed the " Acolhuan " domination of the Mexican valley. Meanwhile the Aztec had
arrived, but being the latest of the migrants they were
also the rudest, and were of little account. Even their
prowess as fighters was counterbalanced by the comparative smallness of their numbers, and for years they
lived under the protection of various rulers who employed their services in the wars which had already
begun to break out between city and city. In the reign
of Nopaltzin, Xolotl's successor, they are said to have
been settled at Chapultepec, but, being oppressed by
the chief of Xaltocan, they removed to securer, though
less comfortable, quarters on the group of islands called
Acocolco at the south end of the lake. Here they remained for half a century, until they were transferred
to Colhuacan by the ruler of that city. By this time
their numbers had increased, while their fighting qualities had not deteriorated, and after giving proof of the
latter fact by defeating the Xochimilca, with whom the
Colhua were at war, they felt their position sufficiently
strong to insist on leaving Colhuacan for Mexical-
tzingo. Here however they did not reside for long, but
moved north first to Iztacalco and finally to Tenochtitlan. Even yet they were not strong enough to stand
entirely by themselves, probably partly because they

c

were not yet under a single chief who could lay claim
to kinship with the ruling houses of other cities, and
they were now under the protection of Azcapotzalco,
to the ruler of which they paid tribute. Not long after
their settlement, dissensions broke out among themselves, and certain clans removed to the small island of
Tlaltelolco adjoining Tenochtitlan on the north. The
split however was not final, and the two sections remained in close alliance, though under separate administration. The question of the dates of these various
events is by no means easy to determine. Tenochtitlan,
according to the Mendoza codex, which gives a continuous chronicle from this point, was founded in the
year 2. *calli* (two house), or 1325, and this date may, I
believe, be taken as reasonably exact. We are told that
the Aztec were subject to Colhuacan for about twenty-
five years, and that they spent half a century before
that on the islands of Acocolco. If we allow about
twenty years spent at Chapultepec and in the migration
from Colhuacan to Tenochtitlan, we get 1230 as the
approximate date of their arrival at the former city. At
this time, according to legend, Nopaltzin, the successor
of Xolotl, was ruling at Tenayocan, and the commencement of his reign cannot be put much earlier than 1225,
since we are told that Tlotzin, his successor (called
Huetzin by Ixtlilxochitl), died in the year in which
Tenochtitlan was founded. Xolotl, the founder of the
" Chichimec " power, seems to have reigned long, and
indeed the Mexican rulers as a whole seem to have been
singularly long-lived. But in any case Xolotl cannot
have led his followers into the Mexican valley much
before the second half of the twelfth century. If the
annals of Quauhtitlan are correct in assigning the year
1064 to the destruction of Tulan, then the statement
that the Chichimec migration occurred some thirty
years later must be an error. It is true that if the statements of Sahagun as to the length of the reigns of the

Acolhuan and Chichimec kings be correct, the error is not nearly so considerable, but in that case the association of these kings with certain epochs of Mexican history becomes impossible. I am inclined to believe that far more reliance is to be placed on associations of this kind in tradition than upon mere numbers of years, and it is possible that some mistake may have arisen between Sahagun and his informants regarding the length of a king's life on the one hand and the length of his reign on the other. I have therefore given premier importance to statements regarding associations in my scheme of dates. Moreover it seems far more likely from several points of view that at least a century must have intervened between the downfall of Tulan and the immigration headed by Xolotl, though there must have been a steady drift of " Chichimec " tribes southward during that period, having its commencement before the former event, to which it no doubt contributed.

For the first half-century after their establishment at Tenochtitlan, the Aztec were ruled by a council, composed no doubt of the heads of clans ; but in the year 1376 they elected a king. Nothing illustrates better the idea among the Mexicans that kingly power was inherent in certain families, than the fact that they elected Acamapitzin, whose mother was a daughter of the ruler of Colhuacan, Coxcoxtli, and therefore of Toltec descent. Simultaneously the inhabitants of Tlaltelolco elected a ruler, Quaquapitzauac, said to be connected with the ruling family of Azcapotzalco. At this time the most powerful cities in the valley were Tezcoco, whither Quinatzin had removed the Acolhuan court, which was now ruled by his successor Techotlala ; Azcapotzalco, ruled by the Tepanec Tezozomoc, descended from Acolhuatzin ; Coatlichan, where a member of Tzontecomatl's family held sway ; and Colhuacan, under the kingship of Coxcoxtli, of the race of Pochotl the son of Topiltzin the last Toltec king.

Acamapitzin was followed in 1396 by Uitziliuitl, and he in 1417 by Chimalpopoca, Tlacateotl having succeeded to the rulership of Tlaltelolco in 1406. Meanwhile Techotlala had died, and Ixtlilxochitl had become ruler of Tezcoco about 1400. The Mendoza codex assigns the conquest of certain cities to these kings, but it is probable that in these expeditions they acted merely as allies of Tezcoco or Azcapotzalco. During this period the power of Azcapotzalco began to expand, and, aided by the Mexicans, Tezozomoc, the ruler of that city, attacked Ixtlilxochitl of Tezcoco. The obstinate war which followed was the commencement of the struggle between the Tepanec and Acolhua for the hegemony of the valley, but for the time the latter prevailed, and a hollow peace was made. This lasted but a short time, and Ixtlilxochitl was eventually killed in an ambuscade by the Tepanec, who had utilized the interval in winning over certain of his allies. The Tepanec thus became masters of Tezcoco in 1418, and Nezahualcoyotl, the legitimate heir, was driven into exile. Tezozomoc, the Tepanec ruler, did not however enjoy his success long, but died about 1425 at an advanced age. So old was he, it is related, that he was at last kept in a basket surrounded with wool for warmth, and his final years were embittered by dreams that Nezahualcoyotl in the form of an eagle devoured his heart, or, as a lion, sucked his blood. His death brought internal dissension upon Azcapotzalco ; one of his younger sons, by name Maxtla, assassinated the heir-designate and seized the power. He seems to have been the most energetic of the members of the ruling house, but lacked his father's political wariness, since he began to quarrel with Mexico. This was a fatal mistake, since it caused the Aztec, secretly at first, to intrigue with the exiled Nezahualcoyotl, who had, moreover, many friends among the cities where the Acolhuan element was strong. In 1417 Itzcoatl succeeded to power in Tenochtitlan ; the Aztec had by this time increased considerably in numbers and prosperity, and the new ruler proved himself a man of action and an excellent general. He definitely espoused the cause of the exile, with the result that the latter, aided by the people of Tlaxcala and Uexotzinco, succeeded in recapturing Tezcoco and killing every Tepanec in the city. At the same time Coatlichan was stormed by the Chalca, who had also offered assistance to Nezahualcoyotl. These events brought matters to a head ; Maxtla, refusing peace, rashly sent an expedition against Tenochtitlan, and the populace in terror wished to submit. But Itzcoatl succeeded in inspiring them with courage, and, aided by Quauhtlatoa, who had just been elected to the kingship of Tlaltelolco, they inflicted a signal defeat upon the invading force. Nor was this all, Itzcoatl followed up his success by attacking Azcapotzalco, which was successfully stormed and Maxtla was killed. Meanwhile the forces of Tlaxcala and Uexotzinco had captured Tenayocan, and the Tepanec domination was at an end. The Aztec were now actually the paramount power in the valley, but Itzcoatl was too wise to insist upon the fact. He recognized Nezahualcoyotl as his equal, and contracted with him an alliance on equal terms, by which means he won the support of the large Acolhua population. He also conciliated the favour of the defeated Tepanec ; Azcapotzalco, it is true, was reduced to the level of a subordinate city, but over Tlacopan, another Tepanec town, he placed Totoquiuatzin, a descendant of Tezozomoc, as ruler and admitted him to the confederacy on the terms that the booty which was won by the allied arms should be distributed in the following proportions ; to Tenochtitlan two-fifths, to Tezcoco two-fifths, and to Tlacopan one-fifth. The one essential of power Itzcoatl retained for himself ; he stipulated that the military policy of the allies should be directed from Tenochtitlan.

But if the political power was concentrated in Tenoch-titlan, Tezcoco under the wise rule of Nezahualcoyotl became the intellectual and artistic centre of the valley. The government was reformed, and a code of laws drawn up which was regarded as the pattern of all legislation; schools were instituted for the study of poetry, astronomy, music and painting, and the city was embellished by the construction of temples and gardens. However the fall of the Tepanec did not bring peace to the valley; many cities began to be jealous of the Aztec and their newly-acquired hegemony, and the Mendoza codex gives a list of cities which were conquered during the reign of Itzcoatl, among them Quauhtitlan, Cuitla-uac, Xochimilco, Chalco, and Quauhnauac (Cuerna-vaca). Yet these " conquests " were not on the same scale as that of Azcapotzalco; from this time forward the Aztec were content with exacting merely a nominal submission from the towns which they subdued, and imposing tribute. As long as the latter was paid punctu-ally no interference was made either with the local rulers or their administration, though theoretically the heir of a " king " who died was supposed to seek con-firmation in his office at the hands of the ruler of Tenochtitlan.

With the advent to the throne of Montecuzoma, the first of that name, in 1440, the Aztec continued to extend their power beyond the valley. After a short campaign against the Chalca, in order to obtain pris-oners to sacrifice at his coronation, this king proceeded to attack the region around Cuernavaca, subduing, among other towns, that of Tepoztlan, where a temple still remains inscribed with his name (S.S.W. of Cuer-navaca), Yauhtepec and Tlaxco (Pl. XIV, 2 ; p. 174). Further south, he conquered Coixtlahuaca in Mix-tec territory, but his operations to the east were more extensive. In 1458 he sent an expedition into the Panuco valley, against the Huaxtec, and in

PLATE II

1

2

MEXICO

1. COLOSSAL STONE HEAD OF COYOLXAUHQUI
2. STONE FIGURE OF CHALCHIUHTLICUE

(Scale : 1, 1/25th ; 2, 1/3rd)

1461 he won Cotaxtla in the Totonac district, penetrating as far as Cozomaloapan and overrunning also the
region of Tuxpan. His foreign conquests were not undisturbed by troubles in the valley, and the same must
be understood of the later rulers also. Revolt was frequent, and encouraged rather than otherwise by the
religious beliefs of the Mexicans, as will be explained
later. In particular those cities which contained a large
percentage of some formerly dominant people were
perpetually seceding, and among them Chalco and
Xochimilco were frequent offenders. To the east the
population of Tlaxcala and Uexotzinco were a perpetual thorn in the side of the Aztec, and were never
reduced to subjection. The Tlaxcalans in particular
succeeded in holding their own, and their hostility to
Tenochtitlan, of more than half a century's duration,
proved of inestimable value to the Spaniards. This
people, who as we have seen were of " Chichimec "
origin, had originally been settled on the east shore of
the lake, but, owing to quarrels with their neighbours,
decided to move their residence. A few went north and
settled in Tulanzinco, but the majority migrated east
through Cholula to the region of Mount Matlalcue,
whence they drove the Olmec and Xicalanga. No doubt
a certain amount of intermingling took place between the
peoples, and it was partly the large infusion of Toltec
blood which rendered them so implacably hostile to
Aztec rule, and usually on such good terms with the
Cholulans. With the Uexotzinca their relations were
variable, but more often friendly than not. As has been
related, they assisted in the overthrow of the Tepanec
power, but the expansion of Mexico under Montecuzoma was by no means to their liking, and friction soon
arose. With the Uexotzinca they assisted the northern
Mixtec against Montecuzoma, and succeeded at first in
checking the Aztec advance in this direction. However,
in twenty-nine years Montecuzoma extended the influ-

ence of Tenochtitlan, on the east to the Mexican gulf, on the south-east and south to the northern portion of the Mixtec territory and the Cuernavaca region, while on the west and north-west he penetrated into the Toluca valley and the country of the Otomi. At home he built the great Uitznauac temple and, on the advice of Nezahualcoyotl, constructed the ten-mile causeway from Atzacoalco to Iztapalapa in order to guard against inundation, besides adding many buildings to the city and enlarging the code of laws. He died in 1469, preceded in 1464 by Quauhtlatoa the king of Tlaltelolco, who was succeeded by Moquiuix. Axayacatl now became lord of Tenochtitlan, and events moved fast in the valley. Totoquihuatzin, ruler of Tlacopan, died the next year, and was succeeded by Chimalpopoca,[1] while the long life of Nezahualcoyotl came to an end in 1472, and Nezahualpilli assumed the power in Tezcoco. The following year Moquiuix intrigued with the Chalca and others against Axayacatl, and the latter stormed Tlaltelolco and killed the traitor. From this time Tlaltelolco was definitely united to its neighbour, and placed under a governor, the kingship being abolished. This reign was signalized, as far as external affairs were concerned, by an expedition to the Zapotec territory, as far as and beyond Tehuantepec, and though no doubt the province cannot be said to have been absolutely conquered, yet it had the effect of opening up the road to the fertile district of Soconusco, rich in cacao, feathers and gems. Archæologically considered the Zapotec country constitutes an extremely interesting region, if only for the reason that they and the smaller tribes immediately in their neighbourhood possessed no legends hinting at immigration, but claimed that their ancestors issued from caves, rocks or trees in the locality. Similar myths were found among the Mixtec also, but

[1] Sahagun states that this prince came to the throne in 1489, but the Codex Telleriano-Remensis assigns that year to his death.

immigration legends are not wanting. For instance, one story relates that the first lords entered the country from the north, after the Mexican migration, and settled between Achiutla and Tilantongo. The relationship which exists between the Mixtec and Zapotec languages suggests a strong common element, but it seems probable that the former people had received an element of some immigrant nationality, possibly akin to the Toltec or Chichimec. This element was not strong enough to influence the local dialects, but gave the Mixtec that superiority in arms which enabled them to encroach upon the Zapotec district. East of the Zapotec were the uncultured Mixe and Zoque, from whom the Zapotec in their turn had won territory, including Tehuantepec.

To return to the conquests of Axayacatl, this king completed the reduction of the Toluca valley, and reconquered the region of Cotaxtla which had revolted, so that his successor Tizoc, who seems also to have sent an expedition to the Mixtec country, was able to lay claim to an empire extending over the valleys of Toluca and the Rio de las Balsas, and the highlands of Mixteca, Huaxteca, Orizaba, Cotaxtla and Teotitlan. Axayacatl died in 1469, and Tizoc in 1482, and Auitzotl became the Aztec ruler. He continued the strenuous foreign policy of his predecessors, and proved a vigorous conqueror, though he was passionate and often cruel in administration. His armies conquered many cities in the Zapotec country, including Mitla (1494), Teozapotlan (1495) and Tehuantepec, and after seizing Tonala, the key to the country further south and east, pursued their victorious course through Soconusco, *via* Mapaxtepec, Escuintla and Huiztla, as far as Huehuetlan. Other expeditions penetrated Chiapas, and even subdued certain cities in Guatemala. Probably however there was nothing like an effective occupation of the country beyond the city of Oaxaca, where a Mexican colony was established. In particular Chiapas can never be said to have been conquered. Still, in this reign the Aztec power reached its furthest extent, and the influence of Tenochtitlan was felt from the Panuco valley to northern Guatemala, and from Tuxpan to Acapulco. In the city itself Auitzotl completed the great pyramid-temple to Uitzilopochtli, the tribal god of the Aztec, which his predecessor had commenced, and also constructed an aqueduct which supplied water from Coyoacan. A severe inundation took place in his reign, and as he was escaping from the lower floor of a building which had become flooded, he struck his head against the lintel, causing an injury from which he eventually died. Montecuzoma, the second of that name, succeeded in the year 1502 ; Nezahualpilli was still ruling in Tezcoco, but Chimalpopoca of Tlacopan had died in 1489 and Totoquiuatzin the second was now the ruler there. Montecuzoma had been trained as a priest as well as a soldier, and though his military abilities enabled him to maintain the empire much in the same condition as he received it, he was particularly superstitious and amenable to sacerdotal influence. Abroad he quelled a rebellion among the Zapotec and Mixtec, and carried on operations in Soconusco and Vera Cruz. Nearer home he seized the opportunity of a quarrel between the Tlaxcalans and Uexotzinca to espouse the cause of the latter and to carry on a vigorous campaign against the former. For many years the Aztec had been able seriously to obstruct Tlaxcalan trade with the coast, so much so in fact that salt was a rarity in that province, but Montecuzoma made an energetic attack upon their territory. Undismayed, the Tlaxcalans fortified the approach to their dominions with a wall six miles long, and succeeded in withstanding the invasion and even in inflicting defeats upon their foes. Meanwhile Nezahualpilli, ruler of Tezcoco, died in 1515, and his son Cacamatzin was elected in his place. A younger son, Ixtlilxochitl, laid claim to the power and succeeded in attracting a number of supporters. He was still haunting the neigh- bouring mountains and carrying on a guerilla warfare with the confederate troops when the arrival of the Spaniards in 1519 brought the development of abori- ginal American civilization to an abrupt close. Monte- cuzoma had emphasized the aristocratic aspect of Mexi- can government, and under him the court ceremonial had been greatly elaborated. He surrounded himself with a semi-divine state, and the rich tribute which now poured into Tenochtitlan enabled him not only to undertake many important works for the beautifying of the city, but to model his personal service on a scale which surpasses even the " Arabian Nights." The mag- nificent "calendar-stone," figured on Pl. VIII, 1 ; p. 74, was brought by him from Coyoacan to serve probably as a sacrificial altar to the sun in the enclosure of the great temple of Uitzilopochtli. He was a strong personality, and though his superstitious training led him to adopt a fatally hesitating policy when the Spaniards landed, he displayed under all circumstances a personal courage and dignity which lend additional pathos to his fate.

Of Zapotec and Mixtec history, apart from that of Mexico, we know practically nothing. We hear of a mythical Mixtec king named Dzahuindanda, who pos- sessed a magic sack which he was wont to take to a desolate mountain and shake, after appropriate incanta- tions, producing thereby as many soldiers as he re- quired. Less legendary are the Zapotec Zociyoeza and his son Zociyopi, the former of whom ruled at Teoza- potlan, the latter at Tehuantepec. Zociyoeza in fact opposed the Mexican advance, and held out against the invading troops for four years entrenched in Quiengola, until at last he was able to conclude an honourable peace. Between the Mixtec and Zapotec, hostilities seem to have been not uncommon, and from a story told by Burgoa it would appear that the Zapotec did not form a very large state. The principal ruler was the chief of Teozapotlan, but his resources could not have been great, since he asked a Mixtec king for troops to defend his city while he was absent upon a campaign against the Mixe in Tehuantepec. The same author relates that after being successful in his operations the chief rashly laid claim to certain Mixtec territory, a demand which resulted in the seizure by the Mixtec of a large slice of the Oaxaca region, and the founding of the Mixtec town of Xoxocotlan.

The history of the Pazcuaro plateau seems to have been very similar to that of the Mexican valley. Originally the shores of the lake were occupied by a population of agriculturists and fishers, probably akin to the pre-Toltec inhabitants around the lake of Tezcoco. Upon them descended, from the hills around Zacapu, certain tribes of wandering hunters led by a tribal hero Ticatamé. The new-comers mingled and intermarried with the original population and adopted their habits, but friction arose, Ticatamé was killed and the idol of the immigrants, Curicaveri, was captured. Sicuirancha, son of Ticatamé, called upon the god for aid, the foe were smitten with a pestilence and the idol recaptured. In course of time the immigrants became a ruling class, and to the whole population the name Tarascan was given, from Taras, another hunting-god who was identified with the Chichimec Mixcoatl. It is possible that this ruling class was originally of Chichimec stock, and its descent upon Pazcuaro was part of that general movement southward which took place among the hunting tribes of the north towards the end of the Toltec rule. If this is so they must have abandoned their own language in favour of the tongue of the original agricultural population with whom they intermarried. It is interesting to find in Michoacan a definite story of a Toltec immigration. A body of Toltec, specified as skilled workers in gold, stone and feather-work, are said to have travelled from Vera Cruz *via* Tehuacan, Coyoacan and Tenochtitlan to Xiuhquillan (Tzitzipu, on L. Pazcuaro), where they settled. The Tarascan of later date bore a high reputation as stone-cutters, mosaic-workers and feather-workers, and this fact, together with the presence in Michoacan of a peculiar class of pottery with polychrome *champ-levé* ornament, which is also characteristic of the pre-Aztec remains of the valley, suggest that Toltec influence had in fact penetrated into Michoacan.

Totonac history is as deficient as that of the Zapotec. Tradition related that they were immigrants into the country where they were found by the Spaniards, and lived there for about six and a half centuries in complete independence. Less than two centuries after their immigration, certain " Chichimec " tribes of lower culture settled on their north-western borders, and in course of time considerable intercourse, and even inter-marriage, sprang up between them. Eventually civil war broke out among the Totonac, much of the country was laid waste and sections of the population emigrated from the district. It is quite possible that the " Tol-tec "who are said to have found their way to Michoacan may have been a body of Totonac emigrants who left their country at this period. The result of the civil strife was that a great portion of Totonac region fell under " Chichimec " domination. Three kings of this nationality held sway, until, in the reign of the last, the Aztec conquered the country and reduced it to the status of a province as related above.

Much light is shed upon the interrelation of the various tribes who combined to form the population of Mexico by the study of their various gods ; and since religion formed the mainspring not only of all public but also of private life, it will be as well to deal as shortly as possible with this complicated subject before proceeding to discuss the manners and customs of the pre-Spanish inhabitants and their archæological remains which have been found scattered throughout the country.

PLATE III

Photo. Prof. Seler   Mexico Museum

MEXICO
COLOSSAL STONE FIGURE OF COATLICUE

CHAPTER II—MEXICO: THE GODS

THE question of the religion of the Ancient Mexicans is by no means easy to approach. At the time of the Spanish conquest the Mexican pantheon was still in a state of great confusion, and the number of tribal cults of which it was composed had not yet been reduced to a homogeneous whole. Gods whose functions were similar or associated had been invested with the attributes one of the other, and there is reason to suspect that the names of deities whose importance was relatively recent had been incorporated in the earlier myths by a priesthood jealous of the dignity of its own particular god. The history of the valley of Mexico, as far as it can be traced, consists, as we have seen, of the conquest from time to time of the sedentary agricultural population by ruder and more warlike tribes from the hills. The victors, conscious of their cultural inferiority, in adopting to the best of their ability the mode of life of the conquered, were careful also to propitiate the local gods, whom they regarded as responsible for the superior culture of the latter ; though they attempted, as far as they dared, to subordinate them to their own chief deity. These hill-tribes of primitive hunters seem to have worshipped each a god of its own, who was regarded as its personal leader, who presided over war and the chase and who appears to have been connected with the stars and occasionally with the sun. This connection with the sun was, I am inclined to think, an afterthought, and not universal, arising from the belief that war was instituted in order to provide the sun with blood-offerings. To this class of deities belong Curicaveri, Tiripemé and Taras, worshipped by the Tarascans, Mixcoatl of the Otomi, Chichimec and Matlatzinca, Camaxtli of Tlaxcala and Uexotzinco, Amimitl and Atlaua of the Chiampanec, and the Mexican Uitzilopochtli (Fig. 3,*f*). The connection is especially close between Mixcoatl, Camaxtli and Uitzilopochtli, in fact they are occasionally identified. Their attributes consist of a spear-thrower and net bag, or bow and arrows, and the arrows are sometimes shown as tipped with down, in allusion to the fact that they are gods of sacrifice, such being the *insignia* of prisoners destined for the sacrificial stone ; Uitzilopochtli is usually shown in the dress of a humming-bird (Uitzitzilin) in punning allusion to his name, and with him is associated a minor deity, Paynal, believed to be his messenger. According to a widespread legend Uitzilopochtli is said to have been conceived by his mother, Coatlicue, from a ball of down which fell from heaven and which she placed in her bosom ; her other sons, the Centzon Uitznaua (Four hundred Southerners, the number meaning "innumerable"), at the instigation of their sister Coyolxauhqui (Pl. II, 1), accused Coatlicue of improper conduct, and attempted to kill her ; but Uitzilopochtli, springing from his mother's body, defeated them, decapitating Coyolxauhqui with the *xiuhcoatl* or "fire-snake" with which he was armed. Coatlicue was an earth-goddess, patron of flower-sellers, and, as her name implies, is distinguished by a skirt woven of snakes (Pl. III) ; the brothers are identified with the stars of the southern heaven. Very similar is the legend of Mixcoatl (Fig. 4, *a*), according to which this god was attacked and killed by the Centzon Mimizcoa (also stellar deities), but was avenged by his son Ce Acatl, who slew the latter with the *tezcacoatl* ("mirror-snake"). In the person of Mixcoatl we find a direct connection with the Tarascan Curicaveri, whose symbol was a stone knife kept in a box by the priest, since the same legend relates that Mixcoatl always carried with him a stone knife as a fetish. It may also be mentioned in passing that the date of Uitzilopochtli's (and Camaxtli's) movable feast was I. tecpatl (tecpatl being the stone-knife day-sign), and, as will be explained later, gods were often known by calendrical names. Mixcoatl's knife was said to be a symbol of the peculiar female deity Itzpapalotl ("obsidian butterfly"), a star-goddess associated with fire and lightning, and occasionally identified with a mythological two-headed deer called Itzcueye which figures in the legends of Mixcoatl and Camaxtli as the captive and wife of the god. This two-headed deer was again identified at Cuitlauac and Xochimilco with the Colhuacan earth and warrior goddess Ciuacoatl (Tonantzin or Quilaztli), invoked in childbirth, whose symbol was an obsidian knife ; but, and here is a good instance of the confused nature of the myths with which we have to deal, Ciuacoatl was regarded as the mother of Mixcoatl (as also the other earth-goddess Coatlicue the mother of Uitzilopochtli), and as sister of the Mimizcoa. The planet Venus was a war-god in Michoacan, and, under the name Urendequa Vecara, was the especial deity of Curinguaro, a town hostile to the votaries of Curicaveri. In Mexico this planet was known as Tlauizcalpantecutli, and was connected in some respects with prisoners destined for sacrifice. Representations of Uitzilopochtli are very rare in Mexican art of pre-Spanish date, but we are told that his facepaint consisted of blue and yellow horizontal stripes. Mixcoatl and Camaxtli are usually shown with black paint around the eye, rather in the form of a highwayman's mask, and Uitzilopochtli also appears with this occasionally. The distinguishing feature of Tlauizcalpantecutli is a series of five dots, arranged quincunx fashion on a dark ground, with the central spot on the nose (Fig. 4, c).

D

FIG. 3.—Mexican deities from various MSS.

A. Tlazolteotl.
C. Xiuhtecutli.
E. Tezcatlipoca.

B. Tlaloc.
D. Ciuapipiltin.
F. Uitzilopochtli

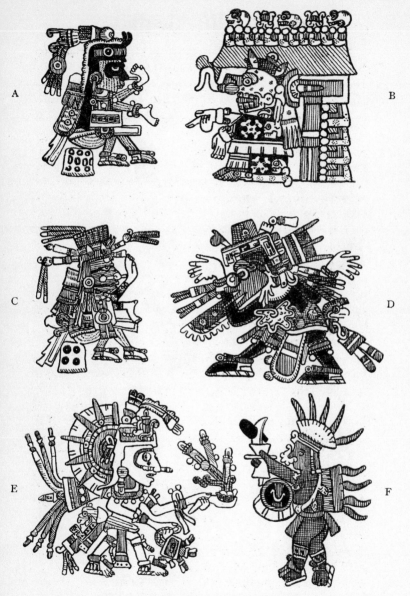

FIG. 4.—Mexican deities from various MSS.

A. Mixcoatl.   B. Mictlantecutli.
C. Tlauizcalpantecutli.   D. Quetzalcoatl as Eecatl.
E. Tonatiuh.   F. Ome Tochtli.

For the sedentary tribes of the valleys, dependent chiefly upon agriculture and fishing for a livelihood, the deities presiding over vegetation, rain and earth were the most important ; and after the Aztec had become settled and devoted themselves to intensive cultivation, they readily adopted these gods and gave them a high place in their pantheon. Most important of all was Tlaloc, the god of rain and thunder (Fig. 3, *b*) ; his worship appears to have been extremely widespread, and his images are found in numbers among the remains of pre-Aztec date at Teotihuacan (where he is the only god who can be identified with certainty), in the Huaxtec country, at Teotitlan, at Quiengola in the Zapotec district, and at Quen Santo in Guatemala. It is even related that when the Acolhua first arrived in the valley in the reign of the first Chichimec ruler Xolotl, they discovered on a mountain a figure of this god, which remained an honoured object of worship until it was broken up by order of the first bishop of Mexico. Tlaloc is one of the most easily recognizable of Mexican deities, since he is represented with snakes twined about his eyes (the snake being throughout practically the whole of America the symbol of lightning and rain), with long teeth, and often with a trunk-like nose. According to legend he was one of the first gods created, and lived in a kind of paradise, situated in the east, called Tlalo-can, where he presided over the souls of the drowned and those who in life suffered from dropsical affections. He was supposed to be assisted in his duties by a number of subsidiary rain-gods, called Tlaloque, who distributed the rain from magical pitchers and caused the thunder by striking them with rods. In the courtyard of Tlaloc's palace four great jars were supposed to stand, which contained rain of varying quality. In the first was the good rain which produced fertile crops ; in the second, rain which gave being to cobwebs and mildew ; in the third were stored ice and sleet ; and in

the fourth, rain after which nothing matured or dried.
Thus Tlaloc combined two aspects, a beneficent and a
terrible ; and this is not unnatural, for rain in Mexico
is more often than not accompanied by thunder, and
the fertilizer is therefore also the smiter. As the god of
fertility maize belonged to him, though not altogether
by right, for according to one legend he stole it after it
had been discovered by other gods concealed in the
heart of a mountain. The great importance of Tlaloc
and the Tlaloque in the worship of the Ancient Mexicans may be gathered from the fact that no less than
five of the twenty month-festivals were dedicated to
them, and that Tlaloc shared with Uitzilopochtli the
great pyramid at Tenochtitlan. The most important of
the Tlaloque was Opochtli, a fishing and hunting god,
the inventor of nets and the bird-spear. Closely connected with Tlaloc was his wife Chalchiuhtlicue (Pl. II,
2), goddess of running water, said also to be sister of the
Tlaloque and mother of the Mimizcoa. This goddess,
under the name Matlalcue, was especially worshipped
at Tlaxcala, and is easily recognized by her tasselled
headband and cape, and often by a stepped nose-
ornament. The most important festivals to these
deities took place on mountain-tops, for it is there that
the rain-clouds gather before they sweep over the
plain, and closely associated with them was the worship
of mountains represented by small figures called Tepic-
toton, with hair dressed in two horns, whose sacrificial
victims were similarly adorned. The valley-dwellers of
Michoacan around Pazcuaro revered a goddess of fertility and rain, named Cueravahperi, casting the hearts
of her victims into certain hot springs which were supposed to give birth to the rain-clouds. In connection
with her worship we are first brought into contact with
a strange and gruesome rite, peculiar to this part of
America, and performed exclusively in honour of agricultural deities. The victim was flayed, and the priest

performed a ceremonial dance wrapped in the fresh skin. The practice seems to be symbolical of vegetation in the early spring, apparently dead, but containing within the germ of life and fertility, and no doubt was originally intended to assist by imitative magic the process of nature in renewing the food-supply. Corresponding to this goddess, and, like her, regarded as the mother of the gods, was the Mexican Teteoinnan or Tozi, a deity held in especial reverence by the Tlaxcalans and Olmec, and perhaps borrowed from the latter people. She was in particular the goddess of ripe maize and healing herbs, patroness of doctors, midwives and bath attendants (for the steam-bath played an important part in childbirth) and diviners. She too was connected with the flaying-sacrifice, and was sometimes pictured as clad in the victim's skin ; otherwise her attributes are the same as those of Tlazolteotl (see below) and she carries a broom. The maize-god *par excellence* was Cinteotl, her son (though occasionally mentioned as a female deity), who appears originally to have been a Totonac god. He is usually shown with a vertical line leading down his cheek, probably representing tears and symbolizing the fertilizing rain. On certain occasions his priest wore a mask made from the skin of the thigh of the victim sacrificed in honour of Teteoinnan. At first sight it is a little surprising to find this god appearing as one of the tutelary deities of the lapidaries of Xochimilco, but no doubt the reason of this is that the ripe maize-cob, nature's mosaic, recalled the incrusted work which formed one of their principal manufactures. Closely associated with all these deities was a maize-goddess, Chicome Coatl, sister of Tlaloc, who presided over agriculture and was honoured with a flaying-sacrifice ; while the young maize-ear had an especial protector in the goddess Xilonen, perhaps the same as the Chichimec Xilo worshipped by the inhabitants of the Amantlan district of Mexico. Another

PLATE IV

1

2

British Museum

MEXICO

1, 2. STONE MASK REPRESENTING XIPE; THE REVERSE SHOWS
THE ENTIRE FIGURE OF THE GOD. TEZCOCO

(Scale: 1/3rd)

goddess who seems to be connected with maize was
Ilamatecutli, also called Cozcamiauh (maize-necklace),
though she appears to have been a star-goddess as well.
She, Teteoinnan and Xilonen were associated in a peculiar form of sacrifice in which the victim was decapitated, and which perhaps represented the reaping of the
maize-ear. The sacrifice by decapitation seems to be
particularly connected with the earth-goddesses, who
are sometimes shown in the MSS. with head almost
severed from the body, and with two snakes, perhaps
representing streams of blood, issuing from the trunk.
Of such a representation the colossal figure in the Mexican Museum (see Pl. III) is an example. This deity is
either Chicome Coatl or Coatlicue, probably the latter,
to judge from the skirt of serpents which she wears. In
this case the two snakes which spring from her decapitated body are placed snout to snout, and from the two
profiles is compounded a grotesque face, or rather two
such faces, one in front and one behind. It is worthy of
note that the mask of the goddess Ilamatecutli, apparently another fertility goddess, is said to have been
double-faced.

The god who above all others was connected with
the flaying-sacrifice is Xipe, who is invariably depicted as clad in the victim's skin (Pl. IV). He was
believed to have been borrowed from the Oaxaca tribes,
was worshipped in Jalisco, and finds a parallel in the
sea-god of the Tarascans. Both Xipe and the latter are
characterized by red and white paint (though Xipe's
skin dress is yellow), and the victims of both were forced
to fight for their lives in a gladiatorial combat. At the
great feast of Xipe those warriors who had taken captives in war offered them to the god, and wore their
skins during the ensuing month. He was a god of sowing, but being connected with the warrior's death by
sacrifice was also a war-god, and his livery, including a
drum as back-device, was worn in battle by the Mexi-

can kings. In invocations his ceremonial name was
" Night-drinker," and he was prayed to give moisture
to the crops. " Put on your golden garment ; why does
it not rain ? It might be that I perished, I, the young
maize-plant." In this connection another form of
sacrifice was practised in his honour ; a captive was tied
to a scaffold and shot with darts so that his blood
streamed down upon the ground (Fig. 5, *a*). This
proceeding may be regarded in the light of imitative
magic, to secure fertilizing rain for the earth. It was
first performed, so the legend says, in honour of the
earth-deities, and occurred also in South America
among the tribes of Colombia. In the illustration, the
victim is shown wearing the peculiar form of head-dress
associated with Xipe. A particular emblem carried
by the water and fertility deities is the *chicauaztli*, or
rattle-staff (see Pl. IV, 1), often seen in the hands of
Xipe, Chicome Coatl and Cinteotl, and associated in invocations with Tlaloc. This instrument, like the rattle-
staves of West Africa, may almost certainly be regarded
as a charm to bring rain by imitating its sound. Besides
the functions already mentioned, Xipe also exercised
that of protector of goldsmiths, since the yellow skin in
which he was clad was supposed to typify an overlay of
gold foil.

Among the fertility gods must be mentioned the goddess of flowers, love and pregnancy, Xochiquetzal (Pl. IX,
6; p. 82), especially worshipped by the Tlalhuica (also at
Tlaxcala), and mentioned as the wife of Cinteotl, though
one legend makes her the first wife of Tlaloc, stolen by
Tezcatlipoca, the Mexican Jupiter. Her distinguishing
insignia are two large feather plumes upon her head,
and she seems to be akin to the Tarascan goddess of
Tzintzuntzan, Xaratanga, who was associated with
Curicaveri as his wife. The functions of this deity however were rather more extended, since she was also regarded as an earth- and maize-goddess, and was con-

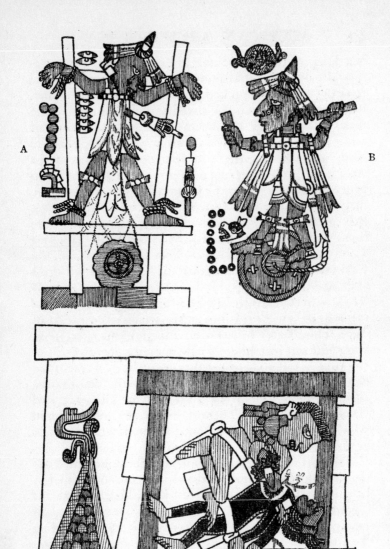

FIG. 5.—Mexican methods of Sacrifice.

A.   Arrow sacrifice.
B.   Gladiatorial sacrifice.
C.   Ordinary sacrifice.

(*Zouche MS., British Museum*)

nected with the game *tlaxtli*. Xochiquetzal was the especial patroness of weaving and embroidery, of which arts she was the supposed inventor. The male equivalent to this goddess was Xochipilli, god of flowers, dance, song and games (Pl. V, 1). He is figured with the high crest of the coxcoxtli bird on his head, a white butterfly painted on his mouth, and occasionally with the tear face-paint. He appears to have been introduced from the Xelhua district on the Oaxaca border, and in one of his manifestations was known by the calendrical name of Macuil Xochitl (Five Flower), in which case he bears a hand painted across his mouth (a constant feature of gods into whose name the number five enters). He was further regarded as identical with, or as the son of, Pilzintecutli, a sun-god, who again was thought to be the son of Mictlantecutli, the lord of the underworld. During recent excavations in Mexico city, a stone figure of Xochipilli was found with a large number of miniature musical instruments in stone and pottery.

Among the gods of fertility must be reckoned those who presided over *octli* (Fig. 4, *f*), the intoxicating drink obtained from the maguey (the American aloe, *Agave americana*). These deities were connected with the harvest, and also bore a relation to the moon; they were regarded as innumerable, a fact explained by an early chronicler as typifying the countless forms of drunkenness, and were spoken of collectively as Centzon Totochtin or the "Four hundred (i.e. innumerable) Rabbits." Many names of these gods have come down to us; they were all regarded as brothers, and it is possible that each one represents a section of the Mexican population, especially as their names seem taken from the names of places. If so their number would point to an early date for the discovery of octli. Tezcatzoncatl is said by some to be the chief, by others Izquitecatl, or again Ome Tochtli, (Two Rabbit, a calendrical name taken from the date of

PLATE V

British Museum

MEXICO

1. STONE FIGURE OF XOCHIPILLI (THE CHARACTERISTIC HIGH CREST OF HIS HEAD-DRESS IS MISSING)

2. STONE WITH FIGURE OF A XIUHCOATL (FIRE-SNAKE IN RELIEF

(Scale : 1, 1/8th ; 2, 1/9th)

the principal feast). The two former are Chichimec
gods, and Coatlicue was assigned to both as wife.
Tepoztecatl was the octli god of the Chichimec inhabitants of the Amantlan quarter, while Patecatl was
connected with the Huaxtec, a people popularly supposed to be especially given to drunkenness. Indeed
one legend makes the tribal father of this people the
first drunkard. In invocations the Totochtin were related to Colhuacan. Their principal *insignia* consisted
of red and black face-paint, and a semi-lunar nose-
ornament which appears also on their shields, while
Tepoztecatl, the god to whom most probably the
temple at Tepoztlan was erected, carries an axe. As
sister of the Totochtin we have Mayauel, the agave
goddess, wife of Patecatl, who, like the Ephesian Diana,
was supposed to have four hundred breasts. An interesting myth attaches to Tezcatzoncatl, who was fabled
to have been killed and revived by Tezcatlipoca, by
which action the sleep of the drunken, so similar to
death, became harmless for men. No doubt it was this
awakening after heavy sleep, as much as anything else,
which connected the octli gods with the waxing and
waning of vegetation and the moon. The Tarascans of
Cumachan also worshipped an octli god, who was
believed to be lame, since he disgraced himself by becoming intoxicated in heaven, and was thrown thence
to the earth. The supremacy which Tlaloc was supposed to exercise over the deities of fertility is well seen
in the fact that at the great feast to the mountains four
women and a man were sacrificed to him, named after
five of these divinities, Matlalcue, Mayauel, Tepexoch,
Xochitecatl (the two latter connected with flowers), and
the male god of snakes, Milnauatl. One other goddess
connected with the food-supply deserves mention here,
namely Uixtociuatl, the deity of salt, who bore a certain relation to Chalchiuhtlicue.

The earth-goddesses Teteoinnan and (to a less degree) Chicome Coatl have already been mentioned, but another most important female divinity, an earth-goddess, but not associated with vegetation, was Tlazol-teotl (Fig. 3, *a*). This deity seems originally to have come from the Olmec, and was identified with the Huaxtec Ixcuina. She is at times identified also with Teteoinnan, and was occasionally honoured with a flaying-sacrifice, but her chief province was the superintendence of carnal sin, confession and penitence. She is shown with a black mouth and chin, a semi-lunar nose-ornament, and a cotton headband in which are stuck two spindles. The cult of this goddess was practised by the Huaxtec, Olmec and Mixtec, but not by the Chichimec or Taras-cans.

We must now consider one of the most interesting and important gods of the Mexican pantheon, Tezcatlipoca (Fig. 3, *e*). It is difficult to give a short, and at the same time clear, account of his manifold functions and mani-festations, since there were few departments of native life with which he was not intimately connected. In the first place he was the all-powerful god of the Nahua-speaking tribes, worshipped by them in common ; as such he was superior to the tribal war- and hunting-gods such as Mixcoatl and Uitzilopochtli, and in actual practice he seems to have been regarded with even greater awe. In typical form he appears with face banded with yellow and black, a shell ring breast-orna-ment, and a mirror from which a spire of smoke issues. This smoking mirror is his especial sign, and constitutes the rebus of his name ; in it he was supposed to see all that was occurring on earth, for one of his main func-tions was the distribution of rewards and punishments. He bears this mirror on his head, or very often in place of one of his feet, a peculiarity explained by the idea that in his capacity of god of the setting sun he lost his foot owing to the premature closing of the doors of the underworld. Sometimes the missing foot is replaced by a stone knife, and in this manifestation he was known as Itztli, the knife-god. He is thus brought into intimate relation with the hunting deities, of whom this weapon was a symbol. Besides this, attempts seem to have been made by the various tribes to dignify their respective gods by actual identification with the supreme deity. One legend states that he became Mixcoatl, and in this personality invented the production of fire from flint. Or again, he appears under two forms, a red and a black Tezcatlipoca, and the latter is identified with Camaxtli and Uitzilopochtli. This distinction of colour recalls the yellow and black Tiripemés of the Tarascans, of whom the former was identified with Curicaveri. One of the many names of Tezcatlipoca was Yoalli Eecatl, the night-wind, and he was supposed to wander through the streets after dark in search of evildoers. Seats were placed for him at crossroads, and a cross-road is often shown as one of his attributes in the manuscripts. When portrayed with bandaged eyes he bore the name of Itztlacoliuhqui, and presided over sin and cold.

As the god of divine punishment he was also a god of confession, and as such was associated with Tlazolteotl, while his connection with war is seen in the fact that he was regarded as the especial patron of the warrior-school, or Telpochcalli. In his dual capacity as a night- and warrior-god he was supposed to appear in all sorts of grisly shapes in order to test the courage of those he might meet. To flee from one of these phantoms was fatal, but the brave man who seized the apparition and wrestled with it until it gave him one or more spines of the maguey, was rewarded with a similar number of prisoners in his next battle. One of the forms which the god assumed on such occasions was a headless body with two doors in its chest which opened and shut, making a noise like the sound of an axe upon a tree. At the same time this deity possessed a lighter side ; as

Omacatl (a calendrical name, "Two Reed") he was the god of banquets and festive entertainments, and as Tlamatzincatl he was regarded as endowed with perpetual youth. His relation to the produce-goddesses is seen in the fact that the four women given as wives to the victim, identified with the god himself, who was destined to be sacrificed at his principal feast, bore the ceremonial names of Xilonen, Xochiquetzal, Uixtociuatl and Atlatonan, the last-named being a goddess associated with Teteoinnan and honoured with a flaying-sacrifice.

Another important deity, whose relations are peculiarly difficult to unravel, was Quetzalcoatl (Pl. VI, 2). He was the especial god of the Toltec, inventor and patron of the arts and crafts, and originator of the calendar and priestly ritual. In studying the extremely confused legends concerned with this divinity it is important to remember two facts which have probably given rise to much misunderstanding. First that the high-priest of the god bore his name, secondly that the last Toltec king, in whose reign occurred the fall of Tulan and the scattering of the Toltec, was called Topiltzin Quetzalcoatl. The relation of this god to the Maya deity Kukulkan, whose name is an exact equivalent (quetzal-=kukul, the quetzal bird; coatl=kan, snake), is discussed below (p. 226). It is said that after giving laws to the people he departed eastward, and on reaching the sea put off his feather dress and turquoise snake-mask and immolated himself upon a funeral pyre, his soul becoming the morning star; or, according to another account, he sailed away eastward, promising to return in a year of similar date. As a god of the morning star he bore the calendrical name of Ce Acatl ("One Reed"), one of the dates marking the periodical appearances of Venus. It will be remembered that we have seen a deity named Ce Acatl as a warrior-god, slaying the Mimizcoa who had killed his father Mixcoatl. But this deity is certainly not to be identified with Ce Acatl Quetzalcoatl, who was essentially a god of peace, averse to human sacrifice. Among the hunting peoples, as can be seen especially from a study of the Tarascan tribes, the morning star was a war-god, while the association of Quetzalcoatl with this planet was due to the fact that it was the regulator of the solar calendar as explained subsequently. In the second legend the promise of the god to return in a year ce acatl had very far-reaching effects. Quetzalcoatl was regarded as white and bearded, and the arrival of the Spaniards in a year bearing this date seemed to the Mexicans to possess a religious sanction which proved of inestimable service to the invaders. Indeed, but for this legend it is more than doubtful whether the almost incredible exploit of Cortés would have been successful. Quetzalcoatl is usually shown with black paint, the priestly colour, and wearing a pointed head-dress of the form associated with the Huaxtec, and hook-shaped ear pendants. As Eecatl the wind-god he bears a mask with a long snout, and a spirally marked shell breast-ornament, typifying the eddies of the wind (Fig. 4, d). In this capacity he was associated with the rain-gods, for whom he was said to sweep the road, and in one place he is given the same title as Tezcatlipoca, Yoalli Eecatl, the night-wind. As a god of ceremonial purification he is generally shown with the bone implement for piercing the ears, sometimes stuck in his head-dress, and, as a patron of education, children were presented to him at the public school or Calmecac. His legendary connection with Tezcatlipoca is interesting. In one myth the two are mentioned as creating-gods, who raised the heavens after they had fallen upon the earth at the end of the last mythical period. In another they are shown as foes, and it is Tezcatlipoca who by his machinations drives Quetzalcoatl from Tulan. The latter story probably represents the retirement of the Toltec before the advancing waves of Nahua migration. As might be expected, Quetzalcoatl is closely associated with the peoples of the eastern coast, he wears Huaxtec dress, and the Olmec are mentioned as his children ; further, he was worshipped at Tlaxcala and Uexotzinco, and especially at Cholula, cities in which the Toltec at their dispersal had settled in numbers. Cholula was in fact the centre of his worship in later times, and his great pyramid there, greater even than that of Uitzilopochtli in Mexico, was regarded with particular veneration by the surrounding peoples, even by the Aztec conquerors. One legend makes Quetzalcoatl the chief agent in the final creation of man. According to this story he goes to the underworld to fetch bones ; as he returns he falls, the bones drop to earth and quails gnaw them. Finally Ciuacoatl pounds them up and makes a paste from which men are formed. The same myth shows him as the discoverer of maize, which was concealed in the mountain Tonacatepetl. All the gods were searching for it, but the way was known to the ants alone. Quetzalcoatl turns himself into a black ant, and a red ant guides him thither, but the mountain is too heavy to lift, so the god Xolotl (in his manifestation as Nanauatzin) splits it open. This god Xolotl, who will be mentioned later, is closely associated in dress and attributes with Quetzalcoatl, as also are the octli-gods, and he is sometimes given as the hero of the creation-myth quoted above. But the maize was not destined to remain the possession of Quetzalcoatl, for it was stolen by Tlaloc, to whom since that time it belongs. In many of the invocations given by Sahagun, Quetzalcoatl is mentioned as a creator-god. A peculiar point in connection with this deity is seen in the practice of professional thieves, who were accustomed to make an image of Quetzalcoatl which they carried with them when they set out to rob a house. The explanation may be sought in the fact that the wind-god was naturally typical of mutability, and so was patron of sorcery and might be supposed to aid the magical precautions taken by robbers to cast sleep upon the inmates of the house which they wished to attack, as related below. A peculiar legend accounts for the feather-work garments and mask worn by Quetzalcoatl ; from two sources we learn that this god was extremely ugly, and one of them adds that when Tezcatlipoca showed him his reflection in his mirror, Quetzalcoatl was so ashamed that he adopted these aids to concealment. The other states that his image was always kept covered.

Besides Tezcatlipoca, there were also other high gods, whose functions related to creation and generation, but, like many high gods among primitive peoples, the amount of active worship paid them was relatively small. Such were Tonacatecutli and his wife Tonacaciuatl, dwellers in the highest heaven, who were said to be Toltec deities, and were identified with Ometecutli and Omeciuatl, also associated with Tulan. The creation once over, they received little direct worship, save that appeals were made to them in invocations relative to pregnancy and birth. Tonacatecutli was also identified with Chicome Xochitl (" Seven Flower," a calendrical name), in which manifestation he appeared as a fertility-god, and Tonacaciuatl was at times likewise identified with Xochiquetzal and Chicome Coatl. Attention has already been called to the manner in which the Aztec tried to add to the dignity of their tribal god by transferring to him the functions of other deities, and it is not therefore surprising to find in one passage that Uitzilopochtli is identified with Tonacatecutli. Connected with the creator-deities are two interesting personalities, Oxomoco (male) and Cipactonal (female). These were the prototypes of all magicians, patrons of the magical arts, assistants in the creation of men and in the discovery of maize, and general advisers in the migration of the Nahua tribes. The material attributes

E

of these personages are not clear, and it is difficult to find a pictorial representation which can be said with certainty to portray either of them. As regards Mictlantecutli, the god of the underworld, the case is quite otherwise ; he is very frequently shown, and nearly always takes the form of a skeleton, often with a stone knife in place of his nose (Fig. 4, b). Skulls and bones are his inevitable accompaniments, the owl is his bird, and his feminine partner was named Mictlanciuatl. Other elemental divinities, of rather nebulous attributes, were the sky-gods Citlalicue and Citlaltonac, who were associated with the creator-gods, the sun and the morning star ; and also Yoaltecutli and Yoalticitl, night-deities, of whom the former seems to be identified with the sun and the constellation Gemini, and the latter with Teteoinnan.

We now come to a deity of great importance, the sun, called by the name of Tonatiuh, and the calendrical name of Naui Olin ("Four Movement," Fig. 4, e). This god is easily recognizable by the sun-disc, set about with divergent rays, which he carries, and by his nose-ornament and long quetzal-feathers. Mexican legend recognizes no less than four previous suns, each marking a world period, and each terminating in a convulsion of nature which resulted in a universal destruction. Accounts differ as regards the order of these suns, but the authentic version is probably that which is supported by the so-called " calendar-stone " figured on Pl. VIII, 1, and Fig. 8. According to this version, when all was dark, Tezcatlipoca transformed himself into the sun to give light to men. This sun, known by the calendrical name of Naui Ocelotl (Four Ocelot), terminated in the destruction of mankind, including a race of giants, by jaguars. Quetzalcoatl became the second sun, called Naui Eecatl (" Four Wind "), and the age terminated in a terrible hurricane, during which mankind was transformed into

PLATE VI

2

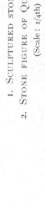

MEXICO

1. SCULPTURED STONE VASE

2. STONE FIGURE OF QUETZALCOATL
(Scale : 1/4th)

1

monkeys. The third sun, Naui Quiauitl ("Four Rain"), was Tlaloc, and the destruction came by means of a rain of fire. The fourth was Chalchiutlicue, Naui Atl ("Four Water"), and mankind was finally destroyed by a deluge, during which they became fishes. The present sun, Naui Olin (" Four Movement ") is destined to conclude with an earthquake.

A fuller account of the birth of the historical sun runs as follows. All the gods were assembled at Teotihuacan, waiting for the appearance of the planet and performing penance. A great fire was prepared, into which, after some hesitation, the syphilitic god Nanauatzin (a manifestation of the dog-headed sun- and lightning-deity, the patron of twins, Xolotl) leaped, reappearing later as the sun. Fired by his example, Tecociztecatl leaped after him, but he failed to spring into the glowing heart of the fire and he reappeared as the moon, the surface of which is clouded with the black ashes of the pyre. A variant myth makes Quetzalcoatl cast his son into the fire to become the sun, while Tlaloc throws his son in later and he becomes the moon. The sun once created, some nourishment had to be found for him, and various gods sacrificed themselves so that he might obtain sustenance from their blood and hearts. A variant legend narrates the special creation of the Centzon Mimizcoa who by fighting might provide the sun with the necessary blood-offerings. The connection of the sun with the war-gods is therefore very close, for war in Mexico was in the main of a ceremonial nature, undertaken with the express purpose of obtaining prisoners for sacrifice, and not necessarily with the intention of inflicting mortal hurt upon the foe. It is in this sense that in a ceremonial invocation to Uitzilopochtli, the warrior-god, the deity is made to exclaim " Through me has the sun risen." From this point of view the sun is closely connected with the souls of warriors perishing in war or on the sacrificial stone, who escorted the orb from the eastern horizon to the zenith ; and also with the souls of women dying in child-birth, the female counterparts of the warriors, who accompanied it from the zenith to its setting. These female souls were deified under the name of Ciuapipiltin or Ciuateteo, and were supposed to descend to the earth on certain dates and inflict maladies on children (Fig. 3, *d*). They are included under the general term of Tzitzimimé, lightning-demons, of whom Itzpapalotl was one, and whose advent to destroy the world was greatly feared during eclipses and at the end of each fifty-two-year period. Associated with the sun as escort was Xolotl, the dog-headed god of twins and monstrosities, and, in invocations, the earth-god Tlaltecutli, who, like him, was supposed to be

nourished with the blood of warriors killed in fight and sacrifice. The creation of the moon, Meztli, in the person of Tecociztecatl has already been mentioned, but other deities were connected with it, especially those associated with vegetation. The waxing and waning of the moon was supposed to typify the process of nature, and

FIG. 6.—The moon.
(*Borgia MS., Rome*)

the moon was supposed to exercise an influence over vegetable growth ; it is even possible that the phases of this satellite may have possessed a calendrical significance before the invention of the solar year. Consequently we find the earth-goddess Tlazolteotl associated with Meztli, and also the harvest-gods, the Totochtin. Probably the connection with the Totochtin was emphasized by the fact that the Mexicans, instead of the " man in the moon," saw the figure of a rabbit (tochtli) in the disc (Fig. 6). Both Tlazolteotl and the Totochtin wear semi-lunar nose-ornaments, exactly similar to the outline of the moon as shown in manuscripts, which often portray it as a curved bone filled with water. A more or less constant emblem of the moon-god is a spiral sea-shell, which he bears partly in his capacity as a god of birth.

Another elemental god of great importance in domestic as well as public worship was the fire-god, known to the Aztec under the name of Xiuhtecutli (Fig. 3, c). His worship probably dated from a very early period, and he also bore the name of Ueueteotl, "the old-old god." Among the Tarascans, this deity was the centre of the domestic cult, and the Tepanec and Otomi worshipped him under the name of Otontecutli. Under this name he was invoked in historic times by the inhabitants of the Tepanec cities of Azcapotzalco and Tlacopan and of Colhuacan. At Xochimilco the fire-deity appears as a goddess, under the name of Chantico or Quaxolotl. Xiuhtecutli is generally shown with a horizontally-banded face (in this respect the illustration in Fig. 3, c, is not typical), and his prevailing colour is yellow. On his back he bears the fire-snake, xiuhcoatl (see Pl. V, 2), and a butterfly, papalotl, frequently appears in his hair. It may be mentioned that in general horizontal face-paint seems to be characteristic of the gods of the immigrant hunter tribes, the vertical of the agricultural gods of the sedentary tribes of the valley. The butterfly is closely connected with fire, since the fluttering flight of this insect was supposed to resemble the flicker of a flame. Mexican mythology is full of poetical imagery of this sort, which constitutes a welcome relief to the gruesomeness of many of their rites. The fire-god was connected with perhaps the most horrible of their sacrifices ; at his most important feast the victims were cast living into a huge brazier, and dragged thence with hooks before death brought a welcome relief, to have their hearts torn from their bodies in the customary manner. An unexpected feature of this god is exemplified in the belief that he was supposed to dwell in the water. As mentioned above, Tezcatlipoca is connected with fire, in so far as he is supposed first to have produced it from flint, after assuming the form of Mixcoatl.

Besides the gods mentioned above there were a number with special functions, a few of whom may now be mentioned. Gods connected with, or invoked during, pregnancy and at birth, besides Chalchiuhtlicue, Ciuacoatl, Teteoinnan, Xochiquetzal and the creating deities, were Chalchiuhtlatonac, associated with Chalchiuhtlicue, and Ayopechtli, the goddess of birth proper, who, like Mayauel, is usually represented as seated on a tortoise. To Ixtlilton, the black god, brother of Macuil xochitl, a sacrifice was made when the child first spoke, and he was regarded as the medical god for children. Other gods, already mentioned, with medical functions were Amimitl (dysentery), Macuilxochitl, Xochiquetzal and Nanauatzin (genital affections), Tlaloc (dropsy), Xipe (skin-diseases), Cinteotl (leprosy), Tezcatlipoca and Tlauizcalpantecutli (senders of sickness), Teteoinnan (goddess of healing herbs), and Tzapotlatenan (who discovered the healing properties of turpentine). The various guilds in Mexico, constituted by members of particular trades, held special rites in honour of those gods who were supposed to preside over their daily activities. Space forbids the inclusion of a complete list, since most can be identified from the details given above. One god however deserves especial mention, Yacatecutli, the god of the Pochteca or travelling merchants, who formed a guild of enormous political importance as will be shown later. Every night while on a journey the merchants, who travelled in companies, burnt incense before their staves which, fastened in a bundle, represented his image, and elaborate rites were held in his honour before their departure and on their return. He was associated in worship with Coyotlinauatl, the god of the guild of feather-workers who in-

habited the quarter of Amantlan, which was contermin-
ous with the quarter of the Pochteca. Finally a peculiar
god, whose function, other than calendrical, is indeter-
minate, may be mentioned ; the bear-headed Tepeyollotl, the " heart of the mountain," a cave-god. He is
often shown with Tezcatlipoca's mirror, and may be a
manifestation of that omnipresent deity.

Such were the principal gods worshipped in the
Mexican valley at the time of the conquest ; there
were many minor deities also, but sufficient has been
said to give some idea of the Mexican pantheon, and to
indicate its composite nature. Most of the gods were
supposed to dwell in supernatural regions such as Tlalocan, the eastern paradise and home of Tlaloc which has
already been mentioned, and Mictlan, the underworld
and home of Mictlantecutli, which consisted of nine
spheres in the lowest of which was a ninefold stream.
Above were thirteen heavens, in the first of which were
certain planets, in the second the Tzitzimimé, in the
third the Centzon Mimizcoa, in the fourth birds, in the
fifth fire-snakes (comets) created by the fire-god, in the
sixth winds, in the seventh dust, in the eighth the gods.
The rest were reserved for Tonacatecutli and his
consort, whose especial home was the thirteenth and
highest heaven.

The elements of Mexican religion then are twofold,
and consist of three classes of supernatural being, each
bearing a direct relation to the mode of life of their especial worshippers. These consist of the rain- and fertility-deities of the agricultural peoples; the stellar war- and
hunting-gods of the nomadic tribes who were regarded
in the light of personal leaders ; and the omnipotent
creating-gods, such as Tonacatecutli and Tezcatlipoca,
common to both. The tribal gods of the nomadic
peoples seem to partake of the nature of fetishes in their
original forms, and to have been evolved from the
" medicine bundles " familiar to the student of North

American ethnography. The more cultured section of the first immigrants, who separated from the main body and departed eastwards, are represented as taking with them their god and leader, whose image was kept veiled in cloth ; and allusion has already been made to the statement that Quetzalcoatl's image was in early days kept similarly covered. Moreover a legend dealing with the Aztec migration states that at an early stage of their wanderings two bundles appeared miraculously in their camp, each of which was appropriated by a section of the migrants. In one was found a jewel, and its possessors finally became the inhabitants of Tlaltelolco, while the other contained fire-sticks (continually associated with hunting and stellar deities), and fell to the eventual inhabitants of Tenochtitlan. Further evidence of the fetish nature of such gods is seen in the stories which tell of struggles between different tribes for the possession of a certain god. Thus we have the story of the capture of the god of the immigrant hill-hunters by the sedentary population around lake Pazcuaro in Michoacan ; and the seizure by the Chichimec of the two-headed deer of Camaxtli which was his war-fetish. The same idea survived in the provision by the Mexicans within the temple precincts of a prison-house where the idols of conquered tribes were kept in durance ; and it was no doubt based upon the belief that once a people was deprived of the god who was its personal leader, its prestige and power must necessarily vanish.

The worship of so many deities involved a cult of no little elaboration, and it must be remembered that apart from the festivals which were observed universally, each tribe, each province, each quarter in Mexico, each guild (often the remains of a former tribe), and each family were punctual in the observance of various domestic and private rites ; and though most of the literature which has come down to us is concerned with the national worship, yet no doubt the domestic cults, for the most part unchronicled, were regarded by the individual as of greater importance, from the point of view that they had a more direct bearing upon his personal prosperity.

Naturally the worship paid to the divine powers varied very greatly in nature according to the mental and cultural status of the worshippers. Many of the myths are extremely crude, and evidently the product of a very low stage of civilization ; but on the other hand, many of the prayers given by Sahagun show a high degree of spirituality. The existence of a professional priesthood carefully trained in astronomy and letters, together with the natural bent of the American mind towards poetic imagery, fostered the evolution of beliefs among the more educated which no doubt differed as much in quality from the superstitions of the populace as those of the higher classes in Peru or in India. Rites which in appearance were crude and savage possessed for the adept a symbolic and esoteric meaning which transformed, even if it did not entirely excuse, their barbarity. Symbolism is the keynote of American ritual, and it is this symbolism which makes the religious manuscripts so difficult of interpretation.

Though practically all the supernatural powers were personified in human form, yet traces are found of more direct worship of nature in Tlaxcala, where, according to Motolinia, altars were erected to trees, and four altars might be found arranged round a spring. Indications of tree-worship were also found among the Mixtec who were said to make offerings to the shadows of lofty trees. In Oaxaca, among the Mixtec and Zapotec, traces of a different kind of religion make their appearance. It is true that here too (in parts of the Mixtec territory) we have immigration legends, pointing to the supposition that a portion of the population came from the north ; but other, and probably older, myths exist which narrate the birth of the human race from trees, rocks and wild beasts. Myths of this nature are far more typical of Peru as a whole than of Mexico and Central America. Another peculiarity of Mixtec and Zapotec worship is the great number of cave-temples, many of them so holy that they became centres of pilgrimage. Some of these shrines were oracular, and one of them, at Achiutla, held such a high reputation that Montecuzoma sent an embassy to consult it at the coming of the Spaniards. Human sacrifice was practised by both these tribes, though to a far less extent than by the Mexicans, the heart of the victim being held to the lips of the idol of stone or wood. Traces of lake-worship also occur, another point in common with Peru and Colombia, in so far as at Tecomastlahuaca (immediately S.E. of Cuicatlan) was a sacred lake into which the bodies of victims were thrown ; and at Teotitlan was a celebrated idol which was said to have descended from heaven in the form of a bird in the midst of a luminous constellation, a myth which would seem to have certain Maya affinities, as will be seen later. At Cuilapa in the Zapotec country was current a creation legend not unlike some of the Mexican ætio-logical myths. According to this the creator and his progeny bore calendrical names, and these semi-deities built their palaces on a huge rock on the summit of which was a copper axe, with the edge upwards, sup-porting the heavens. This preliminary age was termin-ated by a great deluge, after which the creator re-peopled the world with the human race.

CHAPTER III—MEXICO: THE CALENDAR AND CALENDRICAL FEASTS

MEXICAN ritual was so closely connected with the elaborate calendar that some explanation of the latter is necessary before it is possible to give an intelligible description of the various rites and ceremonies by which the favour of the gods was sought. The origin of this calendar is obscure, and can only be discussed in relation to the Maya calendar, with which it is obviously connected; so it will be best to leave this question to a later page, stating here only that in Mexico it was supposed to be the invention of Quetzalcoatl, and transmitted to the Nahua peoples through the agency of the two prototypes of magicians, Oxomoco and Cipactonal. The Mexican calendar is twofold, and comprises a ritual calendar, with a round of 260 days, which was employed in divination and for the fixing of certain " movable feasts," and a solar calendar, with a round of 365 days, according to which the seasonal feasts were held. The method of naming the individual days was the same for both, and consisted in the combination of twenty pictorial signs (Fig. 7) with the numbers one to thirteen. The signs were as follows (see Appendix I):

1. *Cipactli.* The head of a monstrous animal, identified now with the alligator, now with the sword-fish, and appearing in the manuscripts sometimes with legs and sometimes with fins. According to legend, the earth was created from the primordial cipactli, and the irregularities of the earth's surface are due to the scaly prominences on the animal's back. The date 1. cipactli

is given as that of the creation, and the sign is especially associated with Tonacatecutli and fruitfulness.

2. *Eecatl.* The head of the wind-god ; typifying instability.

3. *Calli.* A house, implying rest ; associated with Tepeyollotl.

4. *Quetzpalin.* A lizard, associated with the rising of the water and fertility ; also with a god Ueuecoyotl (the " Old Wolf ").

FIG. 7.—Mexican day signs.

a.	cipactli.	*h.*	tochtli.	*o.*	quauhtli.
b.	eecatl.	*i.*	atl.	*p.*	cozcaquauhtli.
c.	calli.	*j.*	itzcuintli.	*q.*	olin.
d.	quetzpalin.	*k.*	ozomatli.	*r.*	tecpatl.
e.	coatl.	*l.*	malinalli.	*s.*	quiauitl.
f.	miquiztli.	*m.*	acatl.	*t.*	xochitl.
g.	mazatl.	*n.*	ocelotl.		

(*Fejérváry-Mayer MS., Liverpool*)

5. *Coatl.* A snake, typifying poverty and homelessness ; associated with Chalchiuhtlicue.

6. *Miquiztli.* The head of Mictlantecutli, an unlucky sign.

7. *Mazatl.* The head or hoof of a deer ; unlucky because the deer typifies timidity ; associated with Tlaloc.

8. *Tochtli.* A rabbit, good luck and fertility ; associated with Mayauel.

9. *Atl.* Water, unlucky, typifying floods and death; associated with Xiuhtecutli.

10. *Itzcuintli.* A dog (sometimes the ear only is shown), rank and riches; associated with Mictlantecutli.

11. *Ozomatli.* A monkey, implies cleverness and craftsmanship, combined with instability; associated with Xochipilli.

12. *Malinalli.* Grass, sometimes shown as a jawbone with grass hair, unlucky; associated with Patecatl.

13. *Acatl.* A reed, implying emptiness; associated with Itztlacoliuhqui.

14. *Ocelotl.* An ocelot (sometimes the ear only is shown); success in war and love, but suggesting a death by sacrifice (the typical death of a warrior). Associated with Tlazolteotl.

15. *Quauhtli.* An eagle, implying courage in war; associated with Xipe.

16. *Cozcaquauhtli.* A vulture, signifying old age; associated with Itzpapalotl.

17. *Olin.* A sign emblematical of movement (used also to signify an earthquake). Variable in fortune, and associated with Nanauatzin.

18. *Tecpatl.* A stone knife, the emblem of drought and sterility, associated with Tezcatlipoca.

19. *Quiauitl.* The head of Tlaloc, emblem of rain; an unlucky sign.

20. *Xochitl.* A flower, implying good craftsmanship; associated with Xochiquetzal.

These signs ran consecutively in the order given above, one being assigned to each day, and the series was repeated *ad infinitum.* Conjointly with them were repeated the numerals 1 to 13; e.g. 1. cipactli, 2. eecatl, 3. calli, and so on to 13. acatl, which was followed by 1. ocelotl, 2. quauhtli, and so forth. There being no common factor to the numbers 13 and 20, a period of

13 × 20 days, or 260, would elapse before the sign 1. cipactli would recur. This period of 260 days consti- tuted the ritual and divinatory calendar, known as the *tonalamatl*. The tonalamatl was subdivided in various ways ; in some manuscripts each of the twenty thir- teen-day periods, or " weeks," is shown separately, together with the figure of a god who was especially associated with the first day, but whose influence was supposed to extend over the whole " week." The deities presiding over the successive " weeks " of the tonala- matl are given in one MS. (Vaticanus A) as follows, the date preceding the name of each being that of the first day of each " week."

1. cipactli, Tonacatecutli.
1. ocelotl, Quetzalcoatl.
1. mazatl, Tepeyollotl.
1. xochitl, Ueuecoyotl.
1. acatl, Chalchiuhtlicue.
1. miquiztli, Tonatiuh.
1. quiauitl, Tlaloc.
1. malinalli, Mayauel.
1. coatl, Tlauizcalpantecutli.
1. tecpatl, Tonatiuh.
1. ozomatli, Patecatl.
1. quetzpalin, Itztlacoliuhqui.
1. olin, Tlazolteotl.
1. itzcuintli, Xipe.
1. calli, Itzpapalotl.
1. cozcaquauhtli, Xolotl.
1. atl, Chalchiuhtlicue.
1. eecatl, Chantico.
1. quauhtli, Xochiquetzal.
1. tochtli, Itztli.

There is however some variation in the assignment of the week-gods, e.g. Sahagun gives 1. miquiztli to Tezcatlipoca, 1. acatl to Quetzalcoatl, 1. tecpatl to Uitzilopochtli, etc. Within the weeks, many indi-

vidual days were associated with certain deities, such
as 4. olin and 12. itzcuintli with the sun, 5. itzcuintli
and 6. quetzpalin with Mictlantecutli, but for a list of
these the reader may be referred to Sahagun. Apart
from the signs of the days themselves, the presiding
deities of the weeks, and the gods of the individual
dates, the numerical signs also possessed a lucky or unlucky connotation. Three and four were good numbers,
five and six generally bad, seven always good, eight and
nine bad, ten, eleven, twelve and thirteen good. Consequently the diviner was obliged to take into account
all these possible influences, which in many cases might
be contradictory, in considering the fortune attached
to a particular day. In some MSS. the tonalamatl is
arranged on a different system, viz. in five long horizontal rows of fifty-two days each. Each row, and
each vertical column of five days, is provided with a
presiding deity or symbol, the influence of which
must be assessed. Nor have we yet come to an end of
the factors which must be taken into consideration,
but before proceeding it will be necessary to explain
the solar calendar.

The Mexicans reckoned 365 days to the solar year,
which they divided into eighteen months of twenty
days each, and a nineteenth period of five days, considered extremely unlucky, at the end of the year. As
the days were known by their tonalamatl names, it is
obvious that the first 115 days of the year recurred at
the end. But it was possible to distinguish between
two days of the same name which fell in the same year,
owing to the fact that each day was associated with one
of a series of nine deities, called " lords of the night," a
series also repeated *ad infinitum*, save that no " lord "
was assigned to any of the five unlucky days at the end
of the year, which were called *nemontemi* or " useless
days." Thus, since the number 260 is not divisible by
9, it was possible to differentiate between two days of

the same name falling in one year ; and since 9 goes into 360 without remainder, the commencement of the year coincided with the commencement of the series of " lords of the night." These lords of the night are indicated by the heads or symbols of the following gods : 1. Xiuhtecutli, 2. Itztli, 3. Tonatiuh, 4. Cinteotl, 5. Mictlantecutli, 6. Chalchiuhtlicue, 7. Tlazolteotl, 8. Tepeyollotl and 9. Tlaloc. Nor is this all, a corresponding series of thirteen " lords of day," which however is not similarly composed in all MSS., accompanied the days (omitting the nemontemi), and the influences of the day- and night-lord assigned to each day respectively constituted two additional features for the consideration of the would-be interpreter of the tonalamatl. It is perhaps hardly necessary to state that the reading of the book of days was in the hands of a professional priesthood and required much study to perform correctly.

Since each " month " consisted of twenty days, and there were twenty day-signs, it is obvious that each month in a given year began with the same sign ; but since the last month was followed by the five unlucky days, it follows that each year began with a day-sign five days later than the last. Also since 365 is divisible by 13 with 1 as remainder, it follows equally that each year began with a day-number one in advance of the last. Further, since there were twenty day-signs, and five (the least common multiple of 365 and 20) goes into twenty exactly four times, the year began with one of four signs only. Now the year was always distinguished by the sign of the day on which it began, and it is a peculiar fact that the commencement of the year never coincided with the commencement of the tonalamatl. The four signs which give the names to the years are the signs tecpatl, calli, tochtli and acatl, recurring in that order. Whether the day-number entering into the name of the year was that of the first day, as held by most authorities, or of the first day of the fifth month, as Seler tries to prove, need not be discussed here ; the fact remains that the years were named successively, 1. tecpatl, 2. calli, 3. tochtli, and so on, until, after a period of fifty-two years (13×4), the same sign occurred again with the same number as the name-date of the year. This period of fifty-two years constituted the shorter cycle of the Mexicans, the longer cycle consisting of twice that number ; but before proceeding further it will be necessary to say something about the months (see Appendix II).

The first month was called Atlcaualco, and the first day according to Sahagun, who wrote about the middle of the sixteenth century, corresponded with the 2nd of February. This month marked the cessation of the rains,[1] and it was represented in calendars by a figure of the god Tlaloc, to whom, together with Chalchiuht-licue, the religious festivals of the month were especially dedicated. Large numbers of children were sacrificed to the rain-god, chiefly on mountains, but also at a certain deep hole in the lagoon, and it was considered a good omen if the small victims wept on their way to the place of sacrifice, since their tears were supposed to portend a plentiful rain-supply. A gladiatorial sacrifice was also made to Xipe during this month.

The second month, Tlacaxipeualiztli, commencing February 22nd, was dedicated to Xipe, and is indicated in MSS. by a figure of this god. Warriors who had taken prisoners in battle brought them to the temple of Uitzilopochtli, holding them by the hair. Here their hearts were offered to the god, their bodies cast down the temple steps and flayed, and their skins assumed by their captors. In the temple of Xipe, called Yopico, elaborate gladiatorial sacrifices were held during this

---

[1] This is according to Sahagun's statement ; at the present time in the valley of Mexico the rains commence in May–June and end in September–October.

F

month, in which captives, tethered one by one by a
rope to the centre of a circular stone (Fig. 5, *b*; p. 41),
were attacked by four warriors in ocelot and eagle
dresses. If the victim could defend himself against
these, a fifth opponent attacked him, a left-handed
man being selected for this purpose. When over-
powered, the victim was sacrificed, either by having
his heart torn out, or by being fastened to a frame-
work and shot with darts (Fig. 5, *a*). The gladiatorial sacrifice is symbolical of war, and the creation-
myths relate how the gods called into being special
bands of warriors whose blood and hearts should be
devoted to the nourishment of the sun and the earth.
War, therefore, was necessary, in order that the pro-
cesses of nature might continue without hindrance,
and war amongst the Mexicans had thus assumed a
ceremonial character. The arrow-sacrifice was apparently introduced from the Huaxtec country, together
with the worship of the earth-goddesses Ixcuinamé, of
whom Tlazolteotl was the chief. It was practised also
at Tlaxcala and Uexotzinco, as explained above. Both
this and the flaying sacrifice partook of the nature of
imitative magic, and had as their object the promotion of fertility, a matter which at this time of the year
was of considerable importance to the Mexicans. For
the ordinary form of sacrifice (Fig. 5, *c*) the victim,
stripped of his ornaments, was stretched on the
sacrificial stone, which was slightly convex in shape.
Five priests, called Chalmeca, held his arms, legs and
head, while the sacrificer slashed open his breast with
a stone knife, and, inserting his hand in the wound,
tore out the heart, which was held for a moment to
the lips of the idol, or offered to the sun, and then
cast into a stone vase, called quauhxicalli, or burnt.
Many of the so-called " calendar stones " are possibly elaborate quauhxicalli ; a good example of the
normal type is figured on Pl. VII, 1. In most cases

PLATE VII

British Museum

I

Photo. C. B. Waite *Mexico Museum*

2

MEXICO

1. STONE QUAUHXICALLI (VASE IN WHICH THE HEARTS OF VICTIMS
WERE DEPOSITED)
2. STONE QUAUHXICALLI IN THE FORM OF AN OCELOT

(Scale, 1, 1/6th : 2, 1/30th)

the body was hurled down the steps of the temple to the court, where it was seized by certain priests and carried away to be dismembered. For sacrifice was sometimes accompanied by cannibalism, though it is interesting to note that at the festival just described the warrior who provided a captive for sacrifice was debarred from eating his flesh, since he was supposed to stand to the victim in the relation of father to son. At this feast, before the body was cast down the steps, the sacrificing priest inserted a tube in the cavity left after the removal of the heart, and extracted a bowlful of blood, which he gave to the victim's master. The latter with this made the round of certain temples, smearing a little of the blood on the lips of the various images.

The third month, Tozoztontli, began on March 14th, and is signified in MSS. by the figure of a maize-goddess. It was a month of first-fruits ; children were sacrificed to Tlaloc, and the first flowers were offered in Xipe's temple, after which ceremony, but not before, their perfume might be inhaled by mortals. The flower-sellers also held a festival in honour of Coatlicue, and those who had provided victims for the sacrifices during the preceding month, discarded the skins which they had worn until now.

The fourth month, Uei tozoztli, beginning on April 3rd, is also represented by the figure of a maize-god, and the presiding deities were Cinteotl and Chicome Coatl. The ceremonies observed concerned the maize-plant, which was used to decorate the altars and temples, while the selected heads destined to be used as seed were offered by young maidens to the above divinities. A peculiar offering was made to the household images of the harvest-god, consisting of baskets of produce, each surmounted by a cooked frog which bore on its back, in a miniature basket, specimens of each of the varieties of grain which composed the offering.

The fifth month, Toxcatl, beginning on April 23rd, was symbolized by a figure of Tezcatlipoca, and was the occasion of the feast which has so often been described ; at which a young man, identified with the god, was sacrificed to him after a year spent in the enjoyment of every luxury that Mexican civilization could afford. The identification of the victim with the god was a frequent feature of Mexican sacrificial ceremonies, and may have been based on the idea, found in many other parts of the world, that, just as the earthly representative of the deity was never allowed to attain old age, so the youthful vigour of the divinity remained unimpaired throughout the years. It may be remarked in this connection that one of the chief characteristics of Tezcatlipoca was perennial youth. A similar, though less important, ceremony was held in honour of Uitzilopochtli in this month.

The sixth month, commencing on May 13th, was called Etzalqualiztli. It was symbolized by a figure of Tlaloc, and ceremonies took place in honour of the Tlaloque. Aquatic plants were gathered by the priests for the manufacture of mats on which the offerings were placed in the shape of small balls of flour-paste ; great care was necessary in setting out the latter, since if one rolled, the movement was taken as a sign that the officiating priest had infringed some law, and he was severely punished. When the priests set out to gather the reeds, they were permitted by custom to rob any passer-by whom they might meet ; they joined in a ceremonial bath in the lake, imitating the motions and cries of aquatic birds, and finally offered a number of human victims who were adorned in the dress and ornaments of the rain-gods. During these ceremonies severe punishment was inflicted upon priests who had broken any ceremonial rule during the year.

In Tecuiluitontli, the seventh month (June 2nd), typified by the figure of Uixtociuatl, the festival of this, the goddess of salt, was held. Flowers played a large part in the ceremonies, and the sacrifices consisted of a woman, identified with the goddess, and a number of captives.

Uei tecuiluitl, the eighth month (June 22nd), was devoted to Xilonen, and the figure of a noble (or of Xochipilli) appears as its symbol. During the festivals, large distributions of provisions were made by the rich, since this season was wont to be one of scarcity, for as yet it was not lawful to make use of the new crop of maize. Special features of the ceremonials were a dance by accredited warriors clad in all their *insignia*, and the sacrifice, in the temple of Cinteotl, of a woman dressed as the goddess. The victim was taken by one of the priests on his back, and in that position she was decapitated, and her heart offered. The chicauaztli or rattle-staff, a rain-charm, played a prominent part in the ceremonies, which were essentially of the nature of a removal of a tabu from the maize-crop.

Tlaxochimaco, the ninth month (July 12th), was symbolized either by a figure of Uitzilopochtli or of a mummy ; and on this occasion the god appeared in benevolent guise. The festival was a flower-feast, and quantities of blossoms were collected to be offered as first-fruits to the god. It comes as a welcome relief to note that no human victims were offered during these ceremonies, which must have afforded a spectacle of great beauty.

The tenth month, Xocouetzi (August 1st), however, made up in gruesomeness for the simplicity of the last. A festival was held in honour of Xiuhtecutli, the figure of a mummy appearing as symbol, and the terrible fire-sacrifice mentioned on p. 53 was made. A feature of the proceedings was the erection of a lofty pole, surmounted by a figure of the god made of flour-paste, and the final ceremony consisted in a contest on the part of the young men to swarm up the pole and reach the figure, the victor being entitled to certain rewards and *insignia*. Both the last two month-festivals had a certain connection with honours paid to the dead. During the latter the Tlaxcalans especially performed rites in memory of deceased warriors and princes.

Ochpaniztli, the eleventh month (August 21st), was symbolized by a figure of Teteoinnan, in whose honour the ceremonies were held. A woman, dressed as the goddess, was decapitated by a priest of Chicome Coatl, and flayed, the skin from her thigh being made into a mask for the priest of Cinteotl ; she was not told of her fate, since it was of great importance that she should not weep. Sacrifices were also made to Uitzilopochtli, and the proceedings included a battle of flowers and the distribution by the king of military rewards and *insignia*. The skin-mask worn by the priest of Cinteotl was finally deposited on a hostile frontier, and the occasion was often marked by a skirmish with the foe who lay in wait for the escort.

Teotleco, the twelfth month (September 10th), symbolized by a figure of Tezcatlipoca, was signalized by a feast in honour of all the gods, who were believed to have left the country for a season, and were now about to return. Tezcatlipoca, the god of perennial youth, was believed to arrive in advance of the rest, while Yacatecutli and Xiuhtecutli came a day after the main body ; the former because, as the god of travelling merchants, he might be supposed to have wandered further afield, the latter because he was essentially the old god, and could not be expected to travel so fast. For the arrival of the main body, a heap of maize-meal was prepared by a priest, who visited it at intervals until the mark of a footprint announced the arrival of the holy travellers ; this was the signal for universal rejoicing. A large amount of octli was consumed, this proceeding being termed " washing the feet of the

gods." The festival terminated with the burning alive
of a number of slaves.

Tepeiluitl, the thirteenth month (September 30th),
ushered in the festival in honour of the mountain-gods,
and was signified by the figure of a mountain with the
head of Tlaloc. Numbers of snake-figures of wood
(emblems of the lightning) were prepared, as well as
images of the mountains in meal-paste, and certain
victims, identified with fertility-deities were sacrificed
to Tlaloc. The festival was held partly in honour of
those who had perished by drowning or the lightning
stroke, or by some other death which necessitated
burial as opposed to cremation.

In Quecholli, the fourteenth month (October 20th),
was held the festival of Mixcoatl, whose figure appears
as its symbol. A strict fast was observed, during which
large numbers of arrows were made, which were
offered in bundles of twenty to Uitzilopochtli. Miniature arrows were deposited on the graves of the dead,
and, on the tenth day, a great communal hunt was
organized, on the mountain called Zacatepec, in which
various surrounding tribes joined. A victim, the representative of the god, was offered to Mixcoatl, and a
number of slaves to Tezcatlipoca ; some of the latter
being carried up the temple steps bound hand and foot
like captive deer.

Panquetzaliztli, the fifteenth month (November
9th), ushered in the great feast of Uitzilopochtli, whose
figure is shown as its emblem. The proceedings were
symbolical in part of the mythical fight between this
god and his hostile brothers, the Centzon Uitznaua,
since a great ceremonial combat was organized between
the slaves destined as sacrifices. In this one party represented the god, the other the Uitznaua, and a great
figure of the Xiuhcoatl, the mythical weapon of Uitzilopochtli, figured later in the proceedings. During
the fight, the image of Paynal made a rapid ceremonial

tour of certain temples, and the sacrifice which terminated the festival was accompanied by music.

In the sixteenth month, Atemoztli (November 29th),
the first rains usually appeared in the mountains (according to Sahagun, but see footnote on p. 65), and
sacrifices were offered to Tlaloc, who appears as the
symbol. Figures of the mountain-gods were made from
meal-paste, and these were "sacrificed" with a weaver's
sword.

The seventeenth month, Tititl (December 19th),
was symbolized by a figure of Ilamatecutli, whose
representative, a woman, was sacrificed in the ordinary
way in the temple of Uitzilopochtli, though her head
was immediately removed, and carried by the officiating priest in the ceremonial dance which followed.

The last month, Izcalli (January 8th), was dedicated
to Xiuhtecutli, whose portrait appears as emblem.
Various land and water animals were captured by children and young men, who gave them to the officiating
priest to cast into the sacrificial fire before the god.
Human sacrifice was offered only every fourth year,
and the ears of children born in the interval were
pierced in the presence of the god.

The remaining five days of the year, called Nemontemi, were regarded as extremely unfortunate. No
work was done, and the people went out as little as
possible, for an evil omen encountered during this
period was regarded as doubly unlucky. In particular
every attempt was made to avoid quarrelling and dis-
pute, and the time was one of general inaction.

The feasts of the solar calendar have been detailed at
some length in order to give an idea of the nature of
Mexican religious practice, and to show to what an extent religious observances entered into the life of the
people. Those who desire fuller particulars will find
them in Sahagun's great work. Space forbids a description of the various ceremonies relating to certain in-

dividual days of the ritual calendar or tonalamatl, but that performed on the day 4. olin, sacred to Tonatiuh, deserves short mention. A prisoner, in merchant's dress, was taken to the shrine called Quauhcalli and set upon a large stone carved with the image of the sun. Standing thus he declaimed a message to the god, with which he had been entrusted, and was forthwith stripped of his ornaments and sacrificed upon the stone itself. Seler conjectures that the famous so-called " calendar-stone " in the Mexican museum is the stone to which reference is made in this account. This magnificent specimen of the Mexican stone-mason's art is figured on Pl. VIII, 1, and a schematic drawing is seen in Fig. 8. The outer band of decoration is formed by two fire-snakes, each with a human face in its mouth. At the top, in a square cartouche, is the glyph 13. acatl, the date of birth of the historical sun (see p. 51). The day-signs in order form an inner ornamental band, and in the centre is a large olin glyph, accompanied by the number 4, and with a sun-face in the middle. Within the arms of the olin are sculptured the calendrical names of the four previous suns, and in the interspaces are the glyphs 1. tecpatl, the sign used for the name of Montecuzoma, 1. quiauitl, and 7. ozomatli, the significance of which has not yet been satisfactorily explained. Outside the day-signs are seen the pointed emblems which typify the rays of the sun, which enter also into the glyph by which the Mexicans expressed the meaning " year " (Fig. 86, l; p. 356).

Two other special festivals connected with the solar calendar call for mention. The first of these occurred every eight years, in the month of Quecholli or Tepeiluitl ; it was called Atamalqualiztli, and during it only bread and water were consumed, with the intention of letting other food-products rest. An image of Tlaloc was set up, and the worshippers performed a ceremonial dance clad in various animal costumes. An

interesting feature of the ceremonies was the following :
In front of the image of the god was a tank of water,
containing frogs and snakes. A number of men called
Mazateca, perhaps inhabitants of the Mazatec district,
tried to seize one of these animals in his mouth, without
using his hands, and having succeeded, continued to
dance with it in his teeth. The custom has a strange

FIG. 8.—Key to the " calendar-stone " figured on Pl. VIII, I.

resemblance to the snake-dance performed by the
Pueblo Indians up to the present time.

The other festival was that which occurred every
fifty-two years, when the year-date 2. acatl recurred.
The occasion was considered as especially dangerous
to mortal men, since it was feared that the sun might
fail to rise, and the Tzitzimimé demons would descend from the first heaven to destroy mankind and
so bring about the end of the world. The principal

PLATE VIII

I

2

MEXICO

1. THE "CALENDAR STONE"

2. STONE FIGURE OF AN OCTLI GOD

(Scale : 1, 1/50th ; 2, 1/6th)

feature of the ceremonies was the production of new
fire by means of the ceremonial firesticks (Fig. 9),
and it was upon the successful performance of this
operation that the rising of the sun was supposed
to depend. On the eve of the new year all fires were
extinguished, and the priests started in procession to
the top of the mountain Uixachtlan, outside Mexico,
timing their arrival just before midnight. At midnight, which was calculated by observation of the

FIG. 9.—Priests making new fire.
(*Zouche MS., British Museum*)

Pleiads, the high-priest of the Calpulco quarter of
Mexico, kindled the new fire on the breast of a prisoner,
who was sacrificed immediately after in the usual manner. Representatives of the surrounding cities were present, and torches lit at the new fire were rapidly carried
to the chief temples in each city, where the populace
awaited their arrival in the greatest anxiety. From
the temples the fire was distributed all over the city,
and universal rejoicings hailed the commencement of a
new era and the deliverance of the world from universal destruction. Old garments were discarded, and all
household utensils were broken or freshly painted in

token of the new lease of life given to mankind. A peculiar custom in connection with these ceremonies is seen in the fact that women expecting to become mothers, and young children, were made to assume masks of maguey leaves, and the former were shut up in the granaries. It was feared that women in this condition might become monsters and devour their relations, and that the children might be turned into mice, especially if they were allowed to fall asleep. New fire was also made at the dedication of a new temple, or the completion of a new house.

The employment by the Mexicans of a solar year of 365 days brings us to the question whether they at any time intercalated any day or days to make their year square with real solar time. It is quite obvious that a people, most of whose feasts were connected with agriculture, were bound to notice that their festivals gradually failed to correspond with the seasons, and many conjectures have been made regarding the methods which they might have used to rectify their calendar. It must be confessed however that there is no direct evidence that days were ever intercalated in the latter, and Seler has shown that at any rate between the year of the conquest, and the date of Sahagun's writing, some forty years, no intercalation had been made. Moreover the confusion into which the calendar had fallen at the beginning of the sixteenth century seems to be evidence against the practice. It is quite possible that when the discrepancy became too great a new start was made, and it may be that the five " suns " typifying the five ages of the world really represent five attempts to establish a calendar. The sun was not the only body the observation of which served as a check upon the calendar. The planet Venus was also of the greatest importance, and its synodical revolution was closely connected with the 104-year period which constituted the longer cycle of the Mexicans. This revolution occu-

pies practically 584 days, and consequently five such
revolutions are equal to eight years of 365 days. Since
20 when divided into 584 leaves a remainder of 4, it is
obvious that the commencement of a Venus-period will
fall always on one of five of the twenty day-signs.
Further, since 13 when divided into 584 leaves a remainder of 12, it is equally obvious that each successive
Venus-period will open with a day of which the numerical sign is one less than that of the preceding period.
In several of the MSS. we have the Venus-periods set
out in the order in which they occur, viz. on the days
cipactli, coatl, atl, acatl and olin ; 1. cipactli being followed by 13. coatl, the latter by 12. atl, and so forth.
It can be seen that 65 Venus-periods must elapse before
the same sign occurs in conjunction with the same number at the commencement of a period, and this amounts
to 104 years of 365 days, viz. the longer cycle of the
Mexicans. It seems most probable that the Venus-
period was utilized as a means of correcting the 365-
day year, and I am even inclined to believe that observation of this planet was practised before the institution of the solar calendar. But I shall recur to this
point when the subject of the Maya calendar is discussed ; meanwhile it is worthy of note that the signs
of the two last " suns " are atl and olin, signs which
occur as the commencing-days of Venus-periods ; that
the historical sun was supposed to have been born on
13. acatl ; and that the new fire ceremony always took
place in the year 2. acatl. Though the morning star
played such an important part in the regulation of the
calendar, it was not regarded altogether as a beneficent
deity, possibly because of its association with war and
sacrifice among the hunting peoples. However that
may be, its light when it first rose was considered to
exercise a baneful effect upon mankind, and chimneys
were carefully stopped up to prevent the rays from
entering the houses. The cult of Venus was especially

practised at Teotitlan and Tehuacan, where the priests had the reputation of being great calendrical experts. A human sacrifice was performed at the first rising of the star, and offerings of blood and incense were made daily until it commenced to decline. A tradition existed also that the planet was supposed to " shoot " certain classes of individuals in certain signs, and it is interesting to note that in manuscripts the deity in whom it is personified, Tlauizcalpantecutli, is constantly shown hurling darts at other gods and certain animals.

Connected with the calendar was the peculiar regard which the Mexicans paid to the " world-directions." The points of the compass were known by the following names : east, Tlapcopa ; north, Mictlampa ; west, Ciuatlampa ; and south, Uitzlampa. To these a fifth, the central point, was generally added, and, in some cases, the directions up and down. With the east were associated all years with the acatl sign, the paradise Tlalocan, the colour yellow, and the gods Tonatiuh and Itztli. With the north, tecpatl-years, the underworld Mictlan, the colour red, the god Mictlantecutli. In the west was the home of the female deities, especially the earth- and fertility-goddesses, and with it were associated the calli-years and the colour blue. To the south belonged the tochtli-years, the colour white and the god Tlaloc. With the centre the figure of Xiuhtecutli, the god of the hearth-fire, is constantly associated. Other gods are associated also with the four quarters, but the MSS. are often contradictory. The day-signs were divided as follows :

East : cipactli, acatl, coatl, olin, atl.

North : ocelotl, miquiztli, tecpatl, itzcuintli, eecatl.

West : mazatl, quiauitl, ozomatli, calli, quauhtli.

South : xochitl, malinalli, quetzpalin, cozcaquauhtli, tochtli.

In the MSS. the quarters are often typified by four

trees, each springing from the body of the earth-goddess, with a bird perched amidst its branches, and accompanied by the five day-signs belonging to the quarter
which it represents (Fig. 10). In Oaxaca, where the 52-
year cycle was also observed, the years were assigned in
groups of thirteen to the quarters. Those belonging to
the east were supposed to be fertile and healthy ; those

FIG. 10.—The Tree of the West.
(*Borgia MS., Rome*)

to the north, variable ; those to the west, good for
mankind but bad for crops ; while those to the south
were thought to be characterized by excessive heat and
drought.

Among the Tarascans too were found gods associated
with the world-directions, and, as will be seen later,
among the Maya also. The association of the underworld with the north by the Mexicans is interesting as
exemplifying a tendency found amongst primitive
peoples all over the world. The original home of the
Mexicans lay to the north, and consequently it was to
the north that departed spirits took their way, just as
in Polynesia and Melanesia the disembodied souls were

supposed to leap into the sea and disappear in the direction whence their forefathers had arrived.

It is therefore particularly interesting to note that among the Mixtec and Zapotec two spots were pointed out as the entrance to the underworld, and that each of these spots lay in the actual territory inhabited by these tribes respectively. The Mixtec believed that the gate to the region of departed spirits was situated at Chalcatongo, and the place was regarded as a burial-ground of peculiar sanctity. While the Zapotec believed that their sacred city Mitla (or rather Lyobaa, Mitla being the Nahua name) stood on the site of the approach to the spirit-world. This belief, together with the peculiarities in religion mentioned in the last chapter, points to the existence among the population of a large element which may be called indigenous in so far as its beliefs were probably evolved locally and before the advent of the Nahua tribes in Mexico, by contact with whom they were so strongly affected in later years.

In Mexican ceremonial constant attention was paid to the world-directions, and the victim's blood was often sprinkled, and incense offered, in the four directions of the compass.

It will not be necessary to say many words on the subject of Mexican ritual, since much can be gathered from the description of the various feasts given above. In early times human sacrifice seems to have been far from prevalent, and the Chichimec were reputed to have made offerings only of animals and produce until they came into contact with other tribes. But according to the " Annals of Quauhtitlan," human sacrifice had already made its appearance under the Toltec *régime*. The first rite of this nature is said to have been the offering of children to Tlaloc in 1018, while the arrow-sacrifice was introduced from the Huaxtec country in 1058, and the flaying-sacrifice in 1063. But the arrow-sacrifice is mentioned elsewhere at a very early stage of the Nahua migration, in connection with the earth-goddesses. Once introduced into the valley of Mexico, the practice of making human offerings became more and more prevalent, until we find the number of individuals slain during the four-day ceremonies at the dedication of the great temple to Uitzilopochtli by Auitzotl given in two manuscripts as twenty thousand (see Fig. 12; p. 87). The Tezcocan ruler Nezahualcoyotl is said to have forbidden it, and later to have limited it to prisoners of war, but at the time of the conquest it showed no signs of abatement, and Bernal Diaz is constantly referring to the sacrifices which he and his companions were compelled to witness. Spaniards taken prisoner in the hostilities with the Mexicans were invariably devoted to death, and the same chronicler relates the grisly discovery in a temple at Pueblo Morisco of the remains of two of his compatriots, where Sandoval found two " faces which had been flayed, and the skin tanned like skin for gloves, the beards left on, and they had been placed as offerings on one of the altars." The hides of four horses were found at the same place. But terrible as such rites may seem to us, it may be taken as certain that they were regarded almost with equanimity by the Mexicans. Death by sacrifice was considered the normal death of a fighting man, and ensured entrance to the paradise of the Sun. Instances occur where men have deliberately demanded death on the sacrificial stone, notably the king Chimamalpopoca is said to have made arrangements for his own immolation, clad in the *insignia* of Uitzilopochtli. Or again, the Tlaxcalan general Tlahuicol, captured by the Mexicans, who refused his freedom at the hands of Montecuzoma, and subsequently even the rank of general in the Mexican army, and was so persistent in his demands for death on the gladiatorial stone that it was at length granted him.

G

The very cannibalism which, to a limited extent, formed the occasional sequel to human sacrifice, becomes divested of much of its horror when it is remembered that the rite was, in essentials, an act of communion with the deity, with whom the victim was identified. Instances of this identification have been mentioned, and it has been said that the victim, especially he who was condemned to die by the gladiatorial sacrifice, was clad in the *insignia* of the old stellar war- and hunting-deities, Mixcoatl and the Morning Star, *insignia* which are often borne by Uitzilopochtli and the earth-goddesses. The ornament, which was regarded as that typical of the sacrificial victim, was the following : the body and face were painted white with yellow stripes, lips and chin red, and across the eyes was the black " mask " seen in the figures of the star-gods. The hair was covered with down, and the victim carried arrows and a sword tipped and edged with the same material, which also appeared in five bunches on his shield (Fig. 12 ; p. 87).

The act of communion with the god is seen in the many festivals at which an idol of the deity was made of some edible substance, later to be eaten by the worshippers. This custom was followed also by the Totonac.

Human sacrifice was of course reserved for the more important feasts, the offerings on lesser occasions consisting chiefly of incense, quails and the worshipper's own blood. Incense, mixed with tobacco, was offered on every occasion, and the incense-pouch is shown in the MSS. as the invariable accompaniment of priests. It was consumed in pottery braziers (Pl. IX, 1, and Figs. 4, *e*, and 36, 1, pp. 36 and 185), and visitors of great distinction were greeted by censing, a compliment which was continually paid to the Spaniards on their first arrival. Blood drawn by the worshipper from ears, tongue, arms or legs, was offered on most occasions, and this rite was invariably performed as an

PLATE IX

British Museum

MEXICO

1. CENSER OF CHOLULA WARE
2. POTTERY FIGURINE; COATLICUE. MEXICAN VALLEY
3.   ,,   HEAD FROM TEOTIHUACAN
4—5. ,,   HEADS OF WARRIORS. MEXICAN VALLEY
6.   ,,   FIGURINE; XOCHIQUETZAL. MEXICAN VALLEY

MAYA

7—11. POTTERY FIGURINES FROM GRAVES IN BRITISH HONDURAS
(Scale: 1, 1/7th; 2—6, 3/8ths; 7—11, 1/4th)

act of penance
every time that
he wished to at-
tain ceremonial
purity. The usual
implement was a
spine of the aloe,
which, covered
with blood, was
offered to the god,
but implements
of bone were also
employed, especi-
ally for piercing
the ears. An elab-
oration of this
ceremony consis-
ted in passing rods
through the
tongue, and at the
principal festival,
in March, to
Camaxtli at Tlax-
cala, the chief
priest was sup-
posed to pass no
less than 405 speci-
ally prepared rods
through that or-
gan, the other
worshippers be-
ing satisfied with
a smaller number.
This performance
is well illustrated
in a relief from
Huilocintla in the

FIG. 11.—Totonac stone relief, from Huilocintla,
near Tuxpan.

Totonac region (Fig. 11), which bears a distinctly Mayan appearance, and, as will be seen later, the Maya themselves were much addicted to the practice. Upon the proper periodical observance of this penitential act, accompanied by ceremonial fasting, the Mexican believed his material prosperity, to a great extent, to depend. By this means a person born on an unlucky day might avert much of his destined ill-fortune, while a man born under a lucky sign would forfeit by neglect the prosperity which it promised. Fasting played a very important part in all ceremonies preliminary to religious festivals, and was a condition of ritual purity; it consisted in partaking of but one meal a day, of abstinence from flesh and octli, and of rigid continence. Penitential acts and fasting, together with the making of offerings to certain gods, were prescribed by the priests of Tlazolteotl for those who made confession before them. The fact that confession was practised by the Mexicans was especially striking to the Spaniards, and most of the early writers make some comment upon the ceremony. The penitent approached the priest and signified his desire to confess, and the priest consulted the tonalamatl to find a propitious day for the occasion. When this arrived, sacrifice was made to Xiuhtecutli by casting offerings into a fire specially kindled for the purpose, and after an invocation to Tezcatlipoca, uttered by the priest, the penitent made confession of his faults seated before the latter, whom he regarded as the representative of the god. Sahagun states that small offences alone were confessed by the young, and that it was only the elders who made acknowledgment of serious sins, for it was believed that pardon could only be granted once for a particular fault. Absolution, however, was complete, and seems to have freed the penitent from temporal punishment. Sahagun states that in the early days of Christianity, natives would

come to the monasteries to confess, and then ask for a
certificate from the priests which they might show to
the alcade or governor in order that their offence might
be wiped out in the eyes of the temporal law also.
Before confession the penitent took an oath to tell the
truth, by touching the ground with a finger which he
licked. This was the customary manner of swearing, and
the action was usually accompanied by the words, " In
the name of the Sun, in the name of our lady the Earth,
I swear so-and-so, and in ratification thereof I eat this
earth." This action was termed " eating the earth in
respect for the gods," and was performed each time a
temple or shrine was entered.

CHAPTER IV—MEXICO : WRITINGS, PRIEST-
HOOD, MEDICINE AND BURIAL

SO many of the manuscripts have a religious or
calendrical significance, that it may be as well to
say here a few words about the Mexican system of writing. The Indians of the North American plains had
evolved a sign-language, by means of which, under
limitations, a silent conversation could be carried on ;
further, they were in the habit of recording events by
painting figures and scenes on hide, or weaving them in
their wampum belts. The Mexican system was a little
more advanced ; though events were expressed by the
actual depiction of the scenes, yet many of the details
were purely symbolical, and names were expressed by
a figure or combination of figures which constitute a
rebus. Thus the name of the king, Itzcoatl, was written
as a snake (coatl) bristling with obsidian knives (itztli) ;
the town of Tochtepec, by a rabbit (tochtli) on a mountain (tepetl) ; that of Tenochtitlan, by a stone (tetl),
on which grows a cactus plant (nochtli), the syllable
tlan being a place-termination.

To express numbers, as far as the calendar was concerned, since no figure higher than 13 occurred ordinarily, a dot was put for each unit. There was also a
special period-sign meaning a year (Fig. 86, *l*; p. 356,
usually combined with the day-sign from which that
particular year took its name), and another for the
period of 52 years, called *xiuhmolpilli*, or "sheaf of
years." As, however, there was no subsidiary sign by
which one xiuhmolpilli could be differentiated from
another, the reader is obliged to infer from the con-

text the cycle to which a particular year belongs. In the numeration of objects, as in the tribute-lists, higher numbers are expressed by special symbols. The Mexican numeral system was vigesimal, and hence the first special sign was that for 20, a religious banner. 20 × 20,

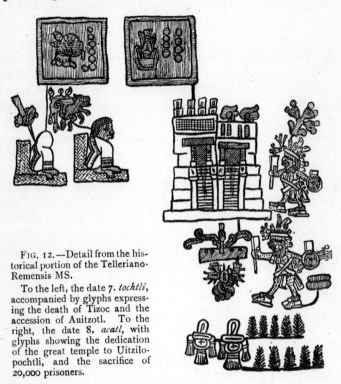

FIG. 12.—Detail from the historical portion of the Telleriano-Remensis MS.

To the left, the date 7. *tochtli*, accompanied by glyphs expressing the death of Tizoc and the accession of Auitzotl. To the right, the date 8. *acatl*, with glyphs showing the dedication of the great temple to Uitzilopochtli, and the sacrifice of 20,000 prisoners.

or 400, was expressed by a tree; and 20 × 400 by an incense-pouch (see Fig. 12). In certain portions of some manuscripts we find the lower numbers simplified by the employment of a bar to mean five. These MSS. present other features which are not typically Aztec in character, and it may at once be said that the use of the bar to express five was universal in the Maya countries, and extended in pre-Aztec times right up through the Zapotec country (e.g. Monte Alban) and Cuernavaca (Xochicalco) to the Mexican Valley (Island of Xico).

In the historical MSS. we have the year-signs in order accompanied by certain figures symbolical of important events. A temple in flames with a place-name attached signifies the conquest of a town ; the sign olin, an earthquake ; a smoking star, a comet ; and so forth. In Fig. 12 appears a small portion of the manuscript known as Telleriano-Remensis ; two year-dates are shown, of which the first, 7. tochtli, is accompanied by two figures, a mummy-pack with the name of Tizoc, and a seated man with the name of Auitzotl. This signifies the death of the king Tizoc, and the enthronement of his successor. Accompanying the next year-date, 8. acatl, is a picture of the great temple to Uitzilopochtli, beneath which is a smoking fire-stick, and the name-sign of Tenochtitlan. The group signifies the dedication of the great temple at Mexico, since new fire was always made at the opening of a newly-constructed building. At the side are two figures clad in the livery of prisoners destined to the gladiatorial stone, each with his name ; these represent two important prisoners sacrificed on that occasion, and below them is a number, reading 20,000, the number of the victims sacrificed during the inaugural ceremonies.

The nature of the calendrical manuscripts has been explained in chapter III, and it will therefore not be necessary to say more about them, except that most, if not all, of the surviving examples seem not to be pure Aztec work. Some are rather in Zapotec style, while others may have been produced at Teotitlan or Tehuacan on the Mixtec border, where the priests were especially skilled in calendrical lore ; of others again the place of origin may be Chiapas. Of great interest are the tribute-lists, of which the best, known as Codex

Mendoza, gives the imperial revenue in the time of
Montecuzoma, together with a list of the tributary
towns; the glyphs, in Fig. 18, p. 118, are taken from this
manuscript. Again, the ownership of land was carefully noted on maps, territory belonging to the king,
the nobles, and the calpulli (or clans) being marked in
different colours ; and plans of towns are also found,
that shown in Fig. 13 in all probability representing the
palace at Tezcoco. Similar documents were prepared

for legal proce-
dure, and at the
landing of the
Spaniards manu-
scripts were taken
to Montecuzoma
on which were
carefully noted
the portraits of
the leaders, to-
gether with pic-
tures of ships,
horses, dogs and
cannon.

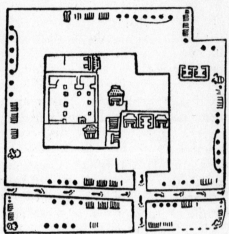

Maps and man-
uscripts were pain-
ted on fine cloth

FIG. 13.—Plan of the palace at Tezcoco.
(*Humboldt MSS., Berlin*)

made of aloe- or palm-fibre, paper made from the aloe,
or dressed skins, the two former being coated with a
kind of size. The colours were applied with a brush,
which was moistened with the lips of the artist, and the
designs were invariably outlined in black. A considerable variety of colours was employed, red from cochineal or log-wood; two yellows, vegetable and mineral;
blue from certain flowers ; white from chalk, and black
from the soot of the ocotl palm. The mixing of colours
was understood, and brilliant greens, purples and
browns are found.

It will be readily understood that the service of so
many gods and so formidable a list of religious festivals
required the services of a large body of carefully trained
priests. The office of priest was one which had under-
gone considerable evolution in Mexico, at least as far as
the immigrant tribes were concerned. At first the priest
was also the temporal leader ; his principal duty was the
care of the image of the tribal god, which he carried
during the wanderings of the tribe ; and since it was
the god who directed those wanderings, and the priest
was the sole interpreter of his wishes, it came about
that the priest was also the director of the tribal policy.
But once the tribe became settled, there was a tendency
for the priest to become less and less a man of action,
and to concentrate his energies on the elaboration of
ritual and the study of astronomy. At the same time
there was no sharp division between the temporal and
religious authority ; the king exercised many priestly
functions, and the priesthood possessed enormous influence in national affairs. Priests even engaged in war,
and there was a special series of *insignia* worn in fight
by those who had distinguished themselves in battle
by the capture of one or more prisoners. In Mexico
itself at the head of the hierarchy were two chief priests,
each of whom bore the title of Quetzalcoatl (since
the god of that name was regarded as the prototype
of all religious orders), and who were distinguished
by the names of Totec Tlamacazqui and Tlaloc Tlamacazqui. The first was the priest of Uitzilopochtli,
the second of Tlaloc ; they were equal in status, and
both were selected from the upper grade of religious
officers in virtue of their wisdom, piety and general
good character, irrespective of their birth. Subordinate
to them was a minister called Mexicatl Teohuatzin,
whom Sahagun terms a " patriarch," and who acted as
general overseer of ritual and of the priestly college
called Calmecac. He was assisted by two other func-

tionaries, the Uitznauac Teohuatzin and the Tepan Teohuatzin, the latter of whom shared his responsibilities as an educational officer. Beneath these dignitaries were ranked an upper grade of priests, called Tlanamacac, and a lower grade, Tlamacazqui; and finally the novices, Tlamacazton. The priests of the upper grade included a number of functionaries with special titles, who were devoted to the services of particular deities, or to the discharge of definite functions, as was the Ome Tochtzin, or overseer of the religious singers, who provided the latter with wine according to the following peculiar practice. After the singing, the Ome Tochtzin produced 303 canes, one only of which was bored throughout its length; the singers drew one each, and he who was lucky enough to hit upon the pierced cane had the sole privilege of drinking octli on that day. It is impossible to enter into details as regards these priests with special functions, and the interested reader may be referred to the work of Sahagun. The Mexican priesthood exercised very little control over the religious life of the subject cities beyond exacting the tribute necessary for the maintenance of the temples and sacrifices, and insisting on expiatory sacrifices in cases of breach of discipline (as in the case of the Totonac of Cempoala for having received the Spaniards). Subject to this very loose supervision, each city was permitted to exercise its own particular form of worship, and, as has been shown, the Aztec were always ready to adopt the worship of the gods of their neighbours. The ceremonial garb of priests in general consisted of black body-paint, sometimes with designs in ochre, and a black mantle; their hair was never cut, and the lobes of their ears were invariably torn in shreds owing to constant practice of the penitential rite of blood-letting. The black-robed priests with their long locks matted with blood and their torn ears made a great impression upon Bernal Diaz when he first met

them in Cempoala. The sacrificial priest constituted
an exception in so far as his garment was red, but his
five assistants, the Chalmeca, wore black, and were
distinguished by a headband ornamented with paper
discs.

The Tarascan priests differed in several essentials
from those of the Aztec. Since the office was hereditary
they formed a caste, their heads were carefully shaved,
and their principal *insignia* were a pair of golden
tweezers, used for epilation, and a calabash containing
tobacco, employed to produce a state of ecstasy during
which they were supposed to hold communion with the
gods. Among the Totonac were two high-priests consecrated to Cinteotl, who were regarded with especial
veneration ; they were widowers, over sixty years of
age, wore garments of jackal-skins, ate no fish, and
their functions were the delivery of oracles, and the
preparation of manuscripts.

In Tehuacan there was an especially holy order of
priests who spent four years at a time in perpetual
prayer (by relays) and observed a continual fast, ab-
staining from meat, fish, fruit, honey and pepper, and
taking but one meal a day. They were supposed to
commune directly with the gods, and were held in
especial estimation by Montecuzoma. But perhaps the
most generally revered priest in Mexico was the priest
of Quetzalcoatl at Cholula, who was regarded as the
direct successor of the god, and who lived a life of particular austerity. Among the Mixtec the high-priest
wore a short coat embroidered with mythological
figures, and over this a garment described as a " sur-
plice," while his head was crowned with feathers inter-
woven with small figures of the gods. But one of the
holiest priests was the high-priest of the sacred Zapotec
city of Mitla, who was kept in retirement, for it was
feared that death would seize any of the ordinary folk
who might set eyes upon him. He was regarded as an

inspired prophet and was supposed to hold converse with the gods.

The functions of the Mexican priesthood were manifold; apart from the general care of the temples and the maintenance of the holy fires, the priests were employed in sacrifice, divination, teaching, astronomy and the preparation of manuscripts. The ceremonial burning of incense at appointed hours absorbed much of their time, for to the sun alone this offering was made four times during the day and three times during the night. They lived in communities, under the strict supervision of their superiors and colleagues ; small breaches of discipline were punished by extra performance of the penitential rite, by pricking with aloe-spines, or by midnight offerings of incense upon a mountain ; more serious offences by beating, especially at the Etzalqualiztli festival, or by death. The provision of wood for the temple fires was a most important duty ; in Mexico it was usually undertaken by the novices, but in Michoacan it was nominally the duty of the king, though in fact the high-priest, as his representative, saw to the matter. The education of would-be priests was a matter of great moment, and the institution at which this was carried out, the Calmecac, deserves a word of description. Parents wishing to dedicate a son to the service of the gods invited the officers in charge of that establishment to a banquet during which they communicated their desires. The child was then taken to the Calmecac and offered to the image of Quetzalcoatl, the patron of the institution, and his ears were pierced. If too young to be entered as a novice forthwith, he was for the time restored to his parents, but his necklace was left with the god, since it was believed that his soul was mysteriously attached to this ornament. At the age of seven or eight the child definitely took up his residence at the Calmecac, where his duties at first consisted in sweeping the building and preparing the black paint used by the priests from the soot of a species of pine. Later on he assisted in the collection of aloe-spines used for blood-letting, and later still in the gathering of firewood and preparation of sun-dried bricks for building (adobes). All the time he was receiving instruction in the cere-monial chants and in ritual, and learning the practice of austerities by rising at midnight to offer incense or to take a ceremonial bath, or by joining in the ceremonial fasts on appointed days. The elder novices occasionally made pilgrimages at night to a neighbouring moun-tain ; they set out alone and nude, carrying a censer, a bag of incense, a torch, a conch-shell trumpet, and a number of aloe-spines. The latter were left at the furthest point of their journey wrapped in a ball of hay. The Tlamacazqui lived with the novices at the Calmecac, all messed and slept together, and were subject to the strictest discipline. A special duty of the Tlamacazqui was the sounding of conch-shells and drums at stated hours of the day and night. A portion of the Calmecac was reserved for girls, also dedicated by their parents to the service of the gods. They were under the charge of elderly unmarried women, and assisted in the sweeping of the temples, the tending of the fires, the preparation of food, and the manufacture of garments and ornaments for the idols. They were compelled to live in strict chastity, but their service was not necessarily life-long. Any girl when she attained a marriageable age might leave the establishment with the permission of her superiors, which was easily ob-tained by means of a present. In fact, many girls entered the service of religion in the hope that their devotion to the gods might be rewarded with a good husband.

An institution similar to the Calmecac existed among the Mixtec at Achiutla.

Other institutions for the religious instruction of the

young of both sexes existed in Mexico, attached to various temples. The mode of life was much the same as in the Calmecac, but the discipline was not so severe.

As said before, one of the principal functions of the priesthood was the exercise of the art of divination, and the principal instrument was the tonalamatl. The priests of Tlazolteotl were supposed to be especially expert in the use of the "book of days"; the horoscopes of new-born children were invariably cast, and a favourable day selected for the baptismal ceremony (as described below, p. 160), in accordance with the various influences attached to the day of its birth. Constant recourse was had to the interpreters of the tonalamatl in almost every emergency, and practically no enterprise of importance was undertaken except upon a propitious day. But there were numerous other methods of divination, and several grades of magical practitioners. Grains of maize or red beans were commonly employed to discover the issue of a sickness. The goddess Tozi was the patroness of the professional magicians who used this means, though the casting of the grains was usually performed in the presence of a figure of Quetzalcoatl, the arch-patron of magic. Twenty grains were usually cast upon a cloth ; if they fell forming a hollow circle, typifying a grave, it was believed that the sick person would die ; but if so that a straight line could be drawn leaving ten on each side, the patient would recover. Or again, if they fell scattered, a fatal termination to the illness was expected ; but if in a heap, health would be restored. At Tlaxcala it was a fatal sign if one grain stood up on end. Grain was also used in divination by the Mixtec, who sowed seed on the nemontemi days, and from its success or failure calculated the prospects of the year's crop. Another method of prognosticating the chances of a patient consisted in winding a string into a knot ; if it could be pulled loose, the patient would recover, otherwise his chances were small. Or again, a sick child would be held over a vessel of water, and his reflection carefully observed ; if the image was dim there was small prospect of recovery. The last method of divination was employed when the sickness was supposed to be due to absence of the child's *tonalli* (which may be translated " soul " or " luck "), and constitutes another instance of the belief, so common throughout the world, that the incorporeal nature of man is closely connected with his reflection or shadow. Snakes were also used in divination, especially to discover a stolen object ; the suspected persons were seated in a circle, and the magician placed a basket containing a snake in the middle. The basket was uncovered, and it was believed that if the culprit were present the snake would indicate the fact by crawling to him. Scrying in a mirror or bowl of water was another method of divination widely employed in Mexico proper, and was found among the Tarascans also. At Tlaxcala a peculiar custom was observed when war was declared in order to estimate the chances of ultimate success. Two sacred arrows were carefully kept in this town, which were supposed to have been brought by the first immigrants from Tulan. These were hurled in the direction of the foe by two specially chosen warriors, and then recovered at all costs. If an enemy was wounded by one the omens were regarded as especially favourable. At Mexico the Naualli was a magical priest of a high order ; he was celibate, had been trained from youth in weather-wisdom and spent much of his time in fasting and purification. He was credited with special powers, such as the assumption at will of animal form, and levitation ; he acted as the general guardian of the city against sorcerers, and gave warning of approaching famine or pestilence. The belief in powers such as these became extraordinarily widespread after the conquest, and resulted in the formation of a regular cult, the members of which were called Nagual. The Nagualists were supposed to have animal familiars, whose shape they could assume, and to hold regular "witches' sabbaths." Many natives confessed to such practices, and the Spaniards experienced great difficulty in stamping out the cult, which had as its avowed object the elimination of Christianity, and penetrated far into Central America. The information available concerning this extremely interesting recrudescence of paganism can be found in a small book by Brinton entitled "Nagualism."

Besides the magical priests already mentioned, there existed a class of professional conjurers, who performed various tricks, often for hire. One would have a number of puppets in a pouch which came out and danced, apparently uninspired by human agency, while another would roast maize on a simple cloth without fire. The Huaxtec were supposed to be particularly expert at such tricks, and among their feats Sahagun mentions the production from space of a spring with fishes, the burning and restoration of a hut, or the dismemberment and resurrection of the conjurer himself. The last proceeding recalls certain of the feats performed by the members of the ritual societies of the west coast of North America during the winter ceremonials. The Ocuiltec of the Toluca valley also possessed a great reputation as magicians. Various forms of domestic divination were practised, such as the sprinkling of octli upon the hearth-fire, auguries being taken from the spluttering. But before saying a word about the popular belief in omens, it will be as well to treat very shortly the subject of sorcery. Individuals born on the days 3. cipactli and 1. eecatl were supposed to be predisposed to the practice of the black art, and days with the number nine, especially 9. itzcuintli and 9. malinalli (but also 4. eecatl), were believed to be especially favourable for their evil prac-

H

tices. They could transform themselves into animal shape, influence the hearts of women, inflict wasting diseases upon their enemies (as implied in one of their names, " heart-eaters "), and bring misfortune. These arts they were ready to place at the disposal of those who were prepared to pay for their services, and they often combined their trade with that of professional housebreaker.   For this purpose their most powerful charm was the arm of a woman who had died in childbirth ; by its means they could cast sleep upon the inmates of the house which they desired to rob, or at any rate deprive them of the faculty of speech and movement. This belief bears a strange resemblance to that once held in this country concerning the magical properties attaching to the hand of an executed criminal. They could however be kept at a distance by placing a stone knife in a bowl of water on the threshold, or thistles in the windows. A bolder method of counteracting the machinations of a sorcerer was forcibly to snatch a few hairs from his head. It was believed that if he could not recover them he was destined to die the same night, unless indeed he could steal or borrow something from the house of his assailant. Practitioners of the black art were punished by the Tarascans by blinding.

Various portents were drawn from the animal world ; the cries of beasts of prey at night were supposed to forebode disaster to those who heard them, and the voices of certain birds were believed equally unlucky. The owl, so closely associated with Mictlantecutli, was especially regarded as the harbinger of ill-fortune and death, and if one of these birds perched upon the house of a sick man his demise was considered certain. It was held unlucky to encounter a skunk or a weasel, and the entry into the house of a rabbit or a troop of ants foreboded bad luck. If a certain kind of spider was found in the house, the owner traced a cross upon the ground, at the centre of which he placed the insect. If it went towards the north, the direction of the underworld, it was regarded as a sign of death for the observer, any other direction foretelling misfortune of minor importance.

Besides these superstitions there were a whole host of popular beliefs, of which only a few can be given here. Many of these were connected with food ; it was customary to blow upon maize before putting it in the cooking-pot, to " give it courage," and it was believed that if a person neglected to pick up maize-grains lying on the ground they called out to heaven to punish the omission. If two brothers were drinking, and the younger drank first, it was thought that the elder would cease to grow ; and it was also believed that the growth of a child was stopped by stepping over it when seated or lying down, but that the effect could be averted by stepping back again. Young girls were not allowed to eat standing, for it was believed that they would fail to get husbands, and children were prevented from licking the grind-stone for fear they would lose their teeth. When a child lost one of its first teeth, the father or mother placed the tooth in a mouse-hole, a proceeding which was supposed to ensure the growth of the second tooth ; and all nail-parings were thrown into the water in the hope that the auitzotl, a mythical water-animal which was believed to eat them, would make the nails grow. Sneezing was thought to be a sign that evil was being spoken of the sneezer, and there was a peculiar belief that the perfume of the flowers which were carried at banquets and in ceremonial dances might only be inhaled from the edges of the bouquet, since the centre belonged to the god Tezcatlipoca.

Magic played a very important part in the treatment of sickness, and many diseases were supposed to be sent by the gods, either in a malignant spirit, or as a punishment for some breach of ritual, such as violation of a public fast. The Ciuapipiltin, the souls of women dying in childbirth, were in particular supposed to be disease-bringers ; they were thought to haunt cross-roads on particular calendrical dates, and to select children principally as their prey. People falling sick on the date 1. ozomatli were generally given up by their doctors as incurable victims of these malignant goddesses. Tezcatlipoca was also regarded as a giver of disease in general, though in his case sickness was a punishment for some fault. Other deities were supposed to preside over special maladies, such as Xipe over disorders of the skin and eyes, and Amimitl over coughs and dysentery. Individuals suffering from the former complaints were believed to obtain relief by wearing the skin of a sacrificial victim during the Tlacaxipeualiztli festival, while the shrine of Amimitl at Cuitlauac was sought by victims of the latter well on into Christian times. Ixtlilton presided over the diseases of children, and in the courtyard of his temple were jars of holy water used as medicine. The mountain-gods were believed to send gout and rheumatism, and sufferers made vows to erect statues to them and to the rain- and water-deities. Another medical divinity was Tzapotlatenan, a deified woman who was revered as the discoverer of the medicinal value of turpentine, while Teteoinnan was the general patroness of doctors and midwives. Certain disorders were supposed to be contracted from the natural world, e.g. by smelling or sitting on certain flowers, while others were attributed to the machinations of sorcerers. The treatment of patients offers two aspects, one of which is purely magical, the other scientific. The Mexicans had a very good knowledge of the properties of certain plants, and used them with much success, both by external and internal application. In surgery they could set bones, and Sahagun states that a badly cut nose was sewed up with a hair, and a mixture of honey and salt applied. But no doubt it was the magical aspect of medical treatment which counted most in popular estimation. The medical priest would often apply suction to the seat of pain, and then produce triumphantly from his mouth some small object, such as an obsidian knife, which he pretended to have extracted from the patient's body. Amulets were frequently worn to banish maladies, especially in the case of children, and many ointments contained ingredients the effect of which was purely imaginary, though the massage which accompanied their application had no doubt a beneficial effect. One such medicament consisted of certain herbs, including tobacco, pounded up with the bodies of various insects, and this was also applied to the body as a protection against poisonous snakes and other wild animals. The idea that sickness could be removed by transferring it to another person was found in Mexico as in many other parts of the world ; in cases of fever the image of a dog would be made of maize dough, and placed on an aloe-leaf in a pathway, and it was believed that the first passer-by would remove the malady in his heel-bones. A remedy which was of almost universal application, and which was of real value, was the steam-bath. The patient was introduced into a small brick-built chamber which had a furnace constructed at one side. Between the furnace and the chamber was a slab of the volcanic stone called *tezontli*, upon which water was poured to produce steam. This building was called temazcalli in Mexico, but the treatment is not peculiar to this area, being found elsewhere in America also. According to Burgoa, among the Zapotec, persons who felt themselves incurably sick would ask to be shut up in a chamber in the holy city of Mitla reserved for the bodies of sacrificial victims and captains killed in war. Here they were left to perish, secure in the knowledge that their lot in the other world would be far superior to that in this.

To the Mexicans, as to many primitive peoples, death

was not an altogether abhorrent idea, being little more than an incident in the continuity between this life and the next. But the manner of death was more important, since it had a direct effect upon the fate of the soul. The most enviable lot was that of the warriors who died either in battle or in sacrifice ; they were supposed to depart to the eastern paradise of the sun, where, assembled on a great plain, they greeted his rising by beating upon their shields, and escorted him on his journey to the zenith. Thence they descended to the earth in the form of humming-birds and other birds of bright plumage, and spent their time among the flowers. Women dying in war or childbirth were equally fortunate ; as the counterpart of the warriors they went to the western paradise of the sun, and bore him in a litter of bright feathers from the zenith to the horizon, when they descended to earth in the form of moths.

Those who were drowned, struck by lightning, or who perished by certain diseases such as dropsy or leprosy, found a home in the terrestrial paradise Tlalocan, the home of the god Tlaloc, where food-plants and flowers flourished in miraculous fertility and summer was perpetual. Those who died of other diseases or old age were obliged to embark upon a difficult journey to Mictlan, the underworld, where the god Mictlantecutli held sway. During this they had to pass between two clashing mountains, to run the gauntlet of a great snake and a huge lizard, to traverse eight deserts and eight hills, and to encounter a wind full of stone knives. Finally, but not until the end of four years, the soul reached the great river of Hades, which must be crossed by swimming. For this the aid of a red dog was necessary, and dogs of this colour were reared in the house and killed at funerals. An interesting parallel to this belief is that current in parts of Peru, that the souls of the dead were escorted to the other world by black dogs, numbers of which were bred for this particular purpose. Though

living in the underworld, the souls of the dead were not
deprived of the light of the sun, since it was supposed
to pass through the infernal regions during the night
on its journey back to the east. The souls of infants
dying still unstained by sin were believed to be received
in a special paradise by Tonacatecutli, where they spent
their time flitting from flower to flower in the form of
humming-birds.

The question of the obsequies of the dead next
arises, and we find two methods of disposal practised in
Mexico, cremation and inhumation. The first of these
appears to be the more characteristic of the hunting
tribes, though the account of Sahagun would seem to
show that the Chichimec originally practised the latter.
This people were said to be extremely long-lived, and
protracted ill-health was regarded as so uncanny that if
a malady lasted over four or five days, the patient was
killed. The Tarascans certainly employed cremation ;
in the case of the king, the body was laid out by the
principal chiefs, who were summoned during his illness,
and carried in state by night to a temple, where it was
burned. A number of slaves accompanied the procession, playing on tortoise-carapaces and rattles formed of
a serrated bone along which a stick was rubbed ; these
slaves were killed while the pyre was burning, and were
buried separately behind the temple. The ashes of the
king were made into a mummy-pack with a false head
and mask, which was buried seated in a large urn at the
foot of the temple steps facing eastward. The grave was
roofed with wooden slabs, and earth was heaped upon
the top. Those killed in war were also burnt with their
bows before the temple, and their ashes buried in urns.
Though the wilder Chichimec, as stated above, appear
to have simply buried their dead, yet the early Chichimec kings in the valley of Mexico, Xolotl, Nopaltzin
and Quinatzin, are said to have been burnt and their
ashes deposited in urns in caves. At Teotihuacan, a site

where the Toltec culture flourished for a considerable period, unburned burials are found, and it is probable, from other evidence, that cremation is not typical of this civilization. The Acolhua practised cremation and buried the ashes. The Aztec practised both forms of disposal of the dead, but cremation, which, according to the early commentator on the MS. known as Vati-

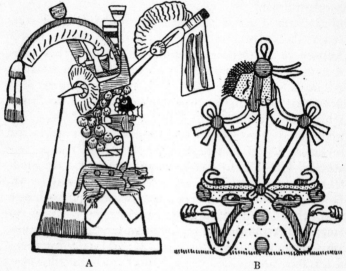

A   B

FIG. 14.—A. Mummy of a warrior prepared for burial.
(*Magliabecchiano MS.*, *Florence*)

B. Mummy supported in the jaws of the earth-monster.
(*Fejérváry-Mayer MS.*, *Liverpool*)

canus A, they learnt from the Otomi, was the more common. The deceased was made up into a mummy-pack with quantities of paper, which was supposed to enable him to pass through the various dangers to be encountered on his journey to the underworld, and decked with appropriate ornaments (Fig. 14, *a*). Water was sprinkled over his head, and a supply for his journey provided in a small vessel; his red dog (shown in the illustration) was killed, and dog and master were burnt together with various articles of personal property which might be wanted in the other world. In many cases this privilege was allowed to slaves destined for sacrifice, and they were permitted to burn their small effects before they mounted the sacrificial stone. The ashes were collected and placed in a vase or stone coffer, together with a small jewel (the lip-plug of the deceased) to serve as a " heart," and buried. Offerings were made on the grave after twenty days' interval, and again after eighty days. These were repeated on the annual feast of the dead for four years, after which the soul was supposed to have completed its journey. The grave, at any rate in the case of individuals of importance, was a vault lined with stone and lime. The obsequies of the king followed the same lines, but were more elaborate, and certain of his personal slaves and wives were killed to accompany him. Motolinia states that in the case of men of high rank, all the clothing which they had worn in life was buried with them. Both the "Anonymous Conqueror" and Francisco de Bologna speak of bodies being placed in the vault seated on a chair, and it is possible that the ashes were occasionally made up into a mummy-pack as among the Tarascans. However, simple inhumation was certainly practised by the Aztec, though it was usually reserved for those whose manner of death entitled them to a place in the terrestrial paradise Tlalocan. In the case of a merchant dying while away from home on a trading expedition, a figure was made by his relations at home and burnt with due ceremony. If he had been killed by a hostile people, the cremation took place in a temple-court, but if he had fallen a victim to disease, in front of his house. Merchants of the Pochteca guild of Tlaltelolco received special treatment ; the body was swathed in paper, the face decorated with the red and black paint of the gladiatorial sacrifice, ornaments, including the lip-plug, were added, and the pack was attached to a carrying-frame and exposed on a mountain-top. As stated before, the souls of women dying in childbirth were deified under the name of Ciuapipiltin, and their bodies were accorded special treatment. The corpse, clad in its best garments, was borne by the husband to the courtyard of the temple dedicated to the Ciuapipiltin, where it was buried. On the way it was escorted by a retinue of midwives armed with swords, and the husband and

his friends kept watch over the grave for four nights. These precautions were necessary to prevent young warriors or sorcerers from seizing the body in order to obtain the left arm, or middle finger of the left hand and the hair of the deceased. It was believed that the finger and hair, if carried in the warrior's shield, would render the possessor invincible, while the hand was a powerful

FIG. 15.—Carved stone slab from Tlacolula, Oaxaca. (*After Seler*)

charm used by robbers to cast sleep upon the inmates of a house, as described on p. 98.

When we come to consider the Mixtec and Zapotec, we find inhumation the rule, indeed the Zapotec abhorred cremation, considering it destructive of the soul. Nor was the method always simple inhumation, but secondary burial. The body was placed in the ground with feet to the east, and the bones were collected subsequently and placed in a vase which was deposited in a stone vault in a mound, the doorway being closed with a sculptured slab (Fig. 15). Both peoples also employed caves to some extent as receptacles of the dead. Simple inhumation in caves seems to have been more common among the Mixtec than the Zapotec, and Burgoa writes of cave burials at Chalcatongo, supposed to be the gate of paradise, where the dead were laid out dressed in rich garments, numbers of small idols in gold, stone and wood being placed in niches in the cave-walls. The same author tells of the Zapotec kings being deposited at Mitla, in a chamber in one of the temples, clad in gorgeous ornaments and holding shield and spear. It is possible that primary burial was reserved for those of high rank.

FIG. 16.—Carved stone slab from Placeres del Oro, Guerrero.

An extremely interesting burial has been found at a place called Placeres del Oro, in the valley of the Rio del Oro, a southern tributary of the Rio de las Balsas. The chief interest of the remains here found lies in the very peculiar art of the sculptured slabs between which the bones were deposited (Fig. 16). The walls of the grave, which was situated at the foot of a mound, were of clay hardened by fire, and of the bones themselves it is said " there is good reason to suspect that at least partial cremation of the body took place at the time this burial was made." This is a most important point, and ought to be definitely settled by careful inspection of the bones. The site is on the debatable land between Nahua, Tarascan and Zapotec, and there are reasons, which will be given later, why I think it most probable, failing definite evidence to the contrary, that the body had not been burnt.

The fine stone coffer from the Huaxtec country shown on Pl. X, 2 ; p. 108, is almost certainly a coffin ; and in the Totonac country both cist-burial in mounds and, occasionally, well-burial are found. Traces of cremation appear to be exceptional, and confined to hill-sites inland, where they are perhaps indicative of Nahua influence.

To speak broadly, it would appear that cremation was typical of the invading hunter-tribes, inhumation of the early sedentary peoples of the valley of Mexico. If this is so, the interment of individuals whose souls were supposed to be destined for the paradise of Tlaloc is easily explained, since that god appears to have been the deity principally worshipped by the agriculturists of the valley, and it is only natural that the form of burial characteristic of his early worshippers should be retained in such cases.

PLATE X

1

3

British Museum

2

HUAXTEC

1. STONE FIGURE; PANUCO RIVER
2.   ,,   CHEST;   ,,   ,,

MAYA

3. POTTERY CENSER; BRITISH HONDURAS
(Scale: 1, 1/10th; 2, 1/8th; 3, 1/5th)

CHAPTER V—MEXICO: SOCIAL SYSTEM, WAR, TRADE AND JUSTICE

IT is difficult to say with certainty what was the social organization of the wandering tribes which, one after the other, found their way into the Mexican valley, but from indications we may gather that there were two centres of authority. No doubt the principal of these was religious ; most of the tribes are mentioned as being under the guidance of their god, and it may be inferred that the priest possessed tremendous influence in directing the tribal policy. If the priest were a fighting-man also, he probably became the sole leader, and it is not unlikely that this was often the case. The fighting-priest was no rarity in Mexico, and in later times there was a special set of *insignia* for priests who distinguished themselves in battle. But normally, it may be concluded, the tribe was led in fight by the best and most experienced warrior, whose authority was probably exercised only during military operations. As amongst practically all nomadic peoples, the heads of families probably constituted a tribal council. The Toltec, upon the ruins of whose civilization the ruder Nahua tribes established themselves, were admittedly a people of higher culture than the immigrants ; and they were living a settled life under the rule of " kings " in whom the priestly aspect predominated. As has been seen above, the Toltec themselves contained an immigrant Nahua element, which presumably had imposed itself upon the prior inhabitants, but, when the later-comers arrived, material prosperity had diminished their warlike propensities, and they were known as a pre-eminently peaceful people. Probably two facts had combined to bring about this result, first that the valley was not at this early period so thickly populated as to render collision between the different cities inevitable ; and second that war was not yet, as it was destined to become, the handmaid of religion. It would seem that the moral effect, upon each wave of rude invaders, of the more cultured, settled tribes whom they were destined to conquer, was enormous. Settlement, increased prosperity, expansion and conquest demanded some form of administration more elaborate than that which a general, a high-priest, and a council of elders could provide. The evolution of a complicated ritual based upon astronomical calculation provided the priesthood with too much work of a highly specialized character to leave it time to undertake temporal rule, especially as that rule now involved the superintendence of an elaborate military system. The result was that the general was replaced by a "king," and, owing to the moral ascendancy which each earlier body of settlers exercised over its successors the first ruler selected either was himself a descendant of some previous ruling house, or received as consort a daughter of such and held his office in virtue of that alliance. So we find that when the Aztec were at Coatlichan, before Tenochtitlan was founded, they elected as leader (he does not seem to have been counted among the " kings ") Uitziliuitl, whose father was an Aztec of no particular rank, but whose mother was a daughter of the ruler of Tzompanco: while Acamapitzin, the first " king " of Tenochtitlan, was, by his mother, grandson of Coxcoxtli, ruler of Colhuacan, and might therefore lay claim to Toltec descent.; also Quaquapitzauac, first king of Tlaltelolco, was son of the Tepanec ruler of Azcapotzalco. Moreover it was Toltec descent which really counted most, as may be seen in the fact that the Mexican " kings " were installed as the representatives of Quetzalcoatl.

The importance of women as the channel by which rank was transmitted is obvious from the genealogy of the Mexican sovereigns. As a rule brother succeeded brother, and in any case it was only the sons of ladies of rank who were elected to the throne. Though, however, the priesthood thus became confined to the exercise of its own complicated profession, it never lost its influence upon temporal affairs. Naturally the degree to which that influence could be exercised depended to some extent upon the personal character of the king, but it was always a power behind the throne, and when the king himself had been trained as a priest, as was the case with the last Montecuzoma, it had few limits, as the history of the conquest shows. The association of the god Quetzalcoatl with the kingly office invested the ruler with a semi-divine character, and the subordination of war to religion gave the priesthood tremendous power in the direction of military policy. The power of the king, apart from his " divine right," was based upon his offices as commander-in-chief and supreme judge, the military aspect of his position being emphasized by the fact that, from the time of Chimalpopoca, only those of the ruling family who had held the position of general were considered as candidates for the throne. In Michoacan however, though here too the king was the chief judge, it was the religious aspect of his office which predominated. The idol of the ruling class was in his especial care, and one of his most important functions was the, at least nominal, provision of sufficient fuel for the sacrificial fires. For the rest, he was supported by a hierarchy of military and religious officers similar to, but less elaborate than, that of the ruler of Mexico.

At the time of the Spanish conquest the Mexican rulers maintained an elaborate court ceremonial and their appointments were truly magnificent. Diaz describes how the lord of Tezcoco came to meet the

Spaniards in a litter richly worked in green feathers, with many silver borderings and rich stones set in bosses of gold. Later, Montecuzoma arrived in a similar vehicle, and after alighting advanced supported by four high chiefs " beneath a marvellously rich canopy of green-coloured feathers with much gold and silver embroidery, and with pearls and chalchiuites suspended from a sort of bordering which was wonderful to look at. . . . He was shod with sandals . . . the soles were of gold and the upper part adorned with precious stones." Cloths were spread before him to tread upon, and all his suite kept their eyes lowered except the four who supported him, who were his nephews. In his palace, his antechamber was kept by a large body-guard, and even the most important chieftains, when they came to visit him, exchanged their rich mantles for garments of poor material and entered his presence barefoot. The magnificence of his service, state apartments and general entourage, his aviaries and collection of wild beasts, have often been described, and by none better than by Prescott, so that it is hardly necessary to enter into detail on this subject. Two quotations will suffice, both from eye-witnesses, one relating to the practice of smoking, the other to the dimensions of the palace. After his meal, which was served on Cholulan pottery, " there were also placed on the table three tubes, much painted and gilded, which held *liquidambar* mixed with certain herbs which they call *tabaco;* and when he had finished eating, after they had danced before him and sung and the tables were removed, he inhaled the smoke from one of these tubes, but he took very little of it, and with that he fell asleep."

Of the palace, the " Anonymous Conqueror " writes, " Several times I entered the residence of the king, simply to see it ; each time I walked about there until I was tired, nevertheless I have never seen the whole of it." The various ornaments and ceremonial dresses of

the king have been described at length by Seler, and
consisted chiefly of mantles decorated with embroidery
and feathers, feather back-devices, lip-plugs and necklaces of particular patterns, and the like, many of them
being divine *insignia* or costumes adopted from other
tribes by right of conquest. The list is too formidable
to be included here, but two are worthy of mention. One
ornament worn by royalty and high officials at festivals
consisted of a band twined
round the hair, to each
end of which a large
bunch of feathers was
attached ; this is shown
in Fig. 17, *a*, where it is
worn by the Tlacochcal-
catl. Diaz mentions an
ornament of particular
interest in the words
" Montecuzoma took
from his arm and wrist
the sign and seal of Uit-
zilopochtli, which was
only done when he gave
an important and weighty
command which was to
be carried out at once."

A   B

FIG. 17.—A. The Tlacochcalcatl in
festival dress.

B. Warrior with *insignia* denoting
that he has taken five prisoners.

(*Mendoza MS., Oxford*)

Unfortunately nothing more is known of this interesting bracelet. The most distinguishing sign of royalty
was a diadem of turquoise mosaic, rising to a peak in the
front, rather after the fashion of a mitre. This was
known as the xiuhuitzolli, and a plainer pattern was
worn by the highest rank of judges.

At the time of the conquest there were several independent states in the neighbourhood of Mexico, of
which the most important were Michoacan, Quauhtitlan, Tlaxcala, Uexotzinco, Cholula and Meztitlan ;
the sovereigns of which held positions very similar to

I

those of Mexico, though their courts were of course considerably less magnificent. The two other states of the Mexican confederacy, Tezcoco and Tlacopan, were similarly administered, and the court of the former was only less brilliant than that of Tenochtitlan. The Tlaxcalan state is often erroneously mentioned as a republic, but it was in fact a confederation of four cities, built, as the population expanded, in the following order : Tepeticpac, Ocotelolco, Tizatlan and Quiauitztlan. Coyoacan, Xochimilco and Chalco were always more or less in a state of revolt against Mexican authority, and must be regarded as quasi-independent ; at any rate they possessed rulers of their own.

When the Mexican throne fell vacant, the nobles and principal officials of the kingdom appointed four electors, usually of royal blood, to select the sovereign from the members of the ruling family. As stated before, in normal cases the choice fell upon a brother of the late king, or on a nephew belonging to an elder branch. The kings of Tezcoco and Tlacopan also acted as electors, but probably only in name.

The election usually took place on the day 1. itzcuintli, and the candidate was conducted in silent procession, clad only in a waist-cloth, to the temple of Uitzilopochtli, where he was clothed in a robe with a design of skulls and other *insignia*, and offered incense to the god. The offering was repeated at other shrines, namely those of the earth-goddess, Xipe, and Tezcatlipoca, and again at the edge of the lake (probably to Tlaloc), and the king, after receiving the homage of his subordinates, retired to an apartment in the temple where he fasted for four days. At the end of this period he was escorted back to the palace, and a great feast was held. At Tezcoco and Tlacopan the rulers were elected by the nobles on similar lines, and the kings-elect were invested by the king of Mexico. In Michoacan the proceedings were similar, save that the king designated his heir during his lifetime and at once admitted him to a share in the government. At Tlaxcala, Uexotzinco and Cholula, the heir-presumptive was overwhelmed with insults to prove his patience and then taken to a temple where he spent one, or even two, years observing a strict fast and performing penance. Finally a day was fixed for the installation ceremony, which must be an uneven number of days from the date of his birth, and his time of trial was over. The final ceremony included the boring of the candidate's nose for the reception of a gold ornament, the badge of his rank. A similar period of penance was endured by the heirs of Mixtec lords before their admission to office.

An interesting variety of government is presented by the constitution of the Matlatzinca district in the days before its conquest by Axayacatl. Here there were three chiefs, the Tlatauan, the Tlacochcalcatl and the Tlacatecutli, ranking in that order. At the death of the first, the second succeeded to his office, and was himself succeeded by the third. The vacant post of Tlacatecutli was then filled up by selection of the most capable son or brother of the deceased, or, if he had no relations, of a prominent noble. Each of these officers was supported by the tribute furnished by particular local clans, similar to the Mexican calpulli described below.

Each ruler confirmed the succession of his subchiefs, and they of their inferiors, but in these cases it was usually a son who inherited, failing sons, a brother, or failing brothers, a nephew. But a very large proportion of the office-holders were merely appointed for life, and their posts at their death became vacant and at the disposal of the king, though in actual fact a relation was often appointed as successor in such cases.

When the Mexicans first adopted settled life, they were brought face to face with a question which they had not before been forced to consider, the land question. In the city itself land was extremely restricted, and the growing importance of agriculture led to an elaborate system of intensive cultivation of the territory around. Land was seized by right of conquest, and assigned by the conqueror to his followers. Thus we read of the Chichimec leader Xolotl giving cities to immigrant chiefs to whom he married his daughters, or whose support he wished to conciliate. In this way certain territories passed into the hands of certain great lords, who apportioned it amongst their dependents, and reclaimed it as they wished. But there was another class of landowner, probably having its origin in later times, consisting of men to whom the ruler made grants of land in return for eminent services, especially in war ; such land was neither alienable nor hereditary, but lapsed to the crown at the death of the holder. Of great interest was the land held in common by the local clans, called calpulli, composed of the descendants of the different families of the invaders, and of the tribes who attached themselves to the latter in early days. The calpulli, which were twenty in number, were the offshoots of the four original tribal divisions, each of which formed a " ward " of the city at its foundation. These wards, named Moyotlan, Teopan, Aztacalco and Cuepopan, survived as administrative divisions in later times, though their functions as holders of land in common were taken over by their sub-divisions, the calpulli. They were even maintained in Spanish times, becoming transformed into the " barrios " respectively of San Juan, San Pablo, San Sebastian and Santa Maria la Redonda. Land belonging to a calpulli was inalienable, though under certain circumstances it could be let to another calpulli; it was vested in the calpulli-chiefs, whose office was nominally elective, but who in fact were usually chosen from one family. Members of a calpulli obtained land sufficient for their needs from their chief, and held it as long as they continued to keep it under cultivation, failing which their tenure lapsed. Land so apportioned was in practice hereditary, but only on these terms, and the man who changed his residence lost his holding. The clan-chiefs possessed considerable power, since they represented the calpulli in all external business, being in fact the descendants of the heads of families who formed the old tribal council, and regulated the inner life of the clan. A land system somewhat similar to that of the Mexican calpulli existed among the Mixtec in so far as land appears to have been hereditary in families but could not pass outside the local group. Below the members of the calpulli ranked certain freemen who farmed the lands of the lords on payment of a rental (in kind), and, finally, a class of serfs who were bound to the soil and probably represented the remnants of the early agricultural population. The Mexican social system therefore comprised a landed aristocracy who paid no definite taxes, but owed service to the king; associated with them was a military nobility who held lands at the king's goodwill, and whose tenants paid royal taxes. Lower in rank were the calpulli freemen, who paid taxes in common; still lower, the tax-paying rent-holders, and finally the serfs, who paid taxes only to their feudal lords. In addition to these there was the official class, their sons and descendants, who, ranking as warriors and noble, paid no definite taxes, but contributed their personal services and formed the suite of the ruler. The office-holders were known by the generic name of Tecutli, and the positions which they occupied were essentially military in origin; four of them were placed as overseers of the four districts into which the city was divided for administrative purposes, and acted as representatives of the Tlacatecutli, or ruler. Besides these there were the judicial officials, treasurers, and a whole host of overseers, of whom the lowest in rank, as in Peru, exercised supervision over a few families only. The

travelling merchants constituted a peculiar and privileged class, and will be considered later when the subject
of trade is discussed.   The expansion of the power of
Mexico brought many other cities under its influence,
and these were obliged to furnish tribute in kind, and
were also liable to military service.   In important cities

FIG. 18.—Various articles of tribute.

a.	Bale of cacao.	*l.*	Chest of maize.
b.	Stone lip-plug.	*m.*	Ceremonial dress.
c.	Jadeite beads.	*n.*	Feathers.
d.	Mosaic ear-ornament.	*o.*	Basket of copal.
e.	Pink shell.	*p.*	Shield.
f.	Amber.	*q.*	Jar of honey.
g.	Salt.	*r.*	Bale of cotton.
h.	Cochineal.	*s.*	Textile with designs.
k.	Burden-frame.		(*Mendoza MS., Oxford*)

a governor, Petlacalcatl, was placed, with a tax-gatherer,
Calpixque, under him; in less important districts a
governor or a Calpixque resided in the principal city, and
the tribute was collected in the surrounding towns by
subordinate officials. Apart from a general supervision
there was very little interference with the tributary
cities; the original rulers were rarely displaced, but continued to govern according to the local laws, and, with
the exception that certain lands were often reserved for

the use of the Mexican crown, the property of the conquered was respected. The rather loose nature of the
suzerainty exercised by Mexico over its dependents made
revolt a frequent occurrence, but this was hardly regarded as a drawback, owing to the ceremonial nature
of war and its function in providing victims for sacrifice. Tribute was generally paid by a town or district in
common, and consisted of local produce and manufactures (Fig. 18). Produce-tribute, which was generally
levied at harvest-time, was furnished by the common
lands, and stored in magazines in the principal cities.
Maize and other grain was contributed in large chests
(Fig. 18, *l*), and cotton (*r*), cacao (*a*) and pepper in bales.
Of manufactured articles, textiles (*s*) and ceremonial
costumes (*m*) were the most common, but the tribute-
lists show a great variety. Many of the town-names in
these lists cannot now be located, but their geographical
position can be roughly assumed from the nature of
their contributions. From Soconusco came lip-plugs,
cacao, feathers and hides, from Oaxaca province, gold
and cochineal (Fig. 18, *h*), from the Tlalhuica, paper
and pottery. Other forms of tribute were honey (*q*),
lime, wood, salt (*g*), copal (*o*), sea-shells (*e*), amber (*f*),
rubber, live eagles, copper axes, chalchiuitl beads (*c*),
turquoise (*d*), swords, shields (*p*), and canes filled with
perfumes for smoking. Tax-gatherers were received
with great ceremony and respect, and the arrival of
these officers at the town of Quiauiztlan, in Vera Cruz, is
described by Diaz. A special apartment decked with
flowers was prepared for them, together with food and
chocolate; they arrived dressed in richly embroidered
cloaks and loin-cloths, their hair bound up on their
heads, each carrying a crooked staff and a bouquet of
flowers which he smelled from time to time. The
Totonac it is true complained to the Spaniards of the
harshness of Mexican rule, probably referring rather to
the Aztec demands for sacrificial victims. Tribute on

the whole seems to have been fairly assessed, and was remitted in years of famine.

While the first step in the evolution of the Mexican constitution is marked by the election of Acamapitzin as king, in place of the old tribal council under a president, yet it was the overthrow of Azcapotzalco which gave the hegemony of the valley to Mexico, and compelled it to provide for the administration of dependent cities. A number of officials bearing titles similar to those at home were sent to Coyoacan, and definite arrangements were made with the allied states of Texcoco and Tlacopan in accordance with which the rulers of these cities became, at least nominally, electors of the Mexican kings, and placed the direction of their military policy in the hands of the latter. It was only in military matters that the two confederate states deferred to Mexico ; they had their own sovereigns, their own laws and provinces, and we are told that Tezcoco exercised dominion over no less than fifteen of the last-named in the direction of the Atlantic coast. Each ruler confirmed the election of their sub-chiefs, and they of their dependents. Of the booty won by the united armies, two-fifths was taken by Mexico, two-fifths by Tezcoco, and one-fifth by the small state of Tlacopan.

The final stage in the development of the Mexican constitution was marked by the conquest of Tlaltelolco by Axayacatl, and the appointment of a governor for this suburb in place of an independent sovereign. The military basis of Mexican hegemony coloured the whole of its domestic economy, and resulted in the formation and rise of a military aristocracy in the hands of which lay practically all the executive offices in the city.

As commander-in-chief the king was of course the head of the fighting-men, and in some cases actually took the field himself, immediately after his installation, for instance, in order to procure the necessary sacrificial victims. He was supported by two principal officers, the Tlacatecatl and Tlacochcalcatl (Fig. 17, *a*; p. 113), of whom the latter was a purely military functionary, while the former exercised certain administrative functions also. The same titles were borne by the chief subordinates of each of these respectively. A propitious date was awaited for the proclamation of a campaign, the day 1. itzcuintli being considered especially favourable; the hostile country was explored by spies, called Tequihua, who brought back to the king various maps and other documents containing information likely to prove of use during the operations. War was formally declared by sending weapons, down and chalk, the *insignia* of sacrifice, to the enemy, and the expedition set forth, on a lucky day such as 1. coatl, in a prescribed order. First marched the priests with the idols of the gods, next the Mexican veterans, followed by the less experienced; following them came the forces of Tezcoco and Tlacopan, and finally the fighting-men of allied provinces. When the forces were drawn up, new fire was made by the priests, and the attack commenced. The actual combat does not seem to have been attended by great slaughter, since the chief object of each individual fighter was not to kill his foe, but to make him prisoner. The first captives were immediately handed over to the priests and sacrificed on the spot, while those taken subsequently were carried back to the city. The ceremonial nature of war is clearly shown in the fact that rewards were conferred upon those who succeeded in capturing prisoners, in proportion to the number of their captives, but no account was taken of those who merely slew their opponents. To this fact the Spanish conquerors owed a large measure of their success, since the foe were chiefly anxious to take them alive, and rather avoided inflicting mortal injuries than otherwise. Diaz comments upon the rapidity with which the Tlaxcalans removed their wounded from the scene of action, but without understanding that the reason was to prevent them from falling alive into the hands of the enemy. The Tarascan customs were similar ; in time of war the priests offered herbs and tobacco at midnight, selecting a date when the position of the stars was favourable, and denounced by name the leaders of the opposing troops. The herbs, together with eagle-down and bloodstained arrows, were taken by spies and deposited within the enemy's territory, a proceeding which was intended as a declaration of war, but also possessed the magical significance of devoting the foe to death. A Mexican army in the field was an extremely gallant sight; the leaders and most distinguished fighters were brilliant in ornaments of gold and the feathers of tropical birds and embroidered tunics. Military *insignia* existed in great variety, each individual wore every decoration to which he was entitled, and the regimental and tribal standards of elaborate feather-work made a brave show. The Mexican standards consisted of an eagle and a jaguar ; that of Tlaxcala was a white heron with outspread wings, and the four Tlaxcalan provinces had each their own badges, Tepeticpac, a wolf with arrows ; Ocotelolco, a green bird on a rock ; Tizatlan, a heron on a rock ; and Quiauiztlan, a green canopy. Standards were fastened securely to the backs of certain officers, and the capture of one of them, or the fall of a general, was invariably the signal for a retreat. Diaz describes the Tlaxcalan levies as " brilliant with great devices, each regiment by itself with its banners unfurled, and the white bird, like an eagle, with its wings outstretched, which is their badge."

Children, as a preparation for military service, were entered in one of the schools called Telpochcalli, which were under the protection of Tezcatlipoca, and there underwent a rigorous training, in part religious, which was not, however, so severe as that of the Calmecac. On first entering they were charged with the duty of sweeping the building and attending to the fires, later of fetching wood and engaging in various constructional works. During this period they took their meals in their own houses, but returned to the Telpochcalli to sleep ; their amusements consisted in attending the dances, in the building called Cuicacalco, which took place between sunset and midnight. The sons of the higher officials who intended to embrace the military profession received the superior education of the Calmecac, and accompanied experienced warriors to battle in the capacity of shield-bearers. As soon as the young man was of an age to go to war, the whole of his hopes centred upon the taking of a prisoner, so that the lock of hair which he wore at the back of his neck as a sign of his noviciate might be removed. If he performed the feat with the aid of several of his companions, all were permitted to wear a side-lock instead, but if single-handed he received at the hands of the king the privilege of wearing certain body-paint and embroidered mantles of particular designs. The capture of two, three, four or more prisoners was also rewarded with special *insignia* (Fig. 17, *b*; p. 113), with promotion in rank, and the gift of privileges including the right to wear a lip-plug of a particular pattern and to sit on a particular seat. A distinction was made according to the nationality of the prisoners captured ; one or more Huaxtec were of comparatively small account, but the taking of even a single warrior of Atlixco or Uexotzinco was regarded as a great feat and received a corresponding reward. Two " orders " existed, which were conferred upon the most prominent warriors, the " eagle " and the " ocelot " ; those who obtained one of these coveted distinctions were allowed to wear dresses representing the animal from which their order took its name. Other dresses and back-devices, each conferring a definite status, existed in numbers, and constituted an important item in the tribute sent by the dependent cities. If after a few fights the would-be warrior had still failed to secure a prisoner, he was disgraced, and usually retired into private life rather than continue to wear the novice's lock, but he was for ever debarred from wearing garments of cotton or ornamenting his clothes with embroidery. Proved warriors were permitted to wear their hair in a lock on one side which they brushed so as to stand upright, while those of higher rank wore the lock above the forehead encircled by an ornamental band (see Pl. IX, 4 and 5).

The distinguishing weapon of the Aztec was the bow, and it was no doubt the possession of this arm which contributed substantially to their success in their fights with the early population of the valley. Manuscripts relating the wanderings of the people before they reached their final home show the Aztec, skin-clad and armed with the bow, fighting with the valley-dweller clothed in cotton and armed with the macquauitl, or wooden sword edged with obsidian. The Chichimec were also wielders of the bow, as well as the Tarascans, but this weapon was especially associated with Uitzilopochtli, who was supposed to have given it to the Mexicans, saying "All that flies on high do the Mexicans know how to hit with the arrow." The bow was plain and of no great dimensions ; the arrows were headed with fish or mammal bone or with flint or obsidian, and, to judge from the manuscripts, each had two feathers attached with the flat sides against the shaft. The macquauitl, a broadbladed club along the edges of which were set flakes of obsidian set in resin, was carried by the ordinary soldier, and, wielded by an expert, was capable of decapitating a horse at one blow; however, it soon lost its edge. The early Nahua and the valley-dwellers seem to have employed the atlatl, or spear-thrower, rather than the bow. This implement, which is found both in North and South America, consists of a staff armed at the

point with a hook, which fits into the butt of the javelin ; Mexican specimens are usually provided with two
rings of shell or other material near the handle through
which the fingers are passed (Pl. XVII, 1). This appliance
gives length to the arm, and enables the javelin to be
hurled with far greater force than by the hand alone.
While Uitzilopochtli and Camaxtli are usually shown
with the bow, most of the other gods appear with the
atlatl, which is often richly ornamented with feathers.
The javelins were pointed as the arrows, or the ends were
simply hardened in the fire; some had two or more points,
and were furnished with a cord like a harpoon by means
of which they could be retrieved ; these were especially
feared by the Spaniards. The only mention of poison
is found in Burgoa who states that the Mixtec applied
it to their javelins. Spears were carried by those of
higher rank, and were furnished with stone heads or
set with obsidian after the fashion of a macquauitl.
Long spears of this pattern, with a fathom of cutting
edge, were used by the Zapotec. Slings were also employed, especially by the Matlatzinca, and though bows
were found among the Olmec and Huaxtec, they must
have been of quite late introduction. Diaz mentions
" three blow-guns with their bags and pellet-moulds,"
which he saw in the treasury of Axayacatl, the blow-
guns themselves being incrusted with mosaic work, but
these weapons were probably used only in hunting.
Quilted cotton corslets, laced up the back and forming
one with the breeches, were worn as defensive armour,
and, according to one of the conquerors, could only be
penetrated by a good arquebus. Nobles wore cuirasses
of gold plates under their feather mantles. The Mexican bucklers were small and circular, usually made of
wicker with a covering of feather-work (Fig. 18, p ;
p. 118) and sometimes gold plates ; tortoise carapaces
were also used, and among the Zapotec larger shields
covering the whole body. Helmets were of wood, with

hide and feather ornaments, and often represented the head of some animal, jaguar or snake, the jaws of which framed the face of the warrior (as Fig. 18, *m*). The defensive armour of the Mixtec was of hide. Clubs with heads of stone or wood were employed by the Tarascans. Defensive works were not very elaborate, though we read of palisades and walls ; but the cities were usually built in some position which afforded natural protection. Thus Tenochtitlan and Xochimilco were situated on small islands in lakes, while the settlements of the Tlalhuica were amidst almost inaccessible barrancas. Of the various nationalities the Aztec were undoubtedly the most warlike, followed at no great distance by the peoples of Tlaxcala and Uexotzinco. Of the peoples of Oaxaca the Mixtec, though inferior to the Aztec, were superior to the Zapotec.

In connection with the military expansion of Mexico, mention must be made of the guild of travelling merchants, or Pochteca. The Pochteca were not peculiar to Tenochtitlan; similar guilds were found in Azcapotzalco, Uitzilopochco and Quauhtitlan, but those of Tlaltelolco were by far the most famous. Membership of the guild was a valued privilege, since the merchants stood high in the royal favour ; only the sons of merchants could become merchants except by permission of the chiefs. Like the other calpulli, the Pochteca were under the direction of headmen, who represented the guild in external business, but they were privileged in so far as they were exempt from agricultural labour and from the ordinary judicial system, delinquents being judged by their own headmen. They worshipped special gods, chief of whom was the deity Yacatecutli, and joined in private ceremonies of a kind, as far as can be judged, far more elaborate than those of the other guilds. To some extent it is true that the importance of the guild grew with the expansion of Mexican power, but it would be almost equally true to say that Mexican power grew with the extension of the merchants' sphere of operations. They acted in fact as the pioneers of Mexican political influence, they penetrated fearlessly into hostile countries either openly and armed, or disguised, and for this purpose learned the speech of foreign nations. They acted as spies of the king, and in one case a body of Pochteca of Tlaltelolco were besieged in a town in Ana-uac Ayotlan, or the district around Tehuantepec, and, after four years, succeeded unaided in reducing the province to submission. For this deed they received special privileges and *insignia* from the king Auitzotl, including the right to wear lip-plugs of gold, while their captains bore military titles. At the time of the Spanish conquest these merchants made extended journeys far into Chiapas and Tabasco, and penetrated even to Guatemala. The gradual extension of their sphere of operations can be seen in the wares which they imported from time to time, and as this has a bearing upon Mexican history it is worth mention. In the reign of Quaquapitzauac, first king of Tlaltelolco, the imports were brilliant feathers from the low countries; under his successor, quetzal-feathers, turquoise, chalchiuitl and cotton textiles were added; in the next reign, lip-plugs of precious stones, gold, skins, and a greater variety of feathers were introduced; and under Moquiuix, the last king, cacao became an article of merchandise. This information is from Sahagun, who, in a later passage, states that precious stones were collected especially in southern Vera Cruz and Tabasco, and quetzal-plumes from the region around the present San Cristobal in Chiapas.

The Pochteca were careful to set out on their expeditions on a favourable day, such as 1. coatl, and before starting they made offerings to their god and the Earth; they also cut their hair and washed their heads, since custom forbade them to do either while on a journey. Their relations were also obliged to remain with head and face unwashed, except at intervals of eighty days, during their absence. They started out in a large body, merchants from various towns combining to form a caravan, as far as Tochtepec. There they divided, some going to Anauac Ayotlan, others to Anauac Xicalanco (southern Vera Cruz and Tabasco). When they returned, often after years of absence, they awaited a favourable day to enter their city, such as 1. calli, or 7. calli, when their home-coming was celebrated by a banquet and various religious ceremonies. Each merchant carried a staff, which was regarded as the image of the god Yacatecutli, and received offerings in his name. When on the march, the company of merchants at night tied their staves together, and offered incense before them, at the same time making blood-offerings from their ears and tongues.

The extraordinary facility with which nomadic hunting tribes adopt a trading profession has many parallels in Africa, where the interests of the wandering merchant are similarly guarded. Just as violence against one of the Pochteca inevitably resulted in a punitive expedition, so in times past the murder of a Bushongo trader by a Basongo Meno village would result in the extermination of the latter, and, at the present day, the death of a Badjok merchant would be similarly avenged by his compatriots. Mexican trade was for the most part carried on by means of direct exchange, and the result provides many difficulties to the archæologist. Once a town became famous for any kind of manufacture, the work of its artisans became spread far and wide, so that the discovery of objects of a particular style in a certain locality can by no means be taken necessarily to indicate that that style is characteristic of the site. Even pottery, which provides such valuable evidence in other parts, is not exempt from suspicion, since the ware of Cholula constituted an important article of export from that town. Certain articles formed a rough-and-ready currency in commerce, such as textiles and maize ; cacao beans also were used as a kind of " small change," and copper axe-blades were employed in certain localities, such as Oaxaca. More than one of the contemporary historians mention quills containing gold-dust as being utilized for the same purpose. The great market in Tlaltelolco moved the wonder of the conquerors ; it is described as being three times as large as that of Salamanca, and one estimate places the daily attendance at twenty or twenty-five thousand persons. One of the conquerors gives the following picture of it. " On one side are the people who sell gold ; near them are they who trade in jewels mounted in gold in the forms of birds and animals. On another side beads and mirrors are sold, on another, feathers and plumes of all colours for working designs on garments, and to wear in war or at festivals. Further on, stone is worked to make razors and swords, a remarkable thing which passes our understanding ; of it they manufacture swords and roundels. In other places they sell cloth and men's dresses of different designs ; beyond, dresses for women, and in another part footgear. A section is reserved for the sale of prepared hides of deer and other animals ; elsewhere are baskets made of hair, such as all Indian women use. Cotton, grain which forms their food, bread of all kinds, pastry, fowls, and eggs are sold in different sections ; and hard by they sell hares, rabbits, deer, quails, geese and ducks. Elsewhere wines of all sorts are for sale, vegetables, pepper, roots, medicinal plants, which are very numerous in this country, fruits of all kinds, wood for building, lime and stone. In fact, each object has its appointed place. Beside this great market-place there are in other quarters other markets also where provisions may be bought." Special magistrates held courts in the market-places to settle disputes on the spot, and there were market officials similar to our inspectors of weights and mea-

K

sures. Falsification of the latter was visited with severe punishment.

The judicial system at Mexico was elaborate and efficient ; justice was administered by a hierarchy of special officials, at the head of whom stood the Ciua-coatl or Chief Justice. This office, however, appears to have had its military aspect, in so far as the holder acted as commander of the Mexican contingent when the confederate forces went out to battle. The Tlacatecatl also acted as a high judicial functionary. The judges were selected by the king and highest officials from past students at the Calmecac, men of middle age full of experience and of unimpeachable integrity, who were " neither drunkards, nor amenable to bribes, nor liable to be influenced by favouritism nor passion." They received state maintenance, and if convicted of taking bribes or of delivering unjust sentences were punished with death. Each of the subject provinces maintained two judges at the three confederate towns, to whom the rulers assigned lands and service, and the ordinary courts opened in the morning, as soon as the judges had taken their seats at the mat-covered tribunal. Their midday meals were brought to them in court, and, after a short rest, they remained sitting until two hours before sunset. The high court sat in an apartment in the palace called Tlacxitlan, and dealt principally with high affairs of state and matters affecting the higher ranks, though it also pronounced sentences upon the cases sent up by the lower court. The latter, composed of representatives of the calpulli, also sat in the palace, in a room called Teccalli, and dealt with the affairs of the general public, sending its decisions to the Tlacxitlan for pronouncement of sentence. Important and difficult cases were reserved for a special court of thirteen judges headed by the ruler, which sat every eighty days. In the provinces there were a number of local courts of limited jurisdiction, from which cases of any importance were sent to the capital for trial, and there existed besides in the capitals a number of small courts, such as the market court, which dealt summarily with small offences, but from which appeal could be made to the higher courts. In the case of offenders of high rank the case was sometimes tried in the home of the criminal who, if found guilty, was executed there in private. Important tributary towns, as stated above, were often allowed considerable independence as regards judicial matters, and the rulers were allowed to judge their own people according to the local laws. Below the judges were a number of minor officials, apparitors and the like, as well as a military town-watch which kept order at night. Penalties varied in proportion to the gravity of the offence, from fines, payable in textiles, and flogging, to mutilation and death by the rod, the strangling-cord or by stoning. At Tezcoco a celebrated code, invented by the king Nezahualcoyotl, was in force, and the Mexican and Tacuban codes were based on this to a large extent; moreover, cases were often sent to Tezcoco for trial. Condemned criminals were shut up in cages to await execution, which usually took place upon some day considered appropriate, such as 1. quiauitl or 4. eecatl. Theft was punished in various ways; in unimportant cases the thief was compelled to make restitution, in cases more grave he became the slave of the complainant; if he had stolen gold or jewels, he was sacrificed to Xipe at the goldsmiths' festival. Stealing corn from the fields was punished with death, and though this sentence may seem severe, the crime was the less excusable because corn was planted along the roadsides for the use of wayfarers. The death penalty was also inflicted for wrongful assumption of the *insignia* belonging to the highest offices, for murder, adultery (by stoning), sorcery (by sacrifice), disobedience or desertion in war, injury to a royal messenger, or shifting a landmark. The laws against drunkenness were particularly strict ; in the case of the young this offence was often punished with death, the accused, if of low rank, being publicly clubbed to death so that his fate might serve as an example. Rank could not save a man, though it gave him the privilege of being executed in private. Less aggravated cases were punished by degradation in the case of a noble, accompanied by public hair-cutting and the destruction of the culprit's house. Only the elderly were permitted the free use of octli, though men over thirty were allowed a moderate supply at festivals and when engaged upon hard manual labour. In other cases special permission had to be obtained from some official superior before the intoxicating liquor could be drunk without fear of punishment. These regulations, though severe, were extremely salutary, a fact which is proved by the outburst of drunkenness which took place after the conquest, when the old *régime* was swept away. Punishment was often inflicted upon a tributary town by demanding victims for sacrifice, as in the case of Quiauiztlan in Vera Cruz, the inhabitants of which were ordered to provide twenty men and women for this fate because they had received the Spaniards. The Tarascan ruler, at the time of the greatest development of the Michoacan peoples, was assisted in government by two ministers analogous to the Mexican Ciuacoatl and Tlacatecatl respectively. The judicial code was much the same, though little definite is known concerning it save that the death penalty was inflicted for the wrongful appropriation of land, the head of the criminal being set up on the violated boundary. Among the Chichimec, adultery was punished with death, each member of the tribal group shooting four arrows at the guilty couple. The Mexicans held slaves, or rather bondsmen, in some numbers, and the slave-class consisted of criminals, prisoners of war, and individuals sold into slavery. Persons in extreme poverty could pledge themselves or their children, and we read that in the reign of Montecuzoma many of the better-class families were reduced to such straits by a famine lasting two years that they fell into slavery. By orders of the king these unfortunates were sought out and ransomed by him at twice the price paid for them. It is said that the sale of a slave required two witnesses, and that slaves could not be sold without their own permission, except those who wore heavy wooden collars as runaways or insubordinate. A peculiar form of slavery existed, in accordance with which an indigent family could bind itself to supply one or more slaves perpetually to some lord, the individual in servitude being changed every few years. If a slave-woman died as the result of an intrigue with a free man, the latter became the slave of her master ; but if a child was born and both survived, it became the property of the father and was free-born. Slaves were well treated on the whole, though they were liable to be sacrificed. They were considered as under the protection of Tezcatlipoca, and at one of his feasts were accorded absolute licence as at the Roman Saturnalia.

CHAPTER VI—MEXICO : CRAFTS, DRESS, AND DAILY LIFE

FOR most practical purposes the Mexicans at the date of the Spanish conquest were living in an age of stone. It is true that they both knew and worked two metals with great facility, namely, gold and copper, especially the former ; but gold is useless as a material from which to make implements, and copper was not sufficiently plentiful to be employed very freely. Both these metals were therefore utilized principally in the manufacture of ornaments, though copper tools were employed in wood-carving and a few minor arts.

Hard stone from which adze- and axe-blades and chisels could be manufactured occurred in quantities in Mexico, and various volcanic rocks were quarried for the purpose of making implements. Chalcedony and other flinty materials were used in the manufacture of knife-blades, and the workmanship of these, especially of some of the specimens from the Mixtec country, are surpassed only by the finest examples of ripple-flaking from ancient Egypt (see Fig. 19,8). Knife-blades of this form were usually thrust into a simple ball of resin to form a handle, though for ceremonial use elaborately carved wooden hafts covered with turquoise and shell mosaic (Pl. XVIII, 1) were fitted to them. But the material which perhaps was of the greatest use to the Mexicans was obsidian. From blocks of this natural glass long flakes could be detached by pressure, each of which came away from the core with a razor-edge. Such flakes were used as knives without further preparation, or were inset along the borders of wooden

swords to form a cutting edge. The flaking-implement
was a pointed stick with a cross-piece at one end; the

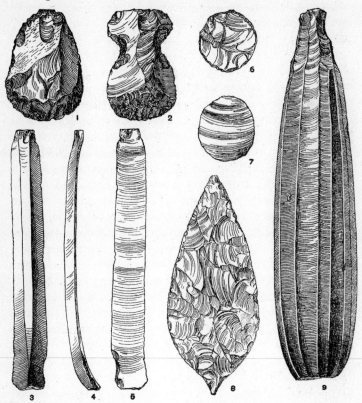

FIG. 19.—Stone and obsidian implements.

1, 2. Obsidian scrapers.
3-5.   ,,   flakes.
6, 7.   ,,   ,, perhaps for inlay.
8. Chert knife-blade.
9. Obsidian core, from which flakes have been struck.

(*British Museum*)

artisan rested the point on a suitable spot on the obsidian block, which he held between his feet, and applied the necessary pressure by leaning his chest against
the cross-piece. The nature of the long thin flakes

which were detached, and of the core from which they were struck, is shown in Fig. 19, 3–5 and 9. Broader flakes were worked up by secondary flaking to form delicate arrow-heads and graceful spear-heads, while large slabs were polished to form mirrors, the surface being carefully finished by continuous rubbing with a handful of reeds. Masks were also made from this material, and details such as teeth and eyes were inlaid with shell and other substances. Stone axes (Fig. 20) were carefully ground by rubbing on a block of hard-stone, probably with sand or emery and water, the surface in the more highly-polished specimens being finished with bamboo. The shapes show some variation, but the implement usually tapers slightly towards the butt, which is rounded off more or less abruptly ; some specimens are long-oval in transverse section, while others are quadrangular. They were hafted by being simply thrust into a wooden handle, as shown in Fig. 4, f; p. 35. The finest specimens are made of some kind of jadeite, and are often beautifully polished, especially those from the Mixtec country. In the Tarascan country, and northward to La Quemada in Zacatecas, are found types closely akin to those of Arizona and California, viz. heavy axes, coarsely ground, with one or two grooves partially or entirely encircling the butt (Fig. 20, 4, 7 and 8). These must have been attached to the haft by thongs, or a stout twig must have been bent round the implement and secured by a lashing below. Such forms as these are not found in the Mexican valley or further south, until Ecuador is reached, but are in reality characteristic of the northern portion of the continent. In the same area are found peculiar blades in animal form, as shown in Fig. 20, 5. Great masses of stone were handled with considerable facility, and it is only necessary to call attention to the objects shown in Pls. III and VI–VIII, as evidence of the skill of the Mexico mason. The large coping-stone with a figure of a fire-snake in high relief illustrated on Pl. V, 2, being an especially fine specimen from a technical point of view.

To speak generally, Aztec sculpture often shows a slight stiffness in style, due in part to its conventional

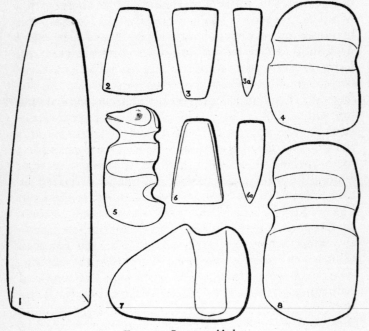

FIG. 20.—Stone axe-blades.

1. Etla, Oaxaca.
2, 3, 6. Valley of Mexico.
4, 5, 7, 8. Michoacan (Tarascan.)

(*British Museum*)

nature, but many specimens exist which exhibit considerable freedom of treatment, notably the figure of Xochipilli on Pl. V, 1 (of which the characteristic crest rising from the head-dress is unfortunately missing), and the magnificent rattlesnake on Pl. XI, A. Characteristic of the stone art of Tulan are caryatid figures (similar to Fig. 84, p. 348) and serpent columns, both of which will be met again when we come to consider the art of Yucatan ; and related to the same culture are figures representing a reclining god, probably one of the octli-gods, holding a vase. One of these, of colossal proportions, has also been found in Yucatan. This type of statue seems to have been copied in Aztec times, and the specimen on Pl. VIII, 2, probably belongs to this later period. Caryatid figures are also found in Tlaxcala. A particular class of sculpture is constituted by the peculiar stone figures found in the Panuco valley, of which a fine series may be seen in the British Museum (Pl. X, 1). These are distinguished by the pointed head-dress associated with the Huaxtec, sometimes combined with the jaws of a monster, or a semicircular crest with engraved snake-design. Most are otherwise nude, and all exhibit a somewhat crude and archaic character. Belonging to the Totonac culture are certain enigmatical stone objects, beautifully carved, of which the principal are the so-called "yokes" and "paddle-shaped stones." The shape of the former is best seen from the illustration, Fig. 21 ; viewed from the side or rounded end (a), the carving in nearly all cases represents a monster or grotesque human being crouching upon the ground, while from above (b), the rounded end represents the upper jaw of a gaping mouth furnished with teeth. The use of these has been much disputed, but I would suggest the following explanation as the simplest. The attitude of the crouching figure shows that the normal position of the object is flat upon the ground, as in Fig. 21, a, while the fact that the yokes are found in graves suggests that they have a funerary significance. It is possible that they were meant to support the corpse in an upright position, and as such the crouching figure typifies the earth-monster, while the gaping mouth represents the jaws of the same creature open to receive the dead, just as the earth-monster is shown in manuscripts supporting a mummy-pack in its open maw (Fig. 14, *b*; p. 104). These carved yokes, many of which suggest Mayan

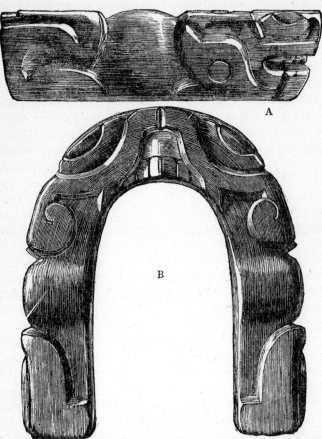

A

B

FIG. 21, A, B.   Stone "Yoke"; Totonac district.
(*British Museum*)

rather than Mexican art, seem to have been carried by trade or otherwise over a large area, since examples have been found in Tlaxcala, Tabasco, Guatemala and San Salvador. The paddle-shaped stones often exhibit great skill in stone-carving, but at present no explanation of their use is forthcoming. These again are Mayan in type rather than Mexican.

In working stone, stone tools were alone employed, copper being quite unsuitable for the purpose. Of smaller works of art attention may be called to the specimens shown in Pl. XI, 3 and 4, which are carved in jadeite or some analogous material. The small seated figures in Fig. 22, and the carved plate in Pl. XI, 4, are particularly characteristic of Oaxaca. Fine alabaster vases were manufactured, especially in the Totonac country around Vera Cruz, the interiors being laboriously drilled out by means of a

tubular drill, probably of bone or bamboo, a practice also followed by ancient Egyptian lapidaries. Small mirrors, with a convex surface

FIG. 22.—Stone figurines ; Mixtec.

to reduce the image, were made from nodules of pyrites, and beads and pendants of all descriptions were manufactured from jadeite and other translucent stones. Fine green jadeite, called chalchiuitl, was highly prized, and its use was allowed only to persons of high rank. Ornaments of this material were given by Montecuzoma to Cortés for transmission to the Emperor, and Diaz quotes his words as follows : " I will also give you some very valuable stones . . . chalchihuites . . . not to be given to anyone else, but only to him, your great Prince." Bead necklaces of this stone formed an important item of tribute from certain subject cities (Fig. 18, c; p. 118). In producing the smaller works of art from crystal, jadeite and amethyst, flint, and sometimes copper, points were

PLATE XI

MEXICO
STONE RATTLE-SNAKE
(Scale : 1/6th)

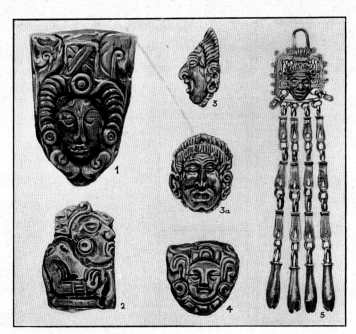

British Museum

MAYA	MIXTEC
1. JADEITE RELIEF	4. JADEITE RELIEF FROM OAXACA
2. ,, ,, FROM TIKAL	ZAPOTEC
MEXICO	5. GOLD LIP-PENDANT FROM
3. JADEITE HEAD	TEHUANTEPEC

(Scale : 1 –5, 2/3rds)

used for engraving and drilling, emery was employed in rubbing down, and small articles were set in wood for polishing. Heliotrope, being very hard, was set in stone. The stone-workers of Xochimilco and Tenayocan enjoyed a particularly high reputation. The most gorgeous works of the lapidary's art were the mosaics, of which two are shown on Pls. I and XVIII, 1. In the first, fragments of turquoise and jet are laid in a resinous matrix on a human skull; the eyes are pyrites encircled with shell rings, and the nose is inlaid with plates of pink shell (pink shells also formed an article of tribute, see Fig. 18, e; p. 118). Some of the teeth have been reset in their wrong places. The knife-handle is similarly incrusted with turquoise, malachite and shell. Masks of the gods, headpieces and ornaments were made in the same materials on wood foundations, and the masks of Quetzalcoatl, Tlaloc and Tezcatlipoca were among the articles sent by Cortés to the Emperor Charles. The Tarascans were especially famed as mosaic workers, and the art extended right up into Arizona, though not in such perfection. It is thought that the turquoise itself passed in trade southwards from the deposits at Los Cerillos in New Mexico. The Toltec were reputed to have been particularly skilful lapidaries, and to have possessed peculiar powers in the way of discovering deposits of precious stones. For this purpose, so it was said, they would take up their position on some elevated spot just before dawn, and at the moment when the sun appeared above the horizon, would note any small cloud of vapour rising from the earth, a manifestation which was supposed to indicate where they might be found.

Copper was used occasionally for axe- and adzeblades, and constituted an article of tribute. Analysis has shown that it was hammered out, and the edge hardened by this means alone. Some of the blades contain a percentage of tin, but the presence of the latter metal may be regarded as purely accidental. The

forms are usually similar to those of the stone implements, and they were hafted by lashing, with wedges, to
a handle, as shown in Fig. 27, *a*; p. 148. "Eared" varieties however occur, though they are rare, and a peculiar
T-shaped type is found in some quantity, extending into
Oaxaca and Guatemala. Most of the last-named are so
thin that it is difficult to see what useful purpose they
could have served, and it is probable that they constituted a form of currency, though the suggestion has
been made that they were used as knives for cutting
feathers in the preparation of feather mosaic. Bells of
copper are common throughout the whole of Mexico,
some in a peculiar technique which look as if they were
made of soldered wire, and animal forms in the same
style have been found in Tarascan territory. Close
examination would seem to show that these are really
cast by the *cire perdue* process, as described below.
Great difficulties however attend the casting of copper,
and it is possible that such articles contain a percentage
of tin. Analyses however are lacking, and it seems certain that the presence of tin must be regarded as accidental, for though deposits of tin were found in Guerrero by Cortés, yet the inhabitants had never deliberately mixed it with copper until shown how to do so
by the Spaniards. Of the mining of copper, little is
known, but ancient workings have been discovered at
Cerro del Aguilar in Guerrero. Abundant traces of fire
are to be seen, and no less than 140 stone wedges have
been collected there. Probably the process consisted in
heating the blocks of ore, and driving the wedges into
the resultant cracks so as to split them up into more
manageable fragments. The Zapotec country was
famed in old times for its copper.

In the working of gold the Mexicans exhibited particular skill, and though great quantities of the wrought
metal were found by the conquerors, yet a very small
percentage of the enormous amount exported since the

conquest has found its way into museums. The greatest
treasure discovered at one time by Cortés was that
amassed by Axayacatl, father of Montecuzoma. Of
this Diaz writes : " Cortés and some of the captains
went in first (into the treasury), and they saw such a
number of jewels and slabs and plates of gold and chalchihuites and other great riches that they were quite
carried away, and did not know what to say about such
wealth. . . . When I saw it I marvelled, and, as at that
time I was a youth, and had never seen such riches as
those in my life before, I took it for certain that there

A   B   C

FIG. 23.—Mexican artisans.
A. Feather-worker.
B. Goldsmith.
C. Stone-bead maker.
(*Mendoza MS., Oxford*)

could not be another such store of wealth in the whole
world." This treasure was subsequently found to be
of the value approximately of one and a half million
sterling. Another of the conquerors relates the finding
of 480 oz. of gold in one grave. But the accounts of
the workmanship of the various articles surpass even
their number. We read of " a very rich necklace of
golden crabs, a marvellous piece of work " ; of " two
birds made of thread and feather-work, having the
quills of their wings and tails, their feet, eyes and the
ends of their beaks, of gold, standing upon two reeds
covered with gold, which are raised on balls of feather-
work and gold embroidery, one white and the other

yellow, with seven tassels of feather-work hanging from each of them " ; and of a fish with alternate scales of gold and silver. Unhappily no such works of art as the two latter have survived. Grijalva describes the getting of gold by picking out the grains from river-sand ; the collector storing them in his mouth and later melting them down on the spot in a pottery vessel, blowing up the fire by means of tubes of reed, as in Fig. 23, b. Gold was also washed from river-sand in small troughs, the water being poured on from gourds. This method was employed both on the east coast and in the Zapotec region, but regular mining was practised by the Zapotec and Chinantec, and gold formed a very important article of tribute, both in dust and plates. The goldsmiths of Azcapotzalco were the most famed in the valley ; and gold-workers in general were divided into two classes, beaters and casters. In beating, stone hammers were used for the most part, and the workmen were very skilful at overlaying with gold-foil (the spear-thrower shown on Pl. XVII, 1, has been ornamented in this way). Wooden beads overlaid with gold have been found in the Totonac country. Casting was carried out as follows : pounded charcoal was mixed with fine clay, and kneaded out into thin discs, on which the details of the desired ornament were engraved with a copper tool. Wax was then prepared by boiling, mixed with copal to give it firmness, and, after clarifying by means of a filter, was rolled out on a polished stone and applied in small strips to the details of the design. Pounded charcoal in solution was added as a covering, and, over all, a coating of clay, also mixed with charcoal. A rod of wax, coated with clay, was added, to form a connection with the wax model within. The whole was baked, the wax run out and the molten gold poured in. Finally the mould was broken, and the casting rubbed with earth mixed with salt, to give it a good colour, and then polished. Objects so prepared often have the appearance of soldered wire, but, in such specimens as the ring shown in Fig. 24, the reverse side plainly shows that the greater portion has been cast solid. In the case of the gold ear- or lip-ornament from Tehuantepec (Pl. XI, 5), some of the details appear to have been soldered on after casting. We are told that the designs applied to beaten gold by engraving were usually traced for the goldsmiths by the feather-workers.

FIG. 24.   Gold finger-ring (*scale* ²/₁).

Of this feather-work (Fig. 25) very few specimens remain, but the description of the methods employed in its manufacture have been preserved in the nahuatl text of Sahagun and translated by Seler. Diaz writes of fine fabrics covered with feather-work made by women, and brought daily " from some towns of the province on the north coast near Vera Cruz called Cotaxtla, close by San Juan de Ulua." In the valley the most renowned feather-workers were the inhabitants of the Amantlan quarter of Mexico, who worshipped gods of their own, and prided themselves on their descent from early immigrants into the valley from the north. The implements used in the craft were a brush and colour-box for sketching designs, a copper knife and wooden cutting-board, and a bone spatula for attaching the feathers when cut into the required shapes. In some cases the feathers were simply sewn to cloth, but the more elaborate mosaics required a lengthier process. Cotton was applied to a strip of maguey by means of paste, and a coating of paste was painted over it ; after drying, the cotton was peeled from the maguey and

L

FIG. 25.—Feather-work mantle (*Berlin*).
(*After Seler*)

pasted to a backing of bark-paper: the design was carefully drawn upon it, and then cut out after the manner of a stencil, through which the design was traced upon a sheet of maguey, backed with cotton, or cotton backed with maguey. To the last a layer of the cheaper kind of feathers of the requisite shapes and colours was applied by means of the spatula, first the outlines in black, and then the body-colours and details. The foundation was then detached and fastened to a board, and the final layer, this time in precious feathers of similar colours, was added. The stencil was used as a check throughout the whole of the process. Every kind of feather ornament was made by these artists, including the elaborate back-devices worn by different ranks of warriors. For many of the latter cane frames were constructed, to which the feathers, carefully marshalled, were attached by threads, layer upon layer being added, each covering the bare quills of the last, the final row consisting of down. In the earlier days obsidian knives were used to cut the feathers, and in reality the art only became of importance after the conquest of various coastal towns brought the plumes of the more gorgeous birds to

FIG. 26.—Pottery spindle-whorls (the top right-hand specimen is of bone), from the Island of Sacrificios.
(*British Museum*)

Mexico in great quantities as tribute. Those workers engaged upon the feather ornaments and mantles used to deck the figure and representatives of the god Uitzilopochtli, lived in a special house, and many of the more important lords maintained artists who worked especially for them.

The textile arts flourished throughout Mexico, though owing to the unfavourable nature of the climate, specimens are practically non-existent. Thread was spun by the women from nequen, the fibre of the maguey or cotton, and the fur of rabbits was also utilized. Girls learnt the art at a tender age, and the ornamented spindle-whorls, usually of pottery, but sometimes of bone, are common in museums (Fig. 26). The spindle was made to revolve in a small pottery bowl, as is shown in Fig. 29; p. 161, and the thread was woven on a loom of simple construction. The warp was fastened to a convenient post, and kept taut by means of a band passing round the back of the weaver, who beat down the weft with a wooden " sword " (Fig. 27, *b*). The loom was in fact almost certainly the same as that used right into modern times, and it is probable that a number of heddles were employed for the more elaborate designs. Cotton was of course grown in the hotter countries, and both textiles and the raw material formed perhaps the most

A   FIG. 27.   B

A. Wood-carver.
B. Woman weaving.
(*Mendoza MS.*, *Oxford*)

important article of import into the valley. Strangely enough it is the inhabitants of the cooler districts who bore the reputation of being the most skilful weavers. Some idea of the designs which were employed may be gathered from the manuscripts, but the patterns there figured form only a very small proportion of the whole. Sahagun gives a long list of names relating to particular types of mantle, unfortunately without further description except in a very few cases. One of these may be cited in illustration of their elaborate nature. " They also made use of cloaks on which were figured beautiful and rich jars mounted on three feet, and furnished with two ' wings ' like those of butterflies (octli-vases). The lower portion of the jar was rounded and coloured red and black (the colours of the octli-gods), the wings were green with a yellow border, and three small dots of the same colour on each. The neck of this jar had the form of the *marquesota* of a tunic, crowned with four small rods embroidered in red and blue feathers. These jar designs were scattered on a white field. This cloak had two red stripes along its front border, passing over white bands grouped two by two " (see the textile in Fig. 18, *s*; p. 118). Many of the details in patterns such as the above were added in embroidery, at which the Mexican women were equally expert. Good polychrome weaving was performed by the Otomi in maguey fibre, and the Tarascan and Huaxtec ranked high as textile artists. The Tarascan women were said to prepare food for a couple of days before starting to weave, so that they might not be disturbed at their task. Weaving and embroidery were under the especial patronage of the goddess Xochiquetzal. Mat- and basketmaking was also an important industry, though of these arts also specimens are lacking. However, the use of mat seats was a privilege of rank, though perhaps less so than in the Maya region, and the mat-makers paid reverence to a special patron-deity, Napatecutli, one of the Tlaloque. The consideration of Mexican pottery will be deferred until the architectural remains have been discussed.

A certain amount of information concerning the dress and ornaments of the Mexicans can be gleaned from the foregoing pages, and repetition will be unnecessary. The ordinary dress for a man, worn by nearly all the peoples mentioned in this book, was a girdle, maxtlatl, the ends of which hung down before and behind, and a shoulder-cloak (e.g. Fig. 23 ; p. 143). The woman's dress, equally universal, consisted of a skirt and a tunic, usually without sleeves (e.g. Fig. 27, *b*; p. 148). The original costume of the Aztec was of skins, but after their settlement in the valley, textiles were adopted, first of nequen fibre, later of maguey and cotton. The last-named material however was reserved for the upper classes, the women of which added to their attire by wearing additional tunics and skirts. Exceptions to the above rule were constituted by the Tarascans, among whom the men, as among the Huaxtec, wore no maxtlatl, and the Chichimec who wore skins. Skin-clothing prevailed to some extent among the Tarascans also, though they were good weavers, and in this district the young wore shorter

FIG. 28.—Designs from pottery stamps; Valley of Mexico.
(*British Museum*)

skirts than their elders. The following garments were considered more or less characteristic of certain peoples; white cloaks with figures of scorpions in blue of the Toltec; striped textiles of the Otomi; duck-feather cloaks of the Tarascans; net cloaks of the Totonac; white cotton mantles of the Zapotec, and polychrome textiles especially representing interlaced eddies (as the shield in Fig. 18, *p*; p. 118) of the Huaxtec. Body-paint was employed by all the tribes, especially on ceremonial occasions; Mexican women were in the habit of painting their faces yellow and impressing patterns in red upon their cheeks with pottery stamps (Fig. 28). Figures of monkeys and coxcoxtli-birds were especially favourite designs. The Tarascans of Tzintzuntzan used black

body-paint, like the priestly orders in Mexico, and the
Tlalhuica red. The question of tatu is more difficult to
settle, certainly this form of adornment was not common.
Sahagun states that in the month of Toxcatl the priests
" with a stone knife made scars on children of both
sexes, on the breast, the stomach, the middle of the
arms and the wrists," and also that the Otomi women
" made on their breasts and arms designs in a blue
colour, by means of small instruments which fixed the
colour in the flesh." The latter statement at any rate
seems to point to the practice of tatu. Sahagun states that
the Huaxtec and Totonac tatued, and the slab illustrated
in Fig. 11; p. 83, shows a man whose limbs are apparently
ornamented in this manner. Otomi women stained the
teeth black, a practice found also among the Huaxtec,
while tooth-filing was found among the latter people,
the Tarascans and the Mixtec. Pottery heads showing
the Maya form of tooth-filing have been found in the
Totonac area. The actual inlaying of teeth seems to have
been confined to those peoples of definite Maya affinities,
such as the Huaxtec, though teeth ornamented in this
fashion have been found in the Mixtec area, at Xoxo.
Mexican women of rank filed the teeth and painted
them red. This practice seems to have been borrowed
from the Huaxtec, and tooth-mutilation as a whole
does not seem to have been a characteristic of the
Nahua-speaking peoples. Methods of dressing the hair
show slight variations, though the ordinary method
was to cut it short on the forehead and temples,
and allow it to grow at the back. The Tarascans however for the most part cropped it close all over, while
the Chichimec did not cut it at all, but wore it in
plaits. Among the Otomi the child's head was cropped
close, men and young girls cut the locks on the forehead,
and women after becoming mothers allowed it to grow
all over the head and dressed it on the top. Zapotec chiefs
and warriors wore long hair gathered at the back in a

pigtail. In Mexico men of rank, being warriors, cut the hair, and brushed it up on the right side (Pl. IX, 4), while chiefs cropped most of the head, leaving a long lock on the forehead which they kept erect by means of a fillet (Pl. IX, 5). Of Montecuzoma we read, "He did not wear his hair long, but so as just to cover his ears." In Mexico women of rank sometimes wore the hair plaited and crossed on the forehead in two " horns," but ordinarily it was allowed to grow and was worn loose. Ear-ornaments were almost universal, in the form of plugs of stone, gold and turquoise; while lip-plugs were found among the Mexicans, Otomi and Totonac (see Fig. 18, b; p. 118). At Mexico the lips of children were pierced on admission to the Calmecac, and the status of a man could be judged by the quality of his lip-plug. Shell and obsidian marked the lower ranks, while gold and gems were reserved for the higher orders of nobility; most prized of all were those of chalchiuitl, or of crystal, the latter being hollow and containing a blue feather. Nose-ornaments were not so common, and were especially associated with the Huaxtec; they are however frequently seen in the representations of Mexican goddesses (especially those borrowed from the Huaxtec) and consisted for the most part of gold plates, often in the form of a butterfly, or of golden tubes. Of the tremendous variety of ornaments worn round neck and arms and attached to the garments, it is impossible to write in detail, but some idea of their variety may be gathered from the following passage of Sahagun, describing the dance performed by men and women of the warrior-class in the month Uei tecuilhuitl. " The women were clad in rich and costly robes and skirts ornamented with elaborate embroidery . . . Of the robes . . . some were white without designs, and the upper opening of these was bordered with deep fringes which covered the whole breast, and the fringes of the

lower border were equally deep. These women danced
with their hair down, confined by plaited bands which
ran from forehead to neck. Their faces were without
ornament, smooth and clean. The men were equally
richly clad ; they wore a cotton cloak of so wide a mesh
that it might almost be called a net. In the case of men
who were distinguished by great valour and who had
the right to wear a plug in the lower lip, these cloaks
were fringed with small white shells . . . those who were
not so distinguished wore black cloaks with (plain)
fringes. All wore ear-plugs of mixed metals, but those
of the higher ranks were of copper with gold pendants,
their lip-plugs corresponding. In some cases these lip-
plugs represented lizards, in others, small dogs, or two
small squares of metal. The youngest who had already
distinguished themselves in action wore in the lower lip
a large disc, containing four others arranged crosswise.
The youngest of all had a plain disc without ornament.
All the ' braves ' wore hide collars with pendants terminating in numbers of small white shells . . . and at
the same time lip-plugs of oyster-shell in the form of an
eagle ; while others who considered themselves of still
greater valour, bought small white spheres found in
certain molluscs. Ordinary folk decked themselves in a
sort of chaplet, yellow in colour, made of other marine
products, and of small value. Among this class, those
who had captured prisoners in war bore an ornament of
plumes on their heads as an indication that they had
taken a captive in battle. The captains were distinguished by feather *insignia* attached to their backs, as a
sign of valour. . . . There were some who carried on
the left foot the hooves of deer attached with strips of
hide of the same animal. All had their faces painted in
various designs ; some painted circles on their cheeks
and stripes on the forehead from temple to temple with
black pigment covered with iron pyrites, others prolonged the stripe to the ears, and others again painted

stripes from the base of the ear to the mouth." Feathers of course, whether applied to textiles or worn by themselves, constituted an extremely important article of adornment, and even the Otomi women wore them on their feet and legs during dancing, a custom found also among the Toluca. Sandals of hide with straps ornamented according to the rank of the wearer were in universal use.

The Mexicans enjoyed considerable variety in food, and though famines were not uncommon, yet the attention paid to agriculture in the valley and the extensive trade-system made the supply plentiful under normal circumstances. The Chichimec hunters lived on game, wild roots and fruits, and honey, but most of the remaining tribes practised cultivation, especially of maize, though the Otomi were said to have been improvident in the use of the crop. To speak generally, maize was the staple food, though free use was made of other grain, yams and beans. From maize a large variety of " bread " was manufactured, mostly in the form of thin cakes differing greatly in quality. The grain was thrown into boiling water, into which a little lime had been sprinkled, to remove the husk; when cool, it was washed, ground on the grinding-stones, called metatl, and kneaded into dough which was cooked in pots, or wrapped in leaves and steamed. Certain flowers were often added to give it a flavour. Maize-meal was often boiled in water, the liquor being strained and reboiled until it was reduced to a kind of gruel, called atolli, which was consumed in large quantities. Venison, rabbits, hares, quails, partridges, ducks, turkeys and geese, provided the most common flesh-foods ; the two latter birds were domesticated and were bred almost as much for their feathers as for their flesh, especially in Culiacan, Jalisco and Michoacan ; eggs were not eaten. The hairless Mexican dog was also bred as a food-animal in some places, such as Jalisco. Meat was cooked wrapped in dough or plainly roasted, and pepper was consumed in great quantities as a condiment, just as in Peru. Fish too formed an important article of diet, and the courier-system in the later days of the Empire was so excellent that it could be brought fresh from the coast for the use of the royal house. Certain marsh-flies which appear in veritable clouds on the lake were pounded and made up into balls and boiled, and their eggs were collected from the reeds and eaten as a kind of caviare ; frogs too were not despised, and the Otomi were credited with eating snakes and rats. A peculiar food seen by the conquerors consisted of " cakes made from a sort of ooze which they get out of the great lake, which curdles, and from this they make a bread having a flavour something like cheese." Honey, both that of bees and that made from the sap of the maguey, was used to sweeten atolli and in many other ways, and salt was prepared by filtering water through certain kinds of earth and evaporating the liquor. The constant hostilities of the Tlaxcalans with the Mexicans had resulted in the almost total destruction of the salt trade as far as the former were concerned ; in fact the inhabitants had practically lost the habit of taking it, and some years elapsed after the conquest before it became common in that district. It is said that neither salt nor pepper was used by the Toluca and Matlatzinca. As regards beverages, two were of great importance ; the first of these was prepared from the cacao, imported from the hotter regions near the coast, and was called chocolatl (whence our own word chocolate). The nut was pounded and boiled in water with a little maize-flour ; the oil was skimmed off, and the mixture strained and poured into another vessel so as to produce a froth ; sometimes honey and vanilla were added, and it was generally taken after food with tortoise-shell spoons. The other national drink was octli (often inaccurately termed pulque, an

Argentine word for the same beverage), prepared from the fermented sap of the maguey. The heart of the plant was cut out (the day 1. tecpatl being considered an appropriate date) and when the sap had collected it was drawn off in long gourds by means of suction applied through a small hole at the end, and stored in skins or calabashes. Fermentation was assisted by the addition of a certain root. The legal restrictions placed upon the use of this beverage in Mexico have already been mentioned. Other fermented drinks were prepared from grain, and a certain mushroom was employed as an intoxicant, especially at a feast organized by the guild of merchants. The effects of the latter are described by Sahagun : " Some sang, others wept because they were intoxicated ; others remained silent, seated in the hall as if absorbed in thought. Some thought that they were dying, and sobbed in their hallucination, while others imagined that they were being devoured by some savage beast. Others again thought that they were capturing an enemy in fight, another that he was rich, another that he possessed a large number of slaves. Some thought that they were taken in adultery, and that their heads were being crushed for this crime, others that they had been convicted of theft and were being executed, and a thousand other illusions. When the intoxication had passed, they entertained one another by relating their hallucinations." The discovery of the properties of this fungus seems to have been made originally by the Chichimec, since its use was common among this people. A kind of chewing-gum was prepared from resin or bitumen, though its use, at any rate in public, was confined by custom to unmarried girls. Allusion has already been made to the practice of smoking ; reeds were collected and after being carefully smoothed were filled with pulverized charcoal mixed with tobacco and other fragrant herbs. The exterior was often richly ornamented with paint and gilding, in some cases in such a way that the design only appeared under the influence of the heat produced by the act of smoking. Pottery pipes are found in Mexico, though not in great numbers, and it is uncertain to what extent they were used before the conquest. Pipes are found more frequently in Michoacan, where tobacco-smoking was commoner than among the Aztec, especially in the case of men of rank.

In general the first meal of the day, taken after a few hours' work, consisted in atolli-gruel, a more substantial repast following at midday, after which the higher classes smoked and took a siesta. Food was cooked in and eaten from pots, bowls and dishes of pottery, often beautifully ornamented. Cups of the same material, and also of gold or stone (such as alabaster), were used for beverages, and a peculiar pattern with two butter-fly-handles and three feet (as shown on the textile in Fig. 18, 5; p. 118) was especially associated with octli, forming one of the devices of the octli-gods.

Maguey-fibre has already been mentioned as a material extensively employed for textiles, and indeed the uses of this plant were manifold. To quote again from one of the conquerors, " This tree is of the greatest utility ; from it is made wine, vinegar, honey, a syrup like boiled grape-juice. They employ it in the manufacture of garments for men and women, for footgear, ropes, the ties used in building houses, the roofing of these houses, for sewing-needles (i.e. the spines), for dressings for wounds, and other purposes. They also collected the leaves . . . and cooked them in subterranean ovens, with wood piled up, in a fashion peculiar to this country. After roasting, the bark and veins are removed, and an intoxicating drink is prepared."

The consideration of Mexican architecture from a comparative standpoint will be deferred until the remains scattered through the country are discussed. But as all these remains consist of buildings devoted to religious purposes, a few words may be said here concerning the actual habitations of the people. Mexico city was utterly destroyed by the Spanish, but from the accounts left by the first visitors a good idea can be gathered of the nature of the buildings. The houses of the chiefs were spacious, built on terraces, and constructed of stone and lime. The buildings usually enclosed a court, and there was often a garden attached where the girls of the household could walk under the supervision of duennas. The women's apartments were separated from the rest ; two storeys were sometimes seen, and in the most important structures the roofs were flat and battlemented. Nezahualcoyotl's palace at Tezcoco, of which a native plan is shown in Fig. 13, p. 89, was constructed on a terrace, and the roof-beams were supported by wooden pillars on stone bases. The terrace formed a court in front, approached by steps, and there were many small buildings for guests, the women of the household, and the retainers. Diaz mentions the palaces of Iztapalapa " how well-built they were, of beautiful stone - work and cedar - wood and the wood of other sweet - scented trees; with great rooms and courts, wonderful to behold, covered with awnings of cotton cloth." He also mentions the " great halls and chambers, canopied with the cloth of the country," of the palace of Axayacatl, and the " beds of matting with canopies above " which were provided for the Spaniards. Earth and unfired bricks (" adobes ") were also used for the walls of buildings, and the houses of the poorer classes were of reeds and mud roofed with thatch of straw or maguey-leaves. In Mexico city, owing to the marshy nature of the ground, a large proportion of the buildings rested on pile foundations, and, in consequence of the growth of the town beyond the limit of land-accommodation, many were built over the water, and could only be reached by boat or draw-bridge. The town itself was intersected by numerous canals, and the inhabitants went about as much in boats as on land. Near the coast, pile-dwellings were constructed so that the inhabitants might be out of the reach of wild beasts, and protecting walls of adobes or wooden palisades were also found. Beds in most cases were made of rushes, with cotton sheets, those of the lords being woven with feathers, and for meals a mat was simply spread upon the ground. The primitive hunting-tribes, such as the wilder Chichimec, lived chiefly in caves, though some of the more advanced constructed rude temporary huts. The Tarascans built the walls of their dwellings of natural stones, and constructed the roof of straw thatch, with, apparently, a clay ridge. Thatch was in fact the principal roofing material throughout Mexico, and even the shrines were usually so covered.

One of the chief features of Mexico city was the series of causeways which connected the island with the mainland. The position of these, according to the most recent ideas, can be seen in Fig. 1, p. 13. In building them a double palisade was first constructed, and the space between filled with stones and earth faced with rubble. The great dyke which ran from Iztapalapa to Atzacualco, built by the first Montecuzoma on the advice of Nezahualcoyotl, was no less than ten miles long, and was perforated by sluices, by means of which an attempt was made to control the inundations to which Mexico was subject. The effect of this feat of engineering was to cause the portion of lake to the west, called the Lake of Mexico, to become fresh, and to be filled with wild-fowl and fish, for the springs which fed it contained no salt, whereas the streams running into the eastern portion still continued to carry into it the salt which they absorbed on their journey. Another work of economical importance was the double stone aqueduct which brought water to the city from Chapultepec. The Mexicans also constructed roads in various directions throughout the country, for the use of merchants, couriers, and others who travelled on state business. Such roads were narrow, of well-beaten earth, and often had a watercourse running along the side. Like the Peruvian rulers, the Mexican kings maintained a system of trained runners established at definite posts along certain roads. Messages and light burdens could be transferred long distances in a short time by this method, and we hear of three hundred miles being covered in a day.

The birth of a child was awaited with great expectancy, and the prospective mother was carefully guarded from all material and supernatural dangers. The steam-bath was an important institution in promoting ease of delivery, and invocations were made to the gods presiding over birth and creation. The child born, the midwife raised the triumph-cry of the warriors, since the woman who bore a child was regarded as the feminine counterpart of such, and congratulatory visits were paid by friends and relations. A fire was lighted in the house and kept burning for four days ; great care was observed that no light from this should be taken outside the house, since it was believed that the luck of the household would follow it, and a number of other precautions were observed. The horoscope of the infant, a most important matter, was cast by a priest, and a day appointed for the baptismal ceremony, a lucky date being carefully selected. This ceremony consisted in sprinkling the infant with water, and giving it a name. Although the water was supposed to have the effect of purifying the child and fortifying it against the perils of life, yet the Mexicans held no doctrine of " original sin," in fact, the midwife addressed the newly born in the terms, " When you were created and sent into this world you were made with-

out stain, and your father and mother Quetzalcoatl
formed you even as a precious stone and as a jewel of
gold of great price." In the case of a boy, miniature
weapons were prepared for the ceremony, as an indication that he was born a warrior, while for a girl a small
set of weaving-utensils was made, the symbols of her

FIG. 29.—-The education of children.

Left. Girl learning to spin, and boy being shown the use of fishing-
implements ; age 7 years ; daily ration a loaf and a half.
Right. Girl being punished with aloe-spines (age 9 years, omitted) ;
boy being held over a fire of pepper (age 11 years, omitted).
Same daily ration.

(*Mendoza MS., Oxford*)

future status as a housewife. Sahagun states that some
ancestral name was given by the midwife, and other accounts allege that the name was first pronounced by certain small children invited for the purpose. Calendrical
names, taken from the child's birthday, were very
common, especially among the Mixtec, but names of
animals were often conferred upon boys, of flowers
upon girls. Animal names were especially common
among the Tarascans. Children, no matter what their

M

rank, were usually nursed by the mother for three or four years, but in cases of inability, a wet-nurse was carefully chosen. Children were educated with great care and according to certain rules. One manuscript shows the progress of children of both sexes, together with the number of bread-cakes allowed for their diet, from the ages of three to fifteen (Fig. 29). The punishments applicable to each year are also shown, starting with a warning, and proceeding to pricking with aloe-spines, beating, holding over a fire on which pepper had been thrown, and tying hand and foot. Parents were in the habit of preaching long homilies to their children, which, however interesting they may be as illustrating the extremely high moral tone of Mexican educational ideas, must have been excessively boring to the child. The Mexicans were greatly addicted to moral discourses, as may be seen from the work of Sahagun, whole pages of which are devoted to the quotation in full of the orations appropriate to particular occasions of public and private interest. Boys as a rule followed the profession of their father, while girls received a thorough training in the domestic arts, such as spinning and weaving and the preparation of food. The part played by the institutions Calmecac and Telpochcalli in the education of the young has already been mentioned.

Marriage took place at about the age of twenty in the case of men, girls being a trifle younger. Intermarriage was allowed between cousins, but forbidden in the case of nearer relatives. The service of female go-betweens was employed by the parents of the man, and it was not considered consonant with a proper dignity for the woman's family to show too much haste in consenting to the match. On the appointed day, selected owing to the auspicious nature of its sign, the go-between carried the bride to the house of the bridegroom, where, after offering incense, the two were seated side by side on a mat, and their garments knotted by a priest. The inevitable homily followed, and then a feast, and the couple observed a fast for four or more days, at the end of which the marriage might be consummated. In some cases a couple might live in concubinage by consent of their parents, and in the event of a child being born, either a marriage was celebrated or the woman returned to the house of her parents with the infant, which was regarded as belonging to her family. Otherwise children belonged to the man and inherited from him, those of the chief wife (for polygamy, limited by the man's means, was practised) having precedence. It was usual for the eldest son in these cases to make some provision for his brothers and their families. When a man married he left the educational establishment where he formerly lived, after asking permission of his superiors and making certain gifts. As a rule widows could not remarry, except with a brother-in-law; divorce was possible with the consent of a magistrate, and the couple could under no circumstances be reunited. Among the Otomi divorce was allowed after the first night of married life, but not later. The Chichimec practised monogamy, and no intermarriage could take place between individuals who were related. Among the Tarascans however, especially those of rank, different ideas prevailed, and endogamy was the rule. Even among commoners, if a girl had given herself to a man against the will of her parents, the union was regarded as legal only if he belonged to the same ward as herself. In normal cases the girl was simply handed over to her suitor by the priest, together with the gift of a wood-cutting axe and the necessary mats and cord for wood-carrying, and a feast followed. The difference between the marriage rules of the Tarascans and Aztec seems accompanied by another sociological divergence, in so far as there are indications that among the former the children were regarded as belonging to the mother's family. The Mixtec ceremony was more like that of the Aztec, but besides the tying together of the garments of the couple, it included also the cutting of part of their hair. Polygamy was also practised in this region.

Much of the time of the more settled peoples of Mexico was devoted to agriculture, and even a few of the Chichimec tribes, who had absorbed something of the culture of their more advanced neighbours, reared a little maize which was tended by serfs. The Otomi also practised agriculture to some extent. Maize was the most important product of cultivation, and the respect in which it was held is seen in the superstition that if a man saw maize-grains lying on the ground and failed to pick them up, they would cry to the gods for vengeance upon him. Circumstances, chief of which must be reckoned the restriction of territory when they first became settled, led to the development of intensive cultivation among the Aztec, and the invention of the celebrated " floating gardens." These were osier rafts, piled with earth and lake mud, which, so it is said, moved about the surface of the lake until they were finally anchored by the roots of the trees which sprang up on their surface. The properties of manure were known to this people, and it was carefully collected for use in the plantations. The implements of agriculture were simple, consisting of a hoe or a spade and a basket. The heavy work, such as preparing the fields, planting and reaping, was performed by the men, while the women assisted in winnowing the crop and weeding. The fields on the mainland were surrounded with adobe walls or aloe hedges, and the crop was stored in wooden granaries. The Mixtec had the habit, when rain was expected, of breaking the maize-stalks so that the heads hung downward ; in this position they were protected by the leaves from excessive moisture, and were easily dried by the sun and wind. Next to maize, cotton, cacao, aloe, pepper, and the grain called *chia* were the most important plants, though the first three could be grown only in districts where the climate was hot. Hunting, both individually and in communal drives, was practised by all the tribes, and the Mexicans generally were expert trackers and huntsmen. We hear of one drive organized for the Spaniards in which eleven thousand Otomi beaters took part, embracing a circle of fifteen miles. The chief weapons employed were bows, darts, blow-guns, nets and snares. Fishing

FIG. 30.—Tlaxtli-court and players.
(*Bodleian MS., Oxford*)

was equally important, in fact more so among the tribes in the neighbourhood of lakes, nets and tridents being the principal appliances used. The invention of these was attributed to the god Opochtli, one of the Tlaloque. Fowling also gave employment to a large number of the population and contributed greatly to the food-supply.

With regard to the lighter side of life it would not be going too far to state that nearly all of the amusements of the Mexicans possessed a religious significance. It is true that the lords maintained jesters and tumblers, and that the performances of conjurers, as mentioned above, were much appreciated. But the national game, tlaxtli, was closely connected with the worship of the gods, and the tlaxtli-courts both at Mexico and in

Michoacan were generally associated with temples. The ground-plan of a tlaxtli-court resembled a double T, as may be seen from Fig. 30, which is taken from a manuscript. The game was played with a rubber ball, and the end walls constituted the goals which were protected by opposing teams of players. At the centre of each side wall, near its upper edge, was fixed a stone ring, the aperture a little greater than the diameter of the ball, and if the latter could be hit so as to pass through the ring, a victory was claimed. The walls were forty or fifty feet long, and twenty or thirty feet apart, and the whole court was carefully plastered. The area was divided by a line, which the ball had to cross for the throw to count ; it is not stated whether this line was longitudinal or transverse, but probability seems to favour the latter. The MSS. often show the two ends of the court distinguished by different colours, though it is only fair to state that they almost as often show it quartered. The players wore special gauntlets, but the most esteemed variety of the game was that in which they were not allowed the use of their hands at all, but struck the ball with their hips, protected by means of a leather shield attached to the girdle. A variety of gods are pictured in association with the tlaxtli-court, principally Tezcatlipoca, Quetzalcoatl, Xochiquetzal and Xochipilli, and in the court connected with the great temple to Uitzilopochtli stood the statues of the gods Oappatzan and Amapan to which sacrifices were made. Seler conjectures that the flight of the ball in its esoteric significance referred to the movements of the moon. The game was usually played for stakes, which often ran very high, and it also served to settle disputed questions, as in the case where Montecuzoma, differing from Nezahualpilli as regards the interpretation of certain omens, challenged him to a game of tlaxtli and was defeated. The origin of the game is discussed later (pp. 302–303).

Other amusements, of a more secular nature, were the game called patolli, played with "men" on a board bearing a cruciform diagram, and tololoque, a variety of dice. Both these were played for stakes.

Music was not highly developed, and there was but little variety in the musical instruments throughout the valley. Rattles of gourd or pottery were common, but the principal instrument of percussion was the gong, teponaztli, formed of a hollow cylinder of wood with two tongues, each of a different note, which were struck with beaters, sometimes headed with rubber. The teponaztli was often beautifully carved, and played an important part in religious ceremonies and dances (Fig. 31). Drums, ueuetl, with skin membranes were also in common use, while instruments of a rather special nature consisted of tortoise carapaces (or their facsimiles in gold), struck

FIG. 31.—Carved wooden gong (*teponaztli*).
(*British Museum*)

with a stick, and serrated bones rubbed with short rods (see p. 103). Wind instruments appear to have been few in variety ; conches, provided apparently with a wooden mouthpiece, like those of the New Zealanders, were sounded in most religious ceremonies, and quantities of whistles and ocarinas have been discovered. The finger-holes do not exceed four in number, and are frequently less in the case of instruments of the flageolet type. Whistles were of frequent use in war, for the purpose of giving signals. Whether the Mexicans, like the tribes of the north-west coast of America, were acquainted with reed instruments is uncertain, at any rate none are known to exist ; it is quite possible that they were known, but that the reeds, constructed of perishable materials, have not survived until our time. Singing was another important accompaniment of religious ceremonies, and there were specially trained temple choirs under the control of responsible officials. Many of the hymns have been preserved, and illustrate well the poetical cast of Mexican thought. A species of primitive drama was said to exist, recited on a terrace in the market-place or temple-court. Dancing was highly developed, and every feast had its ceremonial dance which was carried out with great solemnity and decorum. In some cases the dancers formed large circles, the members of each belonging to one sex and rank. In others, the sexes mingled, and in others again the dancers performed in pairs, with their arms round one another's waists or necks. The last method seems to have been the privilege of the upper classes. In combined figures a long garlanded rope was held by the dancers, who moved their bodies and limbs in unison, as in Peru, while occasionally they danced in threes, two women and one man or two men and one woman.

CHAPTER VII—MEXICO: ARCHITECTURAL REMAINS AND POTTERY

NOW that a sketch has been given of the beliefs and mode of life of the Ancient Mexicans, it is necessary to deal in some measure with the remains of their culture scattered over the country. As far as architecture is concerned, the greater proportion of ruined buildings must be considered to have been either temples or structures associated in some way with religion, and perhaps government. The Mexicans gave of their best to the gods, and though the *corvée* system enabled large numbers of men to be employed at one time on works of considerable magnitude, the rulers seem to have spent more care on the buildings erected for the service of their deities than on their own habitations. The peculiar feature of Mexican architecture lies in the fact that every building of importance was erected upon a substructure, terrace or truncated pyramid, which, though essentially secondary in importance to the building or buildings with which it was crowned, yet represented a vast amount of labour, many hundred times greater than that expended on the superstructure. This feature has been unfortunate, in a sense, for Mexican archæology, since the pyramidal mounds, once the superimposed buildings have disappeared, present a superficial analogy to the pyramids of Egypt. There can however be no real comparison, the Egyptian pyramid represented a building in itself, while the Mexican was in essence a mere accessory. The foundation-mounds must be distinguished from the mounds of the northern Pueblo region, which are formed for the most part of the debris

of buildings which have fallen into decay. True foundation-mounds are rarely found north of a line drawn,
roughly, from La Quemada in Zacatecas to the Gulf of
Mexico in the region of the Panuco valley ; but south
of it, right down to Honduras, they are a characteristic
feature of architecture. There was a large number of
temple pyramids, of varied dimensions, in Tenochtitlan (Sahagun gives a long list), but two were of out-
standing importance, one in Tenochtitlan proper, the
other in the suburb of Tlaltelolco. Both were so utterly
destroyed by the Spaniards that it is not easy at the
present time to fix their exact position. The most
recent, and most successful, attempt to work out the
details of the great Mexican temple from all sources,
literary and archæological, is that of Maudslay, to
which reference can be made by those wishing for
more minute particulars (see also Fig. 12; p. 87).
The pyramid, or teocalli, stood at the eastern end
of a large court, about 300 by 350 yards, surrounded
by a wall on which were carved snakes. It was built
in five tiers, of earth and stones faced with masonry ;
the base measured something over 100 yards, and the
upper surface over 70 yards square. A flight of more
than 100 steps on the west side gave access to the
summit, and on the eastern edge of the latter were two
shrines, each of two storeys, built, as seems most probable, chiefly of wood. These two shrines were dedicated
respectively to Uitzilopochtli (towards the south) and
Tlaloc (towards the north), and faced west, but the
priests and worshippers would face east, the direction
of the rising sun, and there is reason to believe that the
equinox was calculated by observing the rising of the
sun between the two shrines. In front of the latter was
the sacrificial stone, and below, in the court, a number
of other temples, priestly residences, and other ceremonial buildings, including a tlaxtli-court and the
tzompantli, or frame upon which were erected the

PLATE XII

Photo. C. B. Waite

MEXICO

MOUNDS AT SAN JUAN TEOTIHUACAN, SEEN FROM THE "PYRAMID OF THE MOON"

skulls of sacrificial victims. The other temples in the
court included one to Tezcatlipoca, one in circular
form to Quetzalcoatl, and one to the planet Venus
(Tlauizcalpantecutli), whose image was painted on a
pillar in the shrine. The Tlaltelolco temple was
similar, though a little larger, and supported two
shrines dedicated, the one to Uitzilopochtli and the
other to Tezcatlipoca. Larger than either of these
imposing buildings was the teocalli of Quetzalcoatl at Cholula. This still exists, though in sadly
mutilated form ; the length of its base was calculated
by Humboldt as nearly 440 metres. For an example
of an ordinary Mexican shrine, as exemplified in ruins,
it is necessary to go outside what is strictly Aztec territory. Near Cuernavaca, in the Tlalhuica district, among
rocky peaks towering above the valley, is the temple of
Tepoztlan (Pl. XIV, 2), dedicated probably to one of
the octli-gods (Tepoztecatl). This region formed one
of the early Mexican conquests and the temple bears
the name of the Mexican king Auitzotl and the date
of his death. Seen from the east, the building appears
to be a three-tiered pyramid, the upper tier in reality
being the back of the shrine. The walls are of porous
volcanic stone set in mortar, and the roof was similarly constructed. The shrine is a simple rectangular
building with an inner chamber (of the type Fig. 76, 4 ;
p. 327), and the interior is ornamented with carvings.
The front wall is pierced by three doorways, separated
by quadrangular pillars, which are in reality sections of
the wall. In front, on the lower terrace, is a quadrangular " altar," probably corresponding to the
quauhxicalli at Mexico. Another, and somewhat similar
temple, also apparently of Aztec origin, is found at
Teayo, near Tuxpan in the Huaxtec country. This
is a three-tiered pyramid, about forty feet high,
faced with sandstone blocks over which a coat of
stucco has been laid. At the top is a simple quad-

rangular shrine (of the type Fig. 76, 1), with stuccoed and frescoed interior, standing on a low terrace. The stairway is on the west side, and the worshippers therefore faced east, as in the case of the temples already mentioned. This, we are told, was the proper orientation for Mexican temples of the first importance. But of far greater interest and importance than these two small temples are the extensive remains at Teotihuacan, close to Mexico, a site intimately connected with the Toltec and mentioned in Mexican myth as the scene of the rising of the historical sun. At the present day this site presents the appearance of a conglomeration of mounds varying greatly in size and spread over so large an area that their bulk is difficult to realize. The two principal features are two vast pyramids, from the smaller of which runs a depressed road, two to three hundred feet wide, past the other for a distance of nearly two miles in a straight line. This road is interrupted by several low embankments and small pyramids, and bordered by a large number of mounds arranged in series. At the southern end of the road and to the east is a complex of mounds, arranged in a square and including a pyramid of some size. The photograph figured on Pl. XII is taken from the summit of the lesser of the two great pyramids, usually called the " pyramid of the moon," and looks down the sunk roadway, called the " road of the dead." The greater pyramid, or " pyramid of the sun," appears in the centre of the picture, but the complex of mounds towards the southern end of the road is barely visible. The " pyramid of the sun " measures about 700 feet along the base, and the sides rise at an angle of 45 degrees to a platform about 100 feet square. Both it and the surrounding mounds are composed of masses of local earth and stone and adobe (unbaked clay). It was originally faced with roughly dressed stone and received a final coat of stucco. Beneath the outer facing a second

PLATE XIII

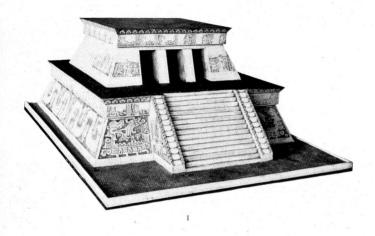

I

Photo. J. Cooper Clark   2

MEXICO
1. TEMPLE AT XOCHICALCO, RESTORED (AFTER HOLMES)
2. TEMPLE AT XOCHICALCO, PRESENT CONDITION

has been discovered at some depth, and it may be that several such were constructed during the process of building in order to give solidity to the mass ; but it is more likely that the outer layer represents an addition to the original building. Other evidence of phases in construction have been discovered in some of the mounds, in cases where an entire building has been filled solid in order to support a later edifice above it. Growth by accretion of this nature was a feature of many of the Maya sites, as will be seen later. It is probable that this mighty pyramid was approached by a stairway on its western face from the " path of the dead." The general assemblage of the lesser mounds seems to exhibit more evidence of design than many Mexican ruins, and the whole site bears the stamp of considerable antiquity as well as long-continued occupation. In particular is to be noticed a tendency to group the mounds round quadrangular courts, a tendency which, as will be seen later, is characteristic of the Zapotec area. The district from early times bore the reputation of a burial-ground of great sanctity, and the lesser mounds were at first believed to be burial-tumuli (whence the name " path of the dead " given to the sunk roadway). Excavation however, as far as carried out, seems to prove that the greater number supported buildings of a residential nature, many of them of an unusually complex ground-plan. The walls were of lava fragments and adobe, dressed with mortar. The roofs of the larger apartments were supported on pillars, probably of wood, of which the rectangular bases, similar in construction to the walls, have been found. Stone-carving is practically non-existent, probably for the same reason that there are no well-dressed stone facings, viz. unsuitability of local material ; but the interiors were ornamented with frescoes in beautiful colours in which plant motives play an important part.

The ruins most nearly resembling those at Teotihua-can are found at Monte Alban in Zapotec territory, on a lofty ridge overlooking the city of Oaxaca. Holmes describes the appearance of the site as it struck him when he had climbed the long ascent from the latter city as follows: " The surface was not covered with scattered and obscure piles of ruins as I had expected, but the whole mountain had been remodelled by the hand of man until not a trace of natural contour re-mained. There was a vast system of level courts en-closed by successive terraces, and bordered by pyramids upon pyramids. Even the sides of the mountain de-scended in a succession of terraces, and the whole crest, separated by the hazy atmosphere from the dimly seen valleys more than a thousand feet below, and isolated completely from the blue range beyond, seemed sus-pended in mid-air." The quadrangular assemblage of foundation-mounds round courts is even more notice-able here than at Teotihuacan, though the limitations of the available building space rendered the arrangement less free on the whole. Most of the mounds seem to have been faced with quartzite blocks, barely dressed at all owing to the hard nature of the stone, and carved orna-ment is not very common. Few traces of buildings have been discovered, but excavation is by no means com-plete; however, the foundations of at least one structure with a complex arrangement of chambers have been laid bare, and it is earnestly to be hoped that some properly qualified archæologist may be entrusted with the task of thorough investigation. Monte Alban is further re-markable for the presence of sculptured grave-slabs and pillars bearing designs and inscriptions in a peculiar style (similar to Fig. 15; p. 106). Many Mexican day-signs can be recognized, but some of the glyphs are enclosed in " cartouches " of Maya style (to anticipate), and are accompanied by numerals in which five is ex-pressed by a bar, another Maya characteristic. Carv-

PLATE XIV

I

Photos. C. B. Waite

2

ZAPOTEC
1. INTERIOR OF CHAMBER AT MITLA, OAXACA *(See Plate XV)*
MEXICO
2. TEMPLE AT TEPOZTLAN

ings in similar style are found at other sites in the Zapotec area. Not unlike Monte Alban are the better preserved ruins at Quiengola, near Tehuantepec, and here the quadrangular arrangement of foundation-mounds round courts takes a very definite form. Some of these mounds are in the form of three-tiered pyramids (Fig. 32, *b*), others of long terraces supporting buildings divided into a succession of simple chambers, each opening on the terrace, and occasionally enclosing a small shrine (Fig. 32, *a*). The latter bear a striking resemblance to Maya buildings, as will be seen later

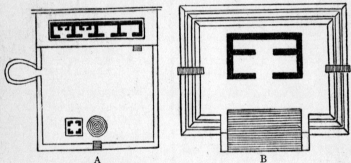

FIG. 32.—Plans of remains at Quiengola, Oaxaca.
A. Court with terrace supporting buildings.
B. Pyramid with Temple.

(compare Figs. 76, *b*, and 77 ; pp. 327 and 329). Adobe was used in large quantities in these buildings, and clay as mortar, and certain groups of structures are found which are decidedly complex in arrangement. At Tlacolula, a site rather similar to Quiengola, cyclopean masonry is found, and at Xoxo in the same district we have mounds built of earthy material with frequent horizontal layers of mortar, a peculiarity also seen at Tlacolula at Monte Alban, and again at Cholula, a city closely associated with Toltec culture. In the same district are found sculptured slabs in a style similar to those of Monte Alban, and in both regions occur stone heads, usually so flattened as to present an axe-like appearance, with a projection at the back for insetting in a wall (Fig. 33, *c*).

The characteristic Oaxaca slabs, with their dates in mixed Mexican and Maya style, have their parallel in the carvings on what must have been an extremely beautiful temple at Xochicalco in the Tlalhuica region. This ruin, though in the same district as the Aztec temple of

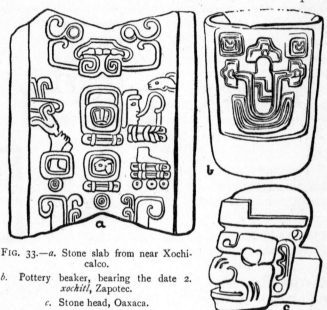

FIG. 33.—*a.* Stone slab from near Xochicalco.
b. Pottery beaker, bearing the date 2.
xochitl, Zapotec.
c. Stone head, Oaxaca.

Tepoztlan, is of an entirely different type and the style of its rich ornamentation bears a close resemblance to the remains at Tulan, one of the Toltec cities. Its present condition is shown on Pl. XIII together with a restoration by Holmes. It is only fair to state that this distinguished archæologist has since modified his ideas regarding its original form, and it should be said that the pillars dividing the doorway would almost certainly have had perpendicular faces. With this exception and with the further exception of some doubt attaching to

the exact form of the roof, the picture gives a very good
idea of what the temple must have been. The substructure, with the noticeable " batter " of its walls and
projecting cornice, is over four yards high, of rubble
faced with andesite ; the carving represents great undu-
lating snakes, between the coils of which are human
figures, and glyphs in the style of those of Oaxaca described above. Originally the details of sculpture were

emphasized by col-
oured stucco and
therefore appeared
far less complicated
than in a photo-
graph. In this build-
ing again the stair-
way was on the west
side.

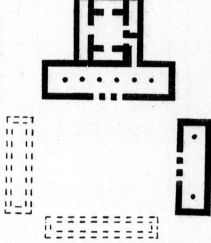

FIG. 34.—Plan of a court and buildings at
Mitla.   The building to the right is
shown on Pl. XV.

To return to Oax-
aca, the most impor-
tant group of ruins
awaits considera-
tion. These are at
Mitla, the sacred Za-
potec city, and are
distinguished by
many peculiarities

which render them almost unique. Here the quadrangular arrangement of buildings round courts attains its most definite form. In two cases one of these
buildings, on the east side, is a pyramid, and therefore presumably approached, as usual, from the west.
The rest consist of long low buildings upon terraces,
opening as a rule only upon the court which they
surround, though in two cases one such building gives
access at the back to another court, entirely enclosed
by similar buildings, which has no other entrance
(Fig. 34). The material is rubble, faced with trachyte

blocks set in mortar ; the wall-surfaces are broken by
sunk panels filled with the mosaic geometrical ornament which gives this site a character of its own (Pls.
XIV, 1, and XV).   Each block constituting the mosaic
bears on its face in relief some detail entering into
the design, but the blocks are not uniform, and
each therefore was cut and fitted to its particular
place, a method entailing enormous labour, especially when it is realized that over eighty thousand
were employed in the ornamentation of one quad-
rangle alone.   The blocks taper somewhat at the back,
so that they were set in the mortar as a tooth in the
gum, a feature seen also in Maya buildings.   The designs
are obviously based on the textile art, and find their
closest parallel in some of the coastal buildings of Peru
(though similar mosaics have been found at Tlacolula,
also in Zapotec territory).   Stucco was not used here for
moulded ornament, though it was employed for finish-
ing defective points in the facing.   Traces of red colour
are found on the mosaic panels.   The durable yet comparatively soft trachyte found in the neighbouring hills
afforded the Zapotec builder far more tractable material than at other sites ;   the result was that large
masses of stone were used in construction, such as lintels from ten to twenty feet long and weighing from
ten to fifteen tons, as well as cylindrical pillars used to
support the roof in the broader buildings.   Indications
show that the roof consisted of logs, probably covered
with canes supporting a layer of masonry and cement.
The quarries of the ancient builders have been discovered in the hills, together with the rude stone picks
by means of which they hewed out the blocks, and, as
Holmes writes, " the feats of engineering necessary to
transport masses of stone many tons in weight down a
thousand feet of precipitous mountain-face, accomplished by these stone-age quarry-men, would be regarded as important undertakings, even by our enter-

PLATE XV

ZAPOTEC

RUINS AT MITLA, OAXACA; PARTLY RESTORED

prising engineers of to-day." It is an interesting fact
that numbers of stone flakes and cores are found in the
mortar of the constructed buildings, and it is possible
that these may have been used in the final dressing of
the stone on the spot. In one of the buildings a fresco
in red and white has been discovered on the cornice.
This is in a style rather resembling certain Oaxacan
and Cholulan pottery, and bears also an analogy to
certain frescoes in British Honduras (compare Figs. 79
and 80; pp. 335 and
336). Various myth-
ological figures are
represented, includ-
ing Mixcoatl (Fig.
35) and his double-
headed deer, and it
would seem proba-
ble that they have
been added at a date
considerably later
than the construc-
tion of the build-
ings. Of the use of
the buildings Burgoa
gives particulars, as-

FIG. 35.—Portion of a fresco at Mitla ; figure
of the god Mixcoatl.
(*After Seler*)

signing one group to the king, another to the priests,
and so forth. But as he speaks of upper storeys, of
which no traces are apparent, his account can hardly be
considered sufficiently trustworthy to be given in detail.
The same author writes also of extensive subterranean
chambers, but with the exception of two cruciform
souterrains of comparatively small dimensions, nothing
of that nature has yet been discovered.

The quadrangular grouping of buildings round courts
recalls at once the statement of Sahagun respecting the
pre-Aztec temples at Tulan. One of these, he writes, was
composed of four buildings, that to the east being orna-

mented with gold, that to the north with red jasper and red shells, that to the west with turquoise, and that to the south with silver and white shells. The other temple was similar, save that the interior decoration of the buildings was of feathers, yellow, red, blue and white respectively. If the tradition is founded on fact, we may safely conclude that the buildings were arranged round a court, and the colours of their ornamentation suggest that this arrangement was connected with the regard paid by the Mexicans generally to the world-directions (see p. 78).

Passing further north, the remains of pyramids and terraces have been found at Placeres del Oro in Guerrero; these are built of natural or roughly-worked boulders, but they have not yet been excavated and it is impossible to say yet what may be their arrangement or what class of buildings they may have supported. The peculiar stone slabs found there (Fig. 16; p. 107) have been mentioned, which bear a certain resemblance to one found in the neighbourhood of Xochicalco (Fig. 33, a; p. 176), which itself appears to be related to those from Oaxaca (Fig. 15; p. 106). The Placeres del Oro slabs, however, are almost more like certain Peruvian work than anything else, and full excavation of this extremely interesting site is highly desirable; it is worthy of note that the latter slabs bear no glyphs. At Pazcuaro in Michoacan we hear of a three-tiered pyramid of flat stones piled together without mortar, the corners being formed of unworked blocks; but in Tarascan territory are found foundation-mounds of a specialized type, consisting of a terrace from the centre of which a spur projects at right angles, terminating in a circular platform. These are known by the name *yacata*, the term applied locally to Michoacan temples, and photographs seem to show horizontal layers of cement in their construction as in the Tlacolula buildings. On the evidence of manuscripts the temple buildings in this district seem to have been of a tower-like nature. Two varieties are shown, one on a square foundation, the other on a circular ground-plan and sometimes with a peculiar domed roof. Further north still, at La Quemada in Zacatecas, occurs an extremely interesting group of ruins, built along a lofty ridge. These remains, the most northerly yet discovered bearing a distinctly " Mexican " character, cover an extensive area and display considerable complexity. The flanks of the hills forming the ridge are built up steeply with terraced walls, and the summits are artificially levelled and broadened with terraces. The lower works seem to be of a defensive nature, and the more important buildings above consist of an intricate series of foundation-mounds, sunk courts, and occasional pyramids. From the summit radiates a system of stuccoed roads, most of which terminate in small pyramids lower down. The quadrangular arrangement of the more important structures is very noticeable, and one of the larger halls evidently possessed a roof supported on large circular pillars, built, like the walls and terraces, of unsquared stone blocks set in earth mixed with grass. The Spaniards found the ruins uninhabited, and the surrounding agricultural and hunting population of Zacatec stated that the inhabitants had migrated in the direction of Mexico after a drought lasting several years.

With the exception of the pyramid at Teayo, described above, which seems to be an Aztec ruin, the architectural remains of the Huaxtec and Totonac appear in certain respects to resemble rather those of the Maya, their linguistic relations to the south. At the same time it is advisable to make some mention of them in this place, firstly because the coastal region in this direction had been subjected for some time to Aztec influences, and secondly because Aztec pottery cannot be adequately described without reference to the ceramic art of the Huaxtec and Totonac. Foundation-mounds occur throughout the whole region from the mouth of the Panuco to Vera Cruz, and afford a splendid field to future explorers. The Panuco district shows abundant traces of settlement from very early times ; the mounds are of earth, sometimes faced with cut stone, but traces of walls are rare throughout the whole of the Huaxtec region. In the Cerro de Nahuatlan, the pyramids are again of earth or rubble, faced with more or less regularly squared sandstone blocks ; some are circular in ground-plan, and the corners of the rectangular ruins are often formed of well-worked monoliths. At Papantla is a remarkable pyramid, faced with cut stone, the distinguishing feature of which is constituted by a series of niches, which may at some time have contained images. This is figured on Pl. XVI, and further description is unnecessary, though it may be said that niches of this character may be found to be a characteristic of Totonac architecture.

In the neighbourhood of Cempoala a very interesting series of ruins is to be found. These consist of mounds on which traces of buildings remain, and which, owing to the lack of stone suitable for building in the district, are constructed of a core of waterworn stones set in concrete with good concrete facing. The highly polished concrete facing of Totonac buildings attracted the notice of the Spaniards, who thought at first that they were ornamented with silver plates. The mounds are either of the normal step-pyramid type, or are built in two very distinct tiers, each with a separate balustraded stairway, of the types Fig. 73, c and e; p. 321. Both are erected on slightly-raised artificial bases, and the buildings found on the summits are rather more complicated than the simple shrines believed to be characteristic of the Aztec temples. In this respect they bear a closer resemblance to certain of the Maya remains which will be described later. One of these

PLATE XVI

TOTONAC

TEMPLE AT PAPANTLA, VERA CRUZ

buildings consists of a series of chambers, like the
buildings at Quiengola described above (Fig. 32, *a*;
p. 175), though on a smaller scale; another consists
of a shrine standing free within an exterior building.
Other similarities to Oaxaca remains include the presence
of pillars to support a roof, found in a building in the
neighbourhood, and again on a foundation-mound at
San Isidro, immediately south of Misantla; and also
numbers of heads, but in this case of clay, which
appear to have been inset in the walls. At Texolo are
mounds some of which are of earth alone, and these are
occasionally arranged in a double row to enclose a court.
Stone facing however is not unknown in this district.

Of architectural remains as a whole it may be said
that the Aztec buildings show a tendency to simplicity
and exhibit on the whole fewer traces of arrangement
on a large and comprehensive plan, such as may be observed at Teotihuacan. Teotihuacan itself, as far as
actual buildings are concerned, has many points in
common with Tulan, and in its general arrangement
shows a considerable similarity to Monte Alban. The
last-named site is obviously closely connected with
other remains in Oaxaca; and Xochicalco, from its
decoration, has similar affinities, affinities which extend
to the pre-Aztec remains of the valley. Mitla stands
practically by itself as far as artistic ornamentation is
concerned, though the arrangement of the buildings is
quite Oaxacan in character. The Totonac ruins display
a certain affinity with the ruins at Quiengola, though
this affinity cannot be said to be direct. The true relation between the two will be more apparent after the
Maya remains have been considered. It is unsafe to
draw any conclusion from structural points alone, since
so much depended upon the presence in the neighbourhood of suitable materials; it was, for instance, the
presence of trachyte in the Mitla region which enabled
its builders to make use of large masses of stone, and pro-

vided the long lintels which distinguish this group of ruins. Where suitable stone was lacking, the deficiency was usually supplied by cement, and much use was made of the latter to correct irregularities in construction, though its employment appears to have been more frequent in Oaxaca and the Totonac region than elsewhere.

The art of pottery was highly developed amongst all the tribes hitherto mentioned, in spite of the facts that the use of the potter's wheel was unknown, and that the method of firing was very primitive. No kilns were constructed, but the pots were fired by means of wood fuel in the open air, perhaps in a hole in the ground. The quality of the potting varies considerably according to locality, but the finer examples, such as the ware from Cholula and the Totonac district, exhibit a very high standard of paste, form and technique, though the potters of this region of America cannot boast such consummate mastery over their material as the early inhabitants of the Peruvian coast. The fact, that in the later years prior to the conquest pottery had become an article of trade and tribute, led to a wide dispersal of local types from centres of manufacture which had acquired a reputation for skill in the art ; and considerable borrowing of forms and ornament had resulted. At the same time, provided that the possibility of importation be not overlooked, the pottery remains afford much valuable evidence as to the interrelation of the tribes and the early history of the country. The coordination of this evidence is however only just at its commencement ; careful excavations with due regard to the stratification of remains have been made at a few points in the valley, and the results have proved of such importance that similar researches throughout the whole of Mexico and Central America are most earnestly desired by all students of American archæology. In the valley of Mexico the local ware manufactured

under the Aztec *régime* is easily recognizable. Fragments of coarse undecorated vessels are found, which
appear to have been made by the simple expedient of
plastering a basket over with clay and then firing, the
basket being destroyed in the process. But the most
characteristic ware falls into two main varieties. The
first is moulded of an orange or reddish yellow clay,

FIG. 36.—Mexican pottery forms (see also Pls. XVII–XIX).
1–3. Valley of Mexico.   4. Oaxaca.
5–9. Island of Sacrificios.
(*British Museum*)

fairly well baked, but often showing a dark line down
the middle of a fracture ; the walls of the vessels are
very thin, and the surfaces carefully smoothed, though
not highly burnished. The commonest forms are
shallow tripod bowls (Fig. 36, 3), standing cups and
jugs with handles, and the ornament consists of small
geometrical designs in black (Fig. 37). Moulded
ornament is not common, though gadrooned bodies
are occasionally found ; incised decoration is confined

to the utilitarian process of scoring the bottoms of bowls for use as graters in the preparation of pepper-sauce (*chilmolli*), and applied ornament is practically non-existent. Miniature tripod bowls with smooth bottoms are found, used to support the revolving spindle in the operation of spinning, and incense-spoons were also manufactured in this ware. The second main type consists chiefly of hour-glass shaped standing cups, of reddish, softer paste, with thicker walls coated with a burnished red slip and painted with black and white linear designs also in slip (Fig. 36, 2).

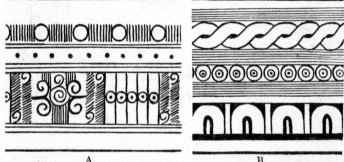

A   B

FIG. 37.—Designs from Mexican pottery ; late valley type.

Less common are bowls of greyish paste with burnished red and yellow slip coating, on which are well-drawn curvilinear patterns in black, or bowls of grey ware with a very highly burnished yellow slip with a matt design in slip of similar colour. Characteristic, too, of this district are two-handled censers, heavy and solid in construction, of grey clay with a black burnished surface, or of reddish clay with a burnished red slip (Fig. 36, 1). Besides vessels, pottery figurines are found in great numbers, in the form of various gods, warriors, miniature temples, and so forth (Pl. IX, 2–6). These are in a hard red ware or a very soft pale cream clay ; some are solid, while others are hollow and form rattles or whistles ; most of these figurines

were evidently made in moulds. Excavations have
shown that the valley type of pottery occurs only in the
surface layers, and is therefore comparatively recent
and represents a period of short duration ; beneath it,
and extending to a considerable depth, are found fragments of a ware which is especially associated with the
ruined city of Teotihuacan. The most characteristic
form belonging to this period is a circular bowl with
vertical, or almost vertical, sides supported on three
feet, either flat or of the cascabel type (Fig. 38). These

vases are usually coated
with a burnished red, yellow, brown or black slip,
and are either plain or
are ornamented with bold
incised curvilinear pat-
terns, or human and ani-
mal masks moulded in
relief. Impressed designs
were also applied by
means of stamps. Flat
shallow bowls of this
ware are also found, and

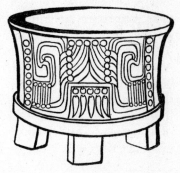

FIG. 38.—Pottery vase from Teotihuacan.

graceful vases with everted lip, but the finest specimens
are covered with polychrome ornament of a peculiar
technique. The design is engraved in the outer slip, and
the background cut away, leaving the former standing
out against the matt colour of the paste ; in some cases
the intaglio portions have received a coating of cinnabar
or vermilion, and in the most beautiful examples the
excised portions have been filled with slip of various
colours, rendering the finished vase a kind of polychrome champ-levé in clay, a vivid blue-green being the
most prominent colour. Vases are also found with a
design produced by the alternation of matt and burnished surfaces. A peculiar feature of Teotihuacan is
constituted by the innumerable small pottery heads

which are found there (Pl. IX, 3). These are in a hard reddish clay, and appear to have been made by hand and not in moulds. Many are without attributes, and among the others only the god Tlaloc can be identified with certainty. One class of head is shown with a turban-like head-dress, which, as will be seen later, is characteristic of the Maya (e.g. Fig. 81; p. 339); a figure with similar head-dress usually forms the support of the circular pattern of censer characteristic of this Teotihuacan culture.

Mixed with the lowest layers of fragments of this type, are ruder remains of a different character. This pottery is yellow or red and often unburnished, though a red or white slip is sometimes found ; it is thick and not so well baked, and moulded rims are common. The ornament consists in bands or knobs in relief, and in series of incised lines or circles. Vase-feet are found in numbers, and occasionally handles, often in the form of a human hand. Pottery figurines are frequent, but of a type different from those of the superior cultures ; they are hand-made, with applied details, the heads are long, the waists narrow and the thighs exaggerated. For the most part they are represented in the nude, and red and white paint is used as ornament. The close correspondence which these remains bear to those of the Tarascans (Pl. XVII, 2–6) described below, seems to prove that before the blossoming of the "Toltec" culture, the valley was peopled by tribes similar in ethnography to the inhabitants of Michoacan. With regard to the relative positions of these three types of remains, it should be mentioned that at Azcapotzalco the earliest and coarsest occupied a stratum of 2·10 metres and it must be concluded that the culture which they represent was of some considerable duration ; while their overlapping with the superimposed Teotihuacan types, indicates a gradual change from the one to the other. The Teotihuacan stratum was found to be no

PLATE XVII

MEXICO
1. SPEAR-THROWER, *ATLATL*

TARASCAN
2—6. POTTERY FROM GUADALAJARA

ZAPOTEC
7—9. FUNERARY VASES, FROM OAXACA

(Scale : 1, 1/6th : 2—9, 1/8th)

less than 3·25 metres in thickness, representing an even
longer period; while the " valley " type occurs on the
surface and to a depth only of 0·40 metres, and shows
no overlapping with the remains below, thus indicating
an abrupt transition.

The Tarascan remains (Pl. XVII, 2–6) which are found
in numbers from Lake Pazcuaro to Lake Chapala, bear
a close resemblance to the fragments from the lowest
strata of the valley. The paste is usually well-mixed, but
not so well fired as the Aztec and Teotihuacan ware, and
constantly shows at a fracture a dark line at the core,
the properly baked portion being in the main a greyish
buff. A burnished red slip is often employed, with pattern in white, the latter being frequently furnished
with an incised outline. The most common shapes are
vases and bowls with three solid or cascabel feet, the
latter enclosing rattles, vases with moulded bodies or in
human or animal form, and plain vases with rounded
bases, a feature uncommon throughout the rest of the
area which forms the subject of this section. Bowls
with incised bottoms, to serve as graters, are common,
and the incised lines are sometimes arranged swastika-
wise, a feature found again in Cuicatlan pottery.
Miniature tripod bowls to use in connection with the
spindle also occur, and the painted ornament of these
and larger vessels shows a tendency to asymmetry. In the
Tarascan area, extending far to the north, are found
occasional vases in the clay " champ-levé " described
above, together with traces of the brilliant blue-green
ornament. Figurines of all sizes are common in this
area, often covered with a red slip and painted black
and white. Many of these represent men and women
engaged in their ordinary occupations, and illustrate
well the shoulder-cloaks, large ear-rings and head-bands
worn by this people. Some are flat and solid, others
hollow, but most show elongated heads, and often exaggerated thighs and slender waists.

We must now consider the finest pottery in Mexico, viz. the ware characteristic of Cholula and Tlaxcala, which seems to bear certain relations to that of Oaxaca on the one hand, and, though less obviously, to that of the Totonac region on the other. The fact that Cholula was recognized as the leading centre of pottery manufacture and exported its wares in considerable quantity in times preceding and up to the conquest, renders the distinction between local types difficult, especially as the Totonac region seems to have been affected by Mexican conquest, and to have furnished tribute in pots. The typical ware of Cholula and Tlaxcala is hard and reddish, very well-mixed and fired, and rarely shows a dark line in the centre of a fracture. Forms include standing-bowls and -cups, tripod bowls and vases, handled jugs, plates and bowls with a slightly flattened base. Footed beakers also occur, but I am inclined to regard this form as one adopted from the Totonac. The vases are usually covered with an even and highly burnished red or yellow slip, on which are painted designs in a variety of colours, red, yellow, white, grey and black (Pl. IX, 1, and Figs. 39 and 40). Geometrical and textile patterns are common, and also figures and emblems of gods and men, animals and plants. The treatment is often bold and free, and though at times the designs suffer from over-conventionalization, they are always highly decorative. Relief ornament is occasionally seen in the shape of

FIG. 39.—Polychrome pottery vase; Tlaxcalan or Cholulan style, found in Mexico city.
(*After Seler*)

animal heads (Fig. 40) or small pierced handles,
and the designs are sometimes furnished with an engraved outline, though I believe both these features to
be characteristic rather of Totonac art. The legs of
tripod bowls, which are found in numbers, are usually
moulded in the form of grotesque faces, or the heads
of birds, beasts and snakes. Peculiar to Tlaxcala are
interesting vases of black ware in the form of a Tlaloc
face or figure, the details of which are applied. The

FIG. 40.—Polychrome pottery vase from Tlaxcala.
(*After Seler*)

scroll-work which constitutes a feature of the painted
art bears a close analogy to the Xochicalco designs, and
it is not surprising to find similar pottery in Oaxaca.
It is quite true that Cholulan pottery may have found
its way in some quantity to the last-named region, by
the great trade-route which ran from Teotitlan to
Oaxaca, but I am inclined to think that much at least
of it must have been manufactured locally, especially
as a certain form of tripod vase (Fig. 36, 4; p. 185)
seems peculiar to this country. Most remarkable of
the finds in the Oaxaca district is that of pottery

designs which any archæologist unaware of their real provenance would attribute unhesitatingly to the Peruvian coast. One of these is illustrated in Fig. 41, and a glance will show how it differs entirely from anything Mexican, and yet is absolutely identical with one of the patterns most commonly found on the polychrome tapestries of the Truxillo district of Peru. A peculiar class of Zapotec pottery may be mentioned here, consisting of figure vases of coarse red-brown or black ware, usually very brittle, found in tombs (Pl. XVII, 7–9). These seem to have been made solely for funer-

Fig. 41.—Design on a vase from Cuicatlan, Oaxaca.
(*After Seler*)

ary purposes, since the figure element has been developed so as almost to eliminate the vase portion. The figures are represented as sitting or standing; they wear mantles with capes, and head-dresses in the form of a monster's jaws with feather plumes. Many of them are shown with a peculiar mouth-mask, rather resembling the mouth-mask worn by the wind-god in Mexico and Guatemala, and also by certain figures on vases from Nasca in Peru; and occasionally the figure represents a bat. Many of them show traces of red paint, and the faces are very skilfully modelled. On the whole they are more Mayan than Mexican in appearance.

From Monte Alban and Xoxo come pottery fragments of rather thick ware, ornamented with broad red stripes on a red or yellow ground, somewhat similar to certain fragments from Teotihuacan ; and elsewhere in the Zapotec country are found beakers with designs incised in outline and the background cut away (Fig. 33, *b* ; p. 176), similar in technique, though not in art, to beakers from the island of Sacrificios described below (e.g. Pl. XVIII, 10).

Quantities of pottery heads have been discovered in Cholula, similar to those of Teotihuacan, though rather coarser in paste, and ornamented in some cases with blue, red and white slip. Polychrome figurines in much the same style have been found at Teotitlan del Camino.

To turn now to the Totonac region ; the island of Sacrificios off Vera Cruz has produced a store of pottery which is in no respect inferior to that of Cholula with the exception that fewer colours are employed in ornament and the surface is not highly burnished. The paste is either pale red, grey or cream, admirably mixed and fired, and the shapes exhibit considerable variety (Fig. 36, 5–9, and Pls. XVIII and XIX). Especially characteristic are footed beakers and vases, tripod bowls with cylindrical or cascabel feet containing rattles, standing-bowls, bowls with slightly flattened bases, and plates. Handles are not common, but a type of vase with single long projecting handle seems confined to this area. Ornament is most commonly applied in the form of slip, white, cream, red (more than one shade), yellow, brown and black. In the most characteristic specimens the designs, monsters or formal patterns, are painted in thick white slip, and usually outlined with red or brown, or, especially in the case of plates, in deep orange on a brown background or *vice versa*. Engraved ornament is far more common in Totonac pottery than Cholulan ; sometimes the engraving merely follows the outline of a painted design, sometimes it constitutes the sole ornament. In more

o

elaborate specimens the entire background is cut away, or an intaglio design produced which is filled with a coloured slip. Fragments of the "champ-levé" ware, with its blue-green filling, have also been found. Moulded ornament again is very common, ranging from the mere gadrooning of a vase-body (Fig. 36, 5) to animal heads in relief, with the other details painted in slip on the sides of the vase (Pl. XIX). The vases with a bird's (or beast's) head in relief, and the details of the body incised, as figured on Pl. XVIII, 2, are very characteristic, and are, further, of particular interest since they, as well as vases in other forms, are often found to be coated with a leaden-coloured glaze hard enough to resist the point of a knife. This is of course an accidental earth-glaze, produced in firing by the action of the smoke or heat on the surface of the slip. Vases, identical in form and with the same accidental glaze, have been found at Atlixco, and also in the neighbourhood of Coban in the Alta Vera Paz district of Guatemala. It seems probable that they have reached these localities as articles of trade. Many vase-feet also are moulded in the form of animal heads (Pl. XIX).

Similar vase-feet are found at Tehuantepec, at Cuicatlan, at Teotitlan and, as we have seen, at Cholula. Of these localities the first pair seem to stand in close relation one to the other, and also the second pair, from the fact that the Cholulan and Teotitlan vase-feet are most commonly in the form of grotesque human heads, those of Cuicatlan and Tehuantepec in the form of heads of snakes. However, the distinction is by no means absolute. As far as the Totonac region is concerned, the beast heads seem to be in the majority. Impressed patterns are found on the bottoms of bowls from Sacrificios (Pl. XVIII, 9), but these form regular designs, instead of being, as in Mexico, mere series of incised lines. Similar bowls are found at Atlixco

PLATE XVIII

MEXICO

1. STONE SACRIFICIAL KNIFE; WOODEN HANDLE ENCRUSTED WITH MOSAIC

TOTONAC

2—10. POTTERY FROM THE ISLAND OF SACRIFICIOS, VERA CRUZ

(Scale: 1, 1/4th; 2—10, 1/6th)

and at Cuicatlan, though at the latter locality they
are made in black ware. An interesting characteristic
of Totonac pottery ornamentation is seen in more
or less naturalistic painted designs, usually in yellow
and brown slip, representing animals, such as the
Mexican porcupine, the coati, monkeys, snakes, bats,
lizards and insects. Quantities of fragments of pottery
figurines occur throughout the Totonac area. These
are made of a ware inferior to that of the vases, and
though the treatment of the bodies and limbs is
apt to be clumsy, yet the faces are modelled with
considerable skill. Many of the details are applied,
such as head-dresses, sandal ties and the like ; the teeth
are often shown filed to a point, or even mutilated in
characteristic Maya fashion. The last peculiarity emphasizes the general resemblance which these figurines
bear to those of British Honduras.

The pottery of the Totonac has been investigated
carefully by Strebel, who distinguishes several local
types within the area. In a general work of this nature
it is impossible to deal at length with minor variations,
and it will be sufficient to state that the careful investigations of this archæologist seem to indicate four
culture centres for the coastal region between the rivers
Nautla and Papaloapan. The two first are in the north,
and close together, and are associated respectively with
sites at Cerro Montoso (E.N.E. of Jalapa, near the
coast) and Ranchito de las Animas (immediately N.E.
of the last). At the former of these the style is akin to
and influenced by the neighbouring highlands and the
district beyond, while the latter is probably more
purely aboriginal. The two second lie to the south, one
including the Rio de Cotaxla, the other extending
thence to the Rio Papaloapan.

The pottery of the Huaxtec (Figs. 42–44) is peculiar
from more than one point of view. The paste of the
most characteristic specimens is hard and well-fired,

of a pale cream colour, and the most typical shape is a handled vase with a spout, rather like a teapot (Fig. 42), with moulded and painted ornament, in red and black, on the body. The latter is frequently in the form of an animal, with a large human face modelled upon its back near the tail. Other vases in human shape, with a spouted handle and similar painted decoration were also moulded from this pale

FIG. 42.—Huaxtec pottery vase; Tanquian.
(*After Seler*)

clay (Fig. 43). The presence of a spout distinguishes Huaxtec pottery from Mexican, though an appendage of this nature is not unknown from the Totonac country, since the tail of the animal vase figured on Pl. XIX is pierced by a hole. Red pottery is also found in the Huaxtec country, in the form of large vases and smaller tripod bowls, often with engraved ornament on the outer surface. Grater-bowls, similar in pattern to those of the Mexican valley, but in the pale cream ware, are also found, together with many figurines and fragments of such which are not mould-made.

To speak generally, the earliest type of pottery of which we have cognizance is similar in type to that manufactured later by the Tarascans. Following this came the far finer ware characteristic of Teotihuacan, the product of the Toltec culture. In pottery-making the mantle of the Toltec seems to have fallen upon the people of Cholula and Tlaxcala, districts associated with them in legend, and upon the Totonac, whose art shows certain affinities with that of Cholula. Between the ware of the Cholula-Tlaxcala region and that of the

FIG. 43.—Huaxtec pottery vase; Panuco.
(*After Seler*)

Mixtec-Zapotec district considerable similarity exists, a similarity which extends to the decoration of the pyramid of Xochicalco. It is usually held that the Cholulan style penetrated into Oaxaca *via* Teotitlan, but I do not feel certain that the reverse may not be truer, and that the real home of the highly-burnished polychrome ware may not eventually be found to lie in Oaxaca. The form of ornament does not seem to be a direct descendant of the Teotihuacan art, and there are found in the Oaxaca region certain original forms, such as the " Peruvian " designs mentioned above, as well as a tendency to elaborate textile motives as ornament (for instance, the wall-mosaics of Mitla), many of which motives constantly recur in the decoration of vases in the " Cholula " style, while they are wanting on the

Teotihuacan pottery. However that may be, Teotitlan is a site of great importance, constituting as it does a meeting-point of the three best schools of pottery, Cholula, Oaxaca and Totonac. Further consideration of the questions involved

FIG. 44.—Huaxtec pottery vase; Tampico.
(*After Seler*)

in the study of Mexican pottery must be deferred until something has been said about the art and culture of the Maya.

PLATE XIX

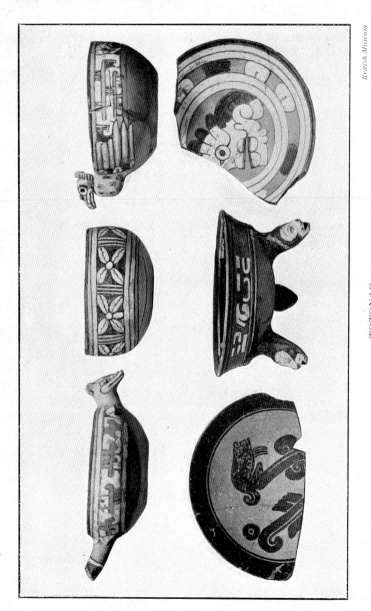

TOTONAC

POTTERY FROM THE ISLAND OF SACRIFICIOS, VERA CRUZ

(Scale: 1/4th)

CHAPTER VIII—THE MAYA: TRIBAL HISTORY

HAVING sketched the archæology of Mexico proper, explained as far as possible by what we know of the religion and customs of the early inhabitants, it now remains to consider the region to the south and east which was the scene of a distinct, but related, culture, that of the Maya. The area involved consists of Tabasco, Chiapas, Campeche and Yucatan in Mexico, British Honduras, Guatemala and the northern portion of Honduras. The task is one of far greater difficulty, since the ruined remains scattered over the country give evidence of a higher culture than that which prevailed at the conquest; but of the people who evolved that culture we know nothing except by implication. The sites which show the greatest architectural and artistic development had been abandoned at any rate some considerable time before the coming of the Spaniards, and the early chroniclers were unable to record anything concerning them. In Yucatan alone were traditions preserved which could be brought into relation with the ancient buildings, and then only with the most modern of them, which bear evident traces of non-Maya influence. The area now under consideration is separated geographically from that which formed the subject of the preceding chapters by the Tehuantepec depression; to the east of the latter, the southern section, including the greater portion of Tabasco, Chiapas, Guatemala (except the extreme north), and Honduras, are part of a mountain system which extends, with interruptions, into South America, and

may be considered a continuation of the Sierra Madre
to the west and north. Campeche, Yucatan and the
part of Guatemala excepted above, constitute a sort of
annexe to the former, formed of limestone, low-lying,
and of comparatively recent elevation from below
the sea. Guatemala (including British Honduras) is
an elevated plateau with its highest and steepest escarp-
ment on the Pacific side, and sloping less abruptly and
in irregular fashion towards the Atlantic. In the south
is a volcanic system, giving rise to scenery of particular
beauty, especially where it includes such highland lakes
as that of Atitlan. The igneous range constitutes the
main watershed, and consequently the only rivers of
importance, the Usumacinta and Motagua, drain into
the Atlantic, while in the low-lying region of Peten a
number of lakes are found. In Honduras the mountain
system decreases in elevation into hilly country, also
with its principal slope towards the Atlantic, traversed
in various directions by ridges branching off from the
central plateau. The volcanic system extends from
Guatemala along the Pacific coast. As in Mexico, climate corresponds with the degree of elevation, and in
Guatemala the same three zones, *tierra caliente, tierra
templada* and *tierra fria*, are found, with similar abrupt
transitions from one to the other. In the lower country
cacao vanilla, rubber, coconuts, bananas and palms grow
freely, while the uplands are covered with oak and pine.
The Atlantic side of Honduras produces a variety of
valuable tropical timber, while the higher ground is on
the whole more open than that of Guatemala, much of
the vegetation being herbaceous and affording good
grazing. The climate of Yucatan is purely tropical, and
the rainfall is very heavy. Under such conditions, more
favourable to vegetable than human existence, the
country is thickly covered with forest which reappears
as soon as cleared and renders exploration a matter of
great difficulty, besides making the country very un-

healthy from the point of view of the European. Indeed, the thick vegetation which clothes the river valleys and lower lying parts of the whole Maya area is the prin-

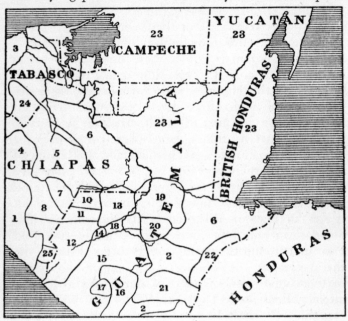

FIG. 45.

1.	Aztec.	16.	Kakchiquel.
2.	Pipil.	17.	Tzutuhil.
3.	Chontal.	18.	Uspantec.
4.	Zotzil.	19.	Kekchi.
5.	Tzental.	20.	Pokonchi.
6.	Chol.	21.	Pokomam.
7.	Chanabal.	22.	Chorti.
8.	Chicomaceltec.	23.	Maya.
10.	Cuje.	24.	Zoque.
11.	Jacaltec.	25.	Tapachula
12.	Mam.		
13.	Ixil.		(1 and 2, Nahuatl ;
14.	Aguacatec.		3–23, Maya ; 24 and
15.	Quiché.		25 Zoquean.)

cipal obstacle in the way of archæological investigation, since not only does it render the ruins extremely diffi-cult to locate, but it also contributes very seriously to their decay. The fauna is rich, and includes birds of brilliant plumage in great variety, jaguar, peccary, deer and alligator ; the deer and the turkey being the most important from the economic point of view of the early native.

Practically the whole of the population of this area, with the exception of an enclave of Nahua-speakers in southern Guatemala, spoke dialects of the language known as Maya in the broadest sense, to which the tongues of the Huaxtec and Totonac also belonged. The distribution of the various tribes is best seen from the accompanying map, after Thomas (Fig. 45), but it is hardly necessary to discuss them in detail, since their present positions cannot be taken necessarily as affording any indication of their positions in pre-Spanish times, and from only a very few have legends been collected which shed any light upon their former history. The dialect spoken in Yucatan is known as Maya in the narrower sense, and seems to bear a nearer relation to that which prevailed among the nations of the older culture, since the Yucatec at the conquest were using a script which corresponded closely with that found upon the monuments. Their dialect extends to the Rio de la Pasion and the western and southern Usumacinta, where it is spoken by the so-called Lacandons who have preserved certain of the ancient customs and beliefs. The Lacandons to the west speak the Chol dialect, though there are indications that both divisions of this people originally spoke Maya, that is to say the dialect of Yucatan. Besides the Yucatec, practically the only tribes of historical importance are grouped around lake Atitlan ; the Quiché occupying the largest area to the north, south and west of the lake, extending from the Pacific to central Guatemala, the Kakchiquel to the west and south of the lake, also extending to the Pacific, and the Tzutuhil wedged in between them on the southern shore of Atitlan. South-east of the Kakchiquel are the Pipil, a Nahua-speaking tribe, and Nahua dialects are

found in San Salvador and even further to the south-
east, as far as Nicaragua and Panama, pointing to a
stream of Nahua migration by an overland route.
The Pipil themselves preserved a tradition that they
had reached their present abode from Tuxtla. The
Maya language as a whole exhibits certain points of
similarity to that of the Mixtec and Zapotec, but its
structure is more akin to that spoken on the islands of
the Mexican Gulf and the northern coast of South
America. A tradition existed in Yucatan that an early
section of the inhabitants had come from the east, and
the Maya of this neighbourhood were certainly good
seamen, since large canoes with sails were met by the
expedition of Columbus, so it is at least possible that a
section of the early population were immigrants from
the Antilles. But at present too little is known of the
languages of Central America to admit of the formula-
tion of definite theories based upon linguistic arguments,
which constitute a class of evidence requiring extreme
caution on the part of those who would make use of it.

The early history of the Maya tribes is by no means
easy to extract from the traditions which have survived until the present day. The chief sources of information are as follows. The traditions relating to the
Tutul-Xiu family, the centre of whose power at the
time of the conquest lay at Mani in Yucatan, which
were reduced to writing, under the name of the " Books
of Chilan Balam " (Chilan Balam meaning Tiger-
priest) in Spanish times. The legends of the Quiché,
who in historical times occupied the plateau around
Santa Cruz and Quetzaltanango, with their capital at
Utatlan, contained in the Popol Vuh. The " Annals "
of the Xahila family of the Kakchiquel tribe, whose
chief city was Iximché near the modern Tecpan Guatemala. Finally the scattered traditions collected from
the natives by such early writers as Landa and Cogolludo. The Yucatec traditions alone can be brought

into any direct connection with the ruined sites of the early and architecturally more advanced Maya culture, but all of them agree in fixing Tulan as the starting-point of their respective migrations. Again the Books of Chilan Balam are the only traditions which are accompanied throughout by definite dates, according to a system which is explained later, and these dates can be correlated with our own time owing to the fact that each version fixes with great precision the death of a certain Ahpula, which occurred in 1536. Unfortunately the different versions do not agree as to the earlier dates, and in some cases extended time-periods appear to have been interpolated. I think however by careful comparison it is possible to reduce the discrepancies to a minimum, and I have therefore drawn up a scheme of chronology, based in the main on the version current at Mani, for which some degree of accuracy may, I think, be claimed. I do not pretend that these dates are more than tentative, but they will at least serve as a frame-work into which the main facts of Maya history may be fitted (Appendix III). The tradition current in Yucatan at the time of Landa was that the country had been peopled by two sets of immigrants, one from the east under a god or high-priest Itzamna, the other from the west under Kukulkan (the Maya equivalent of Quetzalcoatl), who later departed westward in the direction of Mexico. The first immigrants are said to have built Chichen Itza, and Kukulkan is related to have ruled there for a time, though afterwards his votaries built the city of Mayapan, where he reigned as a sort of overlord of the Yucatec. According to this author the Tutul-Xiu entered Yucatan from the south, and joined the Mayapan confederacy. To judge from their own legend the Tutul-Xiu left their original abode, Nonoual in Tulan Zuiva, about the year 418 A.D. (though it is possible that this event may have occurred earlier, viz. in 161, but I think the evidence is in favour of the later dating).

Their leader was Holon Chantepeuh, and their first settlement was at Chacnouitan, and subsequently, under Ahmekat Tutul-Xiu, at Balcalar. Whilst there, they heard of Chichen Itza, and later removed to this site, about the year 496. The fact that they are stated to have heard of Chichen Itza while they were at Balcalar seems to prove that some settlement already existed at the former place, and one version of the tradition represents them as setting out in search of it. For over a century they resided at Chichen Itza, and then removed to Champoton, probably owing to difficulties with their neighbours, since it is stated that Chichen was "destroyed." Their stay at Champoton is estimated at about two centuries and a half, at the end of which period they wandered back to Chichen Itza and again established themselves there. Not long afterwards Uxmal was "founded" by one of the Xiu family, Ahzuitok Tutul-Xiu, about 989, and the famous "league" of Mayapan was formed. For some time, about two hundred years, a central government was maintained at Mayapan, the city associated so closely with Kukulkan, and no doubt the paramount chieftains were satisfied with little more than the bare recognition of suzerainty. But the centrifugal action so noticeable in the political history of the American peoples began to assert itself, the league split up and Mayapan fell. The exact circumstances which led to the downfall of the paramount city are obscure. The family of the Cocomes were the rulers of Mayapan at the time, and it would appear that they had begun to exercise a closer control over their vassals. To support the harsher methods which they introduced they commenced to employ the services of mercenaries, "Mexicans," recruited in Tabasco and Xicalanco, and by their aid levied tribute upon the other members of the league to an extent which the latter were not prepared to suffer. The accounts of the Books of Chilan Balam are obscure, but they agree in

the names of the personages who played the principal
parts in the events which followed. Chac-Xib-Chac
was the " Governor " of Chichen Itza, and it would
appear that he conspired against the ruler of Mayapan,
Hunac Ceel, who drove him out, according to the, no
doubt, partisan account of the Xiu house, by " treachery." This treachery probably implies the employment
of the foreign mercenaries mentioned above, since
Hunac Ceel's agents are called the " seven men of Mayapan," and their names, which are recorded, are Nahua
rather than Maya. Ulil, the ruler of Itzamal, also appears to have been implicated in the conspiracy against
the ruling house. But whatever was the exact course of
events, the net result was that Chichen Itza was de-
populated about the year 1187 ; meanwhile the Nahua
mercenaries had influenced the ethnography of the
country by the introduction of the bow as a weapon.
But the end was not yet, the people of Chichen Itza
nursed their revenge, and about a century later insti-
gated a general rising which resulted in the sack of Mayapan and the slaughter of the ruler and all his sons
except one, who was at the time absent in the Uloa
valley. The survivor on his return collected the remnants of the Cocomes and settled at Sotuta, the Xiu
faction retiring to Mani. The Mexican mercenaries,
who no doubt formed too formidable a section to be
attacked directly, were allowed to form a settlement at
Ahcanul, north-east of Campeche. Itzamal however
survived ; a noble of high rank, Ahchel, who had
married the daughter of a high-priest of Mayapan, took
up his residence at Tikoch near the coast, with his
numerous sons. The family increased in numbers and
importance, and later constituted a ruling house, known
as the Chel, with its capital at Itzamal. Subsequent
history relates various struggles between the Xiu, Cocomes and Chel, the Cocomes preventing the Chel from
obtaining game and cereals from the interior, and the

Chel refusing salt and fish to the Cocomes. But in spite of this the population at large was prosperous, and increased in numbers, until a severe hurricane wrought much damage throughout the land, chiefly by causing the thatched roofs of the houses to catch fire. This disaster was followed by a plague, and then a series of sanguinary wars, after which smallpox appeared. Finally the Xiu, wishing to perform certain ceremonies at their old home, Chichen Itza, asked for a passage through the territory of the Cocomes. This was granted, but the party was enticed into a building which was set on fire and the inmates were massacred. Meanwhile the Spaniards had appeared in the country, and native history had reached its close.

The history of the Quiché exhibits some connection with that of the Kakchiquel, and further displays certain points of resemblance with the early legends of the Mexicans. Though both the Quiché and Kakchiquel accounts give lists of kings who ruled over their respective tribes, yet they furnish no dates, and the lengths of the various reigns can only be conjectured. Quiché history, like the Mexican, begins in myth, with the final or historical creation. The creating-gods fashioned four men out of maize, Balam-Quitzé, Balam-Agab, Mahucutah and Iqi-Balam. Of these the first three were the ancestors of the three Quiché divisions, the Cavek, Nihaib and Ahau-Quiché respectively. The fourth had no descendants, and therefore no place in the later history. We are told that besides these four individuals, the " Yaqui " or " sacrificers " (a name given in later times to the Mexicans) existed in numbers, and further the ancestors of various other tribes to the east (of the original Quiché home) were created, including the Tepeuh Oloman (probably the Olmec), the Tamub and Ilocab (the early inhabitants of the country later occupied by the Quiché), the seven tribes of Tecpan (perhaps the Pokomam and Pokonchi), the Kakchiquel, the

Rabinal (later at Zamaneb), the Tziquinaha (of Atitlan), and others. The four Quiché ancestors however
were too perfect to please the gods, being omniscient,
so the latter dimmed their intellects, but, as some sort
of compensation, provided them with wives. The sun as
yet was not created, all the world was dark, and mankind had no knowledge of ritual. So they set out for
Tulan Zuiva, where each tribe received its god under
whose leadership it commenced its migration. Before
the general separation however the need of fire was
felt, and the Quiché god, Tohil, who was a thunder-god, provided his votaries with a constant supply,
by striking it from his sandal. The other tribes begged
fire from the Quiché, but they, on the advice of a messenger in bat-form from the underworld, Xibalba, demanded in return that the recipients should consent to
be united with their god " beneath their girdles and beneath their armpits." This dark saying implied the gift
of their hearts in sacrifice, and the other tribes, failing
to understand the true import, fell into the trap, with
the exception of the Kakchiquel, whose bat-god stole
fire from the smoke without agreeing to the terms. The
migrations then took place, many of the tribes going
eastward, while the Quiché, together with the Kakchiquel, Tamub, Ilocab, Rabinal and Tziquinaha,
travelled to Guatemala, where on a mountain they
assumed their tribal names and " awaited the dawn,
looking for the morning star." The phrase recalls very
distinctly the Mexican legend related on p. 10. Finally
the morning star made its appearance, followed by the
sun, to which incense brought from Tulan was offered,
but the tribal gods, who had meanwhile expressed the
wish to be secluded in sanctuaries apart from the settlements of men, were turned into stone. After this the
four Quiché leaders withdrew themselves from association with their followers, but were occasionally seen, together with the gods, in the mountains and forests ;

human sacrifice, practised secretly, began to make its appearance, and strife with the other tribes arose. The operations of the hostile tribes seem to have been directed chiefly towards the capture of the Quiché gods, and after the failure of various stratagems, a direct attack was made upon the Quiché, now living in a palisaded settlement in the mountains, but was repulsed with great slaughter. The death of the original leaders next follows in the legend ; they summon the people, sing the song with which they greeted the sun on its first rising and then disappear, leaving behind a bundle afterwards known as "veiled majesty." The song opens, " The king of the deer is ready ; his sign appears in the sky," and the words suggest the stellar god of the Mexican hunting-tribes, Mixcoatl, with his two-headed deer, while the " medicine-bundle " is not unknown to Mexican mythology (see pp. 33 and 55).

The greater portion of the account given at present must of course be regarded as belonging to the region of myth, but at this point the narrative becomes more "historical" in nature. The Popol Vuh naturally exalts the Quiché at the expense of the other tribes, but it appears from other sources that they did actually exercise a certain, though variable, supremacy over their neighbours. Hitherto they had obviously been under a priestly domination, and the leaders of the migration wielded an authority arising from their association with the gods which they received at Tulan. But their sons had no such right to command, and so set out on a pilgrimage to the related tribes in the east, i.e. those who had taken a more easterly route, to obtain the *insignia* of temporal rule. On their return the Quiché began to expand, stone-built cities were constructed to be the centres of ceremonial and political life of the three tribal divisions, the government was organized, and though the Ilocab revolted against the growing Quiché power, they were subdued and the attempt only had the

P

effect of inaugurating the public sacrifice of prisoners. It is interesting to note that one of their early kings, whose name Gukumatz is the equivalent of the Nahua Quetzalcoatl, is credited with the performance of many miraculous feats ; but the first kings important from a historical point of view were Quicab and Cavizimah. Under them the Kakchiquel and Rabinal were con- quered, colonies and garrisons were placed in subject towns and, on their own account, continued to extend the Quiché power by conquest, though many of the leaders broke away from the main stock and set up as independent chieftains. In this reign we first hear of prisoners of war being executed by the shooting sacri- fice as practised by the Mexicans. Quicab appears to have been by far the most important of the Quiché rulers, but the power which he gained was not main- tained even throughout his reign. For the events which commenced the decline of the Quiché domination we must go to the annals of the Kakchiquel, in which it is stated that two of Quicab's sons, who no doubt occu- pied the position of sub-chiefs, took advantage of cer- tain discontent among his subjects to refuse the tribute due to their father and overlord. The sedition seems to have succeeded to the extent that Quicab's authority was considerably weakened, and it was followed by a more serious defection in the form of a revolt on the part of the Kakchiquel as related below. None of Quicab's successors wielded the power which he exer- cised in his most prosperous years, and at the time of the conquest the Kakchiquel, Tzutuhil and other tribes had regained their independence.

In the Kakchiquel annals we find again a list of kings, though five fewer than the corresponding list of Quiché chiefs, but dates are for the most part lacking, though the revolt of a subtribe in the reign of the sixth ruler can be fixed as the starting-point of the chronological system current at the discovery. Again we find Tulan

mentioned as the point of departure, but the statement
is made that there are four Tulans, one in the east, one
in the west (whence the Kakchiquel themselves came),
one at Xibalba (the underworld) and one " where god
is." It is impossible not to see in this a reference to the
four cardinal points, which, as has been pointed out,
were of such ceremonial importance among the Mexicans. The names of the ancestors of the Xahila division
of the Kakchiquel are given as Gagavitz and Zactecauh,
and after the creation they brought tribute to Tulan
together with the Zotzil, the other division, consisting
of jade, silver, feather-work and carvings. All that they
brought away with them were their arms, bows and
shields, and throughout the early portion of the annals
insistence is continually being made on the fact that
the Kakchiquel were warriors of the hills. " Let your
rounded shields be your riches, your bows, your bucklers . . . there in the hills shall you lift up your faces."
Various other tribes are mentioned as starting from
Tulan about the same time, including the Rabinal,
Tzutuhil, and Tukuchi, the last becoming subject subsequently to the Kakchiquel. A number of place-names
occur in the account of the migration, which do not
admit of identification, and at one point the sea is said
to have been crossed by means of a causeway of sand
which miraculously made its appearance. Finally the
travellers come to Tapcu Oloman, where they fought
with those of Nonoualcat, who come against them in
boats, a statement which must surely point to the
Olmec and the region east of the Totonac (between
the rivers Papaloapan and Usumacinta) known to the
Mexicans as Nonoualco. Whilst here they made an
attack upon Zuiva, but were defeated. At this point the
wandering peoples, who included the Quiché, adopted
tribal names, and they then retraced their footsteps over
the route by which they had come, fighting with various
tribes by the way, until apparently they turned south

and arrived in Guatemala. During the journey Zacte-cauh fell into a ravine and was killed, but Gagavitz, whose influence hitherto seems to have been purely priestly, like that of other leaders of migration, was invested with the *insignia* of temporal power and became chief of the Xahila and Zotzil divisions. At this time the tribes were evidently in a neighbourhood which was the scene of considerable volcanic activity, and in one of their wars they captured the ruler of a hostile tribe, by name Tolgom ("Son of the Mud-that-Quivers"), and executed him with arrows. In commemoration of this episode an annual festival was instituted at which children were offered up in an arrow-sacrifice. The tribes then settled, dividing the land amongst themselves, and since Gagavitz remained with the Tzutuhil, the Kakchiquel were left without a chief, and a man named Baquahol succeeded in obtaining the power, apparently by purchase or bribery. Here again the Kakchiquel account is brought into relation with other migration legends, since it is stated that the "dawn" appeared. The actual words used are rather interesting, and they are quoted in full later on. Though Baquahol had obtained the power, yet Gagavitz was not without descendants, and his two sons Cay Noh and Cay Batz took service with a chief named Tepeuh, "king of Kauke, to whom all paid tribute." It has been conjectured with some reason that this ruler is to be identified with the Quiché chief Iztayul, but in any case he appears to have been an overlord of the whole district, and sufficiently powerful to place Cay Noh and Cay Batz as rulers over the Kakchiquel. Cay Noh was succeeded by his son Citan Quatu, but the son of the latter did not rule ; in fact for the time the power appears to have been divided among a number of petty chieftains. However, the tribes were again united by Huntoh and Vukubatz, the former being the grandson of Citan Quatu, though the Kakchiquel had not yet attained complete independence,

since they recognized the Quiché ruler, now Quicab, as
their overlord. But freedom was in sight, and an opportunity was offered by the troubles which marred the
final years of Quicab's reign. The actual excuse of the
Kakchiquel revolt was slender enough, a woman selling
bread had her wares seized by certain Quiché soldiers,
and the Kakchiquel espoused her cause. Quicab appears to have failed to recognize the real nature of the
movement, and neglected to take immediate steps to
suppress it, with the result that the Kakchiquel were
able to declare their independence and now appear as a
rival power. Hostilities between the peoples continue,
and finally the Kakchiquel under Cablahuh Tihax and
Oxlahuh Tzii defeat the Quiché in a pitched battle,
capturing their joint rulers Tepepul and Iztayul, who
have meanwhile succeeded Quicab.[1] The description of
the battle is given in part on p. 292. The power of the
Kakchiquel now appears at its zenith, but their expansion aroused the jealousy of their neighbours. A revolt
occurred of the Tukuchi subject tribe, which was however suppressed, and with such slaughter that the incident became a landmark in history. From this point
in the annals the number of days which elapsed subsequent to the revolt is given, with the result that the
revolt itself can be attributed almost with certainty to
the year 1494. The rest of the history until the arrival
of the Spaniards consists in accounts of fights with
neighbours, which the annals usually characterize as the
suppression of revolts. Two items of information however are of importance. Before the death of Oxlahuh
Tzii, which occurred in 1509 or 1510, we read that certain " Yaqui " (i.e. Mexican traders) were put to death

[1] At this point the Kakchiquel annals prove a useful check upon
the account given by the Popol Vuh. Tepepul and Iztayul, according
to the latter, preceded Quicab, and Quicab was succeeded by Tepepul
and Xtayub. It is evident that some duplication has taken place in
the Quiché legend, that Tepepul and Iztayul are the same as Tepepul
and Xtayub, and that they succeeded Quicab.

for siding with the revolted Akahal, while in 1511 messengers were received by Hunyg and Lahun Noh, then ruling, from Montecuzoma.

It is perhaps impossible in the present state of our knowledge to unravel the myths given above sufficiently to determine with accuracy the routes taken by the different tribes, but still the general trend of migrations may perhaps be gathered from them. The place-name Nonoual, which occurs both in the books of Chilan Balam and the annals of the Kakchiquel, is valuable as a fixed point, since it seems possible to determine the locality with reasonable certainty. The Kakchiquel obviously reached Nonoual from the west, and then retraced their steps before turning southward into Guatemala ; thus they always regarded Nonoual as lying in the east. For the Tutul Xiu however it lay in the west, and this people had settled at Balcalar in southern Yucatan before they moved north to Chichen Itza. If we add to this the information found in the Kakchiquel annals that the inhabitants lived in boats, the conclusion seems inevitable that Nonoual lay somewhere on the coast between the lower reaches of the Papaloapan and of the Usumacinta. This agrees absolutely with the site of the region known to the Mexicans as Nonoualco, and the " sea " crossed by the Quiché and Kakchiquel before they arrived there may be one of the lagoons of the Papaloapan basin. The name of Tulan, the starting-point of the migrations, affords greater difficulties. Tulan is usually mentioned with the addition of the name Zuiva, and the Popol Vuh gives it a further title which means the " seven caverns," and so brings it into direct relation with the Chicomoztoc at which the various Nahua tribes foregathered before they descended upon the Mexican valley (see p. 14). For the Kakchiquel, Tulan was also the starting-point, but Zuiva lay beyond Nonoual, and evidently not far from it ; and this agrees with the Books of Chilan Balam, since in the latter Nonoual ap-

pears to be a district of the realm known as Tulan
Zuiva. A further point in confirmation of this may perhaps be extracted from the fact that certain tribes called
Tepeu Oliman (Popol Vuh), or Tapcu Oloman (Kakchiquel annals), are associated with this particular region, while the inhabitants of the latter were known to
the Mexicans as Olmec. Tulan, the starting-point therefore, cannot be identified with the Zuiva, or Tulan
Zuiva near Nonoual, nor indeed is there any need that
such an identification should be made. The original
Tulan, wherever it lay, was regarded evidently as the
home of a large number of peoples, and there is a tendency, visible all over the world, for migrating tribes to
name their subsequent settlements after their original
or legendary birthplace. Perhaps the best example of
this propensity is presented by the number of Hawaikis
scattered over the Pacific, Hawaiki being the name of
the original starting-point of Polynesian migrations.
That this Tulan Zuiva near Nonoual was an important
kingdom in the youth of the Quiché and Kakchiquel
peoples is obvious ; the Kakchiquel admit defeat at the
hands of its inhabitants, and though it is not expressly
so stated, the account of the Popol Vuh seems to indicate that the *insignia* of temporal power were obtained
from the ruler of this district, a chief named Nacxit.
The name Nacxit is interesting, since Tezozomoc states
that it was an appellation of Quetzalcoatl, and we have
already observed the importance which the Mexican
immigrants attached to Toltec blood as giving the possessor the right to reign, Tulan being closely associated
with this god. That there were more Tulans than one
seems evident from the Kakchiquel statement that
there were four, although the number quoted appears
to have a certain ceremonial reference to the points of
the compass. That the Quiché and Kakchiquel had
come in contact with the later Nahua immigrants into
the Mexican valley seems evident both from certain

points of similarity in their migration legends, and also from the highly important fact that they used the bow, a weapon which was unknown to the Tutul Xiu until a later date. From these considerations, and also from the evidence afforded by the short list of kings which the legends of these tribes furnish, one feels inclined to regard the Tulan from which they started as the region ruled by the Toltec of the Mexican valley, and to conjecture that the Tulan Zuiva with which Nonoual was connected, was perhaps one of the now ruined sites in the Usumacinta basin. The association of the word Zuiva with the original Tulan in the Quiché account may be due to one of two causes. It may on the one hand be the result of confusion, or on the other it is possible that " Tulan " and " Zuiva " may be the same name but belong to different dialects. The question which Tulan gave the name to the other is more complex, and can only be decided after the date of these ruins has been discussed, but it may be mentioned that there is nothing inherently impossible in the suggestion that one of the Usumacinta sites may have been named Tulan, for we do not know the original names of any of them. The net result of a comparison of the migration legends which we possess is therefore as follows. The Quiché and Kakchiquel appear to have been closely connected throughout, and the Tutul Xiu show little trace of connection with either. The former two tribes seem to have been brought into contact with the later Nahua, while the Tutul Xiu were not, and the Tulan from which the Tutul Xiu migration started was not the Tulan which the Quiché and Kakchiquel regarded as their original home, though it is possible that the two were intimately connected. The first stage of Quiché and Kakchiquel migration seems to have been from west to east, through those districts which, from Tuxpan to Tabasco, were regarded as the daughter-states of the Mexican Tulan, and their route, or at any rate some

portion of it, lay along the coast. After this they retraced their steps for a short distance, and then turned
south and west into Guatemala, probably passing
through south-western Vera Cruz, western Oaxaca, and
Chiapas. Further consideration of this complicated
question must be deferred until some account has been
given of the religion, ethnography, and ruined sites of
the Maya area.

CHAPTER IX—THE MAYA : RELIGION AND MYTH

AS among the Mexicans, so too among the Maya, any attempt to reconstruct their civilization must start with a general survey of their religious beliefs. The task of dealing shortly and clearly with this subject is by no means easy ; from the one point of view indeed it is simpler, since the amount of information at the disposal of students is relatively small ; but on the other hand, as far as the builders of the ruins are concerned, we are dealing with a people who had had their day at the time of the conquest, and the meaning of the scenes sculptured on the monuments must be inferred from the religious practices of a people who, though no doubt ethnically and culturally their descendants, had been exposed to influences emanating from Mexico, and had declined in civilization. The different sources of information, moreover, must be kept distinctly apart ; such authorities as Landa and Cogolludo deal only with the Maya of Yucatan as they found them ; the native traditions called the " Books of Chilan Balam " give a few mythical details relating to one Yucatec tribe, and that not the earliest of the Maya immigrants ; while other native chroniclers, the Popol Vuh and Annals of Xahila, relate to the Quiché and Kakchiquel respectively, also comparatively late immigrants, who had fallen under Mexican influence. The native codices give a large number of portraits of beings which, it is safe to conclude, were gods, and these, especially the manuscript known as Troano-Cortesianus, constitute a most important link between the

early Maya sculptures and the accounts of the Yucatec
by Landa and Cogolludo ; but the identification of the
different deities is to a large extent a conjectural matter, impossible of short treatment since it involves the
production of much detailed evidence. The following
account does not pretend to be more than the result of
a careful consideration of most of the sources, and for
the evidence itself the reader must be referred elsewhere. It cannot be denied that many of the conclu-
sions here set forth are controversial, but it may be
claimed that there do exist in all cases certain definite points of evidence in their favour. Mayan religion shows a close fundamental similarity to that of the
Mexicans, so much so in fact that it is fair to argue
from what we know of the latter to the former, always
with proper precautions. Care is necessary, since the
migration legends of the Quiché, Kakchiquel and books
of Chilan Balam all mention Tulan as a resting-place
or starting-point, and there is always the possibility that
the myths contained in them may have been influenced
by " Toltec " beliefs. I hope to show later, however,
that the basis of the Toltec culture was in fact Mayan,
and I therefore think it fair to claim that many, though
certainly not all, of the similarities between the two re-
ligions are due to a common Mayan element. This is
especially true of what we are able to conjecture concerning the beliefs of the builders of the ruins in Honduras, Guatemala and Chiapas.

As among the Mexicans, tribal gods, under whose
leadership migrations took place, are found also among
the Maya. In Yucatan we hear of a god Itzamna, supposed to have come from the east, whose attributes are
much the same as those of Tonacatecutli. Connected
with the sites of Chichen Itza and Mayapan was the
god Kukulkan, of whose name " Quetzalcoatl " is a
literal translation, and who was supposed to have come
from the west. The god of the Quiché was Tohil, and

he was in particular the deity of the Cavek tribe and a thunder-god, while the other principal divisions of the Quiché, the Nihaib and Ahau-Quiché, were under the leadership of Avilix and Hacavitz respectively. A fourth tribal division worshipped a god Nicatayah, but just as the ultimate prosperity of the Aztec raised their deity Uitzilopochtli to a predominating position in the pantheon, so the extinction of this Quiché division resulted in the extinction also of its god. Tohil is in one place definitely identified with Quetzalcoatl, under the name Yolcual Quetzalcuat (i.e. Yoalli Eecatl Quetzalcoatl). The god of the Rabinal was Huntoh, who is probably identical with Tohil. The god of the Kakchiquel was a divinity in bat-form, called Zotziha Chimalcan, and was a deity associated by the Quiché with the underworld, Xibalba. Gods especially associated with certain localities were, Kukulkan with Mayapan and, later, Mani, Ahchun Caan with Tihoo, Ahulneb with Cozumel, Kinich Ahau with Campeche, and Itzamatul (perhaps a form of Itzamna) with Itzamal. The Tzental of Chiapas and Tabasco venerated a culture-hero Votan. But in actual cult, at any rate as far as the Yucatec were concerned, the agricultural divinities were of primary importance. As in Mexico, the god of agriculture and rain was also the thunder-god; in Yucatan he was called Chac, and was assisted in the performance of his functions by a number of subsidiary Chac, just as Tlaloc by the Tlaloque. Another fertility-god was Ah Bolon Tzacab, who, in one creation myth, is represented as taking the seeds of all cultivated plants with him to the thirteenth heaven, a story which recalls the theft of maize by Tlaloc (p. 48). Other patrons of agriculture were the so-called Bacab, the four deities placed by the creator to support the heavens. Their names were Hobnil, Kanzicnal, Zaczini and Hozanek, and they are closely associated with the Chac, so closely in fact that I am inclined to think that they were actually four of

the latter deities. Like the Mexican Tlaloc, the Chac
were supposed to carry axes, the weapon of the thunder-
god, and were closely associated with the snake which
throughout America is the symbol of rain. They have
been identified, I think beyond doubt, with the figure,
called by Schellhas "God B," of the manuscripts, a god
who appears constantly on the monuments throughout
the Maya region (Fig. 46, e). Like Tlaloc he is shown
with a long nose and tusks, the former of which on the
buildings of Yucatan develops into a regular trunk. Seler
identifies Ah Bolon Tzacab with the "God K" of
Schellhas, a god with a foliated nose, who is closely associated with Chac, and appears nearly as often on the
monuments (Fig. 46, b). God K however bears a striking resemblance to the Zapotec funerary figures with
their peculiar elongated mouth-masks, and also to the
Mexican Eecatl, a form of Quetzalcoatl. I think therefore that he is more likely a god of wind, a deity who
would necessarily be closely connected with the rain-
and thunder-gods. But though he may be the Maya
parallel of Quetzalcoatl in the form of Eecatl, I do
not think that he is to be identified with Kukulkan.
This statement may not seem to follow from what I
have said before, but I hope to make it clear later.
Among the Quiché we have Kanel (or Xkanel), Xcacau,
and Xtoh as gods of fertility, and among the Kakchiquel, Kanel also. It is further to be noted that another
name of Hobnil is Kanal Bacab. Hunting- and fishing-
gods existed among the Yucatec, but nothing is known
of them save their names; the hunting-deities were
Akanum, Zuhuyzip, and Tabai, the fishing, Ahcitz, Ah-
kak Nexoi, Ahpua and Amalcum. As gods of the arts we
have Itzamna, the supposed inventor of letters, Ixche-
belyax, goddess of embroidery and painting, a Maya
counterpart of Xochiquetzal, Ixazalvoh, goddess of
weaving, Pizlimtec and Xochbitum, gods of singing
(like Xochipilli and Macuilxochitl), and Htubhtum a

FIG. 46.—Maya gods with their name-glyphs.

A. The Moan bird.
B. The wind-god (God K).
C. Unknown goddess.
D. The maize-god (God E).
E. The rain- and thunder-god (God B).
F. The war-god (God F).

(*Dresden MS.*)

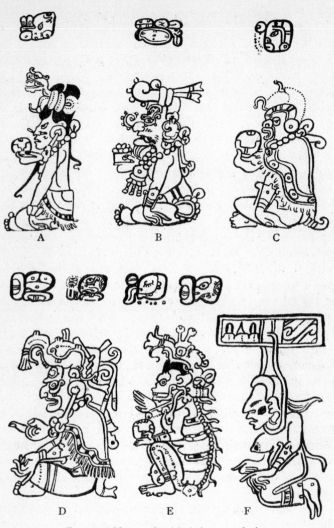

FIG. 47.—Maya gods with their name-glyphs.

A. A water-goddess (Goddess I).
B. The sun-god (God G).
C. The god of the north star (God C).
D. The sky-god (God D).
E. The death-god (God A).
F. The goddess of suicides.

(*Dresden MS.*)

god of gems. There appear to have been four war-deities, Hunpiktok, Ahchuykak, Citchac Coh, and Ahulneb, while the Tzental war-god was called Chinax. Hunpiktok, who had a temple at Itzamal, is identified with Tihax of the Quiché and Kakchiquel, the god of the stone knife, and both were probably sacrificial-deities also. One of these war-gods may be the God F of the manuscripts, who appears to bear a certain relation to the death-god and to sacrifice, and whose face-paint is not unlike that of the Aztec Xipe (Fig. 46, *f*). Like the Mexicans the Maya possessed a god of travellers and traders, Ekchuah, who corresponds to the Mexican Yacatecutli, though he does not seem to have been honoured with so elaborate a cult. Gods of medicine (closely allied with magic) were Itzamna, Citbolontum, Ahau Chamahez and a sun-god, Kinich Ahau, husband of Ixazalvoh. Kukulkan, according to one account, was the god of fevers, and with these deities was associated Ixchel, the goddess of childbirth, wife of Itzamna, whose image was placed under the bed of prospective mothers in order to secure an easy delivery. There was also a goddess Zuhuykak, said to be a deified mortal, who was the special protectress of children. The Quiché venerated a number of disease-gods, connected with whom were the two deities Xpiyakok and Xmukane, counterparts of the Mexican Oxomoco and Cipactonal, who, like the latter, were supposed to have assisted in the creation and were regarded as the prototypes of all magicians.

We come now to the elemental gods, who seem for the most part to have been rather vague personalities, crystallized here and there (and rather robbed of dignity in the process) into more sharply defined tribal protectors. These are the deities whom, I believe, the builders of the monuments chiefly worshipped, and whose portraits or symbols may be identified among the carvings which decorate the ruins. Among these, the most diffi-

cult to treat satisfactorily is
Kukulkan, the Quiché Gukumatz. The name, as stated before in connection with Quetzalcoatl, means "Feathered
serpent," and the conception
of such a divinity is not peculiar to the Maya region, since
a feathered snake, the "Mother
of waters," is worshipped by
the Pueblo Indians far to the
north. But Gukumatz - Ku-
kulkan is not a mere water-god,
and I think that his real
nature is apparent from the
Tzental description of Kukulkan, "the feathered snake that
goes in the waters." It is difficult to see what else this can
typify than the ripple, born
both of wind and water, the
aspect of which suggests feathers, and the motion a serpent. Both as representing
motion, i.e. primordial motion,
and as typifying wind, i.e.
breath, the god represents life,
and so in his highest aspect
becomes a creator-god. In his
snake and water aspect he is
closely connected with the
rain-gods, while in his bird and
wind manifestation he is lord
of the sky and world-directions,
for the winds blow from all
points of the compass. As
this great and vague deity

Q

FIG. 48.—The serpent-bird, from a carved wooden panel at Tikal.
(*After Maudslay*)

he appears in the early part of the Popol Vuh, and also, I believe, on the monuments, where his symbol, the serpent-bird, is not uncommon (e.g. Figs. 48 and 49). But he is not directly represented, for the very reason that primitive peoples (and civilized too for that matter) shrink from expressing their high gods in definite form. It is only when he becomes a tribal protector, as among the Toltec and the rulers of Mayapan, that his attributes become fixed and a definite conception of him is transferred to wood or stone. But once the definite conception is formed, the majesty of mystery is to a large extent lost, and we see in Mexico the god of life and breath becoming Eecatl, the god of the material wind, who sweeps the path of the gods of rain. It is this relation, I believe, that Kukulkan-Gukumatz bears to the Maya god of the material wind, God K. No one who has studied the beliefs of the American tribes will think that such a conception is beyond their psychology. Francisco Hernandez states that the Yucatec chiefs, that is the more highly educated class, worshipped gods which were unknown to the populace, and we know that the religious ideas of the Peruvian rulers were on a very high plane. These higher beliefs, where they occurred, were usually veiled in symbolism to guard them from the vulgar; symbolism thrived in America, and the tendency to esoteric doctrines, evolved by professional priesthoods, adds to the difficulty of interpreting the remains of the earlier civilizations. The degeneration of Gukumatz is seen in the later portion of the Popol Vuh, where he is definitely associated with the Toltec in the additional name " Ah Toltekat," while reminiscences of his former exalted status are apparent in later Mexican beliefs concerning him. His association with the planet Venus, which is not apparent on the monuments, belongs to the later stage, and, together with his portraiture in carvings (e.g. Fig. 87; p. 367), apart from his symbolic representation as a serpent-bird,

PLATE XX

MAYA

STELA 14; PIEDRAS NEGRAS, GUATEMALA

has an important bearing on the origin of the later buildings at Chichen Itza. The god Itzamna, also called
Yaxkokahmut, is again not very easy to fix; he is said to
be the son of the creator Hunabku and to have come
from the east, but since he is regarded as the inventor
of writing, which must have been practised long before
the Maya entered Yucatan, this does not necessarily
mean that he came by sea, but only from some district
lying to the east of the territory occupied by his votaries
at the time when they acquired the art of writing.
A comparison of the manuscripts with the account of
the ceremonies which ushered in the new year given
by Landa seems definitely to identify him with Schellhas'
"God D," the "God with the Roman nose" (Fig. 47, d).
As such he is a sky-god, similar in many respects to Tonacatecutli, and like him is often represented as an old
man with a beard. His head appears constantly upon
the monuments, either as a glyph, or issuing from the
mouths of the double-headed serpent, of which the
body is ornamented with planet-symbols, and which I
believe to represent the sky. In later times in Yucatan
he bore a very close relation to the sun-god, Kinich-
Ahau, and was to a certain extent identified with him, in
so far as we hear of an image of Kinich-Ahau-Itzamna
being prepared for certain ceremonies. A figure exactly
similar to that of Itzamna (identified as God D) is sometimes shown, in manuscripts and reliefs and on pottery,
with a shell (Fig. 68; p. 312), and it may be argued
from Mexican analogies that this deity was also associated with the moon. How far Itzamna may be identified with Itzamatul, the especial god of Itzamal, is perhaps doubtful, but at any rate it is a coincidence that
both were important gods of healing. As regards Itzamatul it is said that his emblem was a hand, and that he
was also known as Kabul, the "Strong Hand"; in this
connection it is extremely interesting to note that two
of the stelæ at Piedras Negras (Pl. XX), one at Copan,

a relief at Palenque, and a fresco at Santa Rita in British Honduras, show a figure with a head-dress in which a hand appears as the central feature. It is stated further that his name implies association with the dew and clouds, and that pilgrimages were made to his oracular shrine from Tabasco, Chiapas and Guatemala.

The sun-god proper in Yucatan was, as stated before, Kinich-Ahau, and at his temple in Itzamal the deity was supposed to descend at midday to consume the offerings " as the macaw with its variegated plumage." The simile is interesting, since it recalls at once the reliefs showing the offerings made to birds perched upon conventional trees (wrongly termed crosses) at Palenque (Fig. 49), and the similar emblems surmounted by birds held by some of the figures at Menché. Still more interesting is the statement, found in the works of Burgoa, that at Teotitlan in the Zapotec country was a temple with a celebrated idol which was said to have come from heaven in the form of a bird in the midst of a luminous constellation. One of the glyphs identified with practical certainty is that of the sun, and figures or heads of deities with his glyph, " kin," upon the forehead are found in the manuscripts and upon the monuments. Such is Schellhas' God G, who differs from Itzamna only in the presence of the kin-mark and of a peculiar curved nose-ornament (Fig. 47, b). On the monuments this god is invariably shown with peculiarly filed teeth, a characteristic which persists even when the kin-mark is absent (see Fig. 72; p. 316, and the cover-design), and a long beard-like appendage beneath his chin which probably represents the rays of the sun (Fig. 55, e; p. 251). But at the date at which the manuscripts were inscribed, as in later Yucatan, the personalities of Itzamna and the sun-god proper were rather confused, and the tendency can be observed even upon the monuments. The association of the sun with war is not so evident among

the Maya as among the Aztec, still I think that it
may be traced in the fact that nearly all the shields
carried by figures carved upon the monuments bear as
a device the face of the sun, distinguished by the peculiar form of the teeth. The magnificent relief in the
temple at Palenque, usually known as the " temple of
the sun," represents in reality one of these shields slung
from two crossed spears, and it is possible that the
temple itself was dedicated to the war-god (Fig. 82 ;
p. 344). Another feature of the sun-face, when shown
thus *en face*, is a twisted snake with the fold upon
the nose, but arranged in the reverse position to that
seen upon certain of the Tlaloc faces in Mexico (compare Fig. 86, *f*; p. 356). It is worth noting, however,
that Tlaloc is often shown with the attributes of Tonatiuh in the Mexican manuscripts. In addition to these
gods, the Yucatec also believed in the existence of a
creator, Hunabku, father of Itzamna, though, like many
creating-deities, he does not seem to have been honoured
with any definite cult. It is possible that he is to be
identified with Hunahpu, a god who held a similar
position in the mythology of the Quiché, and who was
associated in the work of creation with Gukumatz and
Hurakan. The latter was also termed the " Heart of
Heaven," and was a thunder- and lightning-god. As
such he was also a god of fertility. The association of
lightning with fertility is not perhaps apparent until it
is remembered that most rain in the tropics is accompanied by thunder ; for this reason Tlaloc and Chac,
both of them thunder-gods, are gods of agriculture, and
the dualism which makes the god who smites with the
lightning the god also of the fertilizing rain is found in
South America, in Peru, and in the Antilles. Whilst on
this subject the existence of a special maize-god may be
mentioned. This personage does not appear in the
pantheon of the later Yucatec, for whom the Chac were
the agricultural deities, but he is shown constantly in

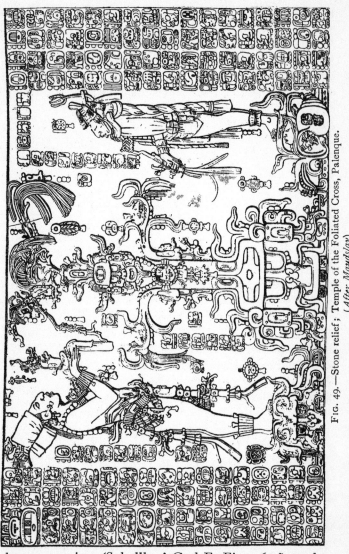

FIG. 49.—Stone relief; Temple of the Foliated Cross, Palenque. (*After Maudslay*)

the manuscripts (Schellhas' God E, Fig. 46, *d*), and on the monuments. But his position is peculiar ; even in the earlier times the rain-gods represented the active principle of fertility, the maize-god being merely passive, and typifying the spirit of the maize, befriended by the beneficent powers and persecuted by the lord of the underworld and the various animals which plunder the growing crop. On the monuments he is distinguished by a foliated ornament, representing the corncob, which forms his head-dress, and he appears most conspicuously in the so-called " foliated cross " at Palenque (Fig. 49), which in reality represents a maize-plant like the Mexican Tree of the West, shown in Fig. 10; p. 79. In the manuscripts he wears a similar head-dress, but is usually shown also with a vertical line running down his face passing across his eye, just as Cinteotl is depicted in the manuscripts of Mexico.

The lords of the underworld held an important position in Maya mythology. The Yucatec recognized two destinations for departed spirits ; one was a sort of paradise, where the souls of the dead rested in the shade of the mythical Yaxché tree, the other was called Mitnal, and corresponded to the Aztec Mictlan. Here presided a god called Hunahau or Uac Mitun Ahau, whose attributes are exactly similar to those of Mictlantecutli. He is usually, though not invariably, shown as a skeleton, and skulls and cross-bones, bell-like pendants and sometimes a feather ruff are his chief *insignia* (Schellhas' God A, Fig. 47, *e*). He is very frequently depicted in the manuscripts, and appears on the monuments chiefly in the form of a skull. The Kakchiquel spoke of him as Mictan Ahau, and associated with him two subordinate deities, Tatan Holon and Tatan Bak (" Father Bones and Father Skull "). The Quiché termed the underworld Xibalba, a word which was also used with the same connotation by the Maya and Kakchiquel. The story of the demi-gods Hunahpu and Xbalanque gives a detailed description of Xibalba. The road to it lies downwards beneath the earth, and its rulers are Hun Camé and Vukub Camé (terms in which we can recognize the Maya word cimi, the name of the day-sign corresponding to miquiztli, symbolized by a skull), whose messengers are the owls. It is expressly stated in the Popol Vuh, however, that the inhabitants of Xibalba are not gods, but beings of a supernatural character who delight in bringing evil upon men and stirring up strife between nations. There are many points about the " harrying " of Xibalba by the two heroes mentioned above which seem to suggest that the original Xibalba was situated in a region at that time inhabited by the Kakchiquel. One of the principal powers there is the Camazotz, a supernatural bat, who nearly compasses the destruction of the heroes in the Zotziha or " bat-house," and, as has been stated, the principal deity of the Kakchiquel was a god in bat-form called Zotziha Chimalcam. Moreover the owl-messengers of Xibalba bear the title of Ahpop Ahchi, a title which also appears at the Kakchiquel court. Connected with the gods of the underworld was the Maya goddess Ixtab, who received the souls of those who committed suicide (by hanging). A figure which probably represents her appears once in the Dresden codex, in the form of a woman with her head in a noose (Fig. 47, f). She was associated however rather with the paradise than with Mitnal, since individuals who hung themselves were considered to be assured of future happiness. A few more gods might be mentioned, but as practically nothing is known of them save their names, and they do not appear on the monuments as far as can be traced at present, they are omitted. But a word must be said concerning certain mythological animals which figure in the sculptures. Chief of these is a monster resembling a dragon, which is furnished with a head at either end of the body (Fig. 50). The head proper is distinguished by an inordinately long upper jaw, and exhibits otherwise certain character-

istics usually associated with the serpent in Maya art.
The mouth is invariably shown wide open, with the
head of a god, usually the sun-god (though sometimes
God B), emerging. The reverse head, often shown
upside-down, is portrayed with a fleshless jaw and
other symbols of death, but is also associated with the
sun in so far as it bears upon the forehead the kin-
glyph, over which are certain ornaments, notably a
flame-like " plume," which are attributes of the sun.
Now the head proper, with the elongated upper jaw,
bears a distinct resemblance to the Mexican cipactli
animal, from which the earth was created, and in a very

FIG. 50.—The two-headed monster ; from a stone carving at Copan.
(*After Maudslay*)

confused creation-myth given in one of the books of
Chilan Balam we find a monster, Itzamkab-ain, who at
the creation is impregnated by a god of fecundity, Ah-
uuk-chek-nale. Further the earth in Mexican symbolic
art is invariably represented by a monster with gaping
jaws, which is often shown as swallowing Tonatiuh or
Tlaloc. I think that it is perfectly just to conclude
that the so-called " double-headed dragon " of Maya
art is the earth-monster. As we have seen, the god who
is usually shown in his jaws is the sun-god, and the
occasional substitution of God B is paralleled in the
Mexican manuscripts which sometimes show Tlaloc in
the jaws of the earth-monster. The head with the
attributes of death and the sun combined, which appears at the other end of the animal (sometimes, as I
have said, upside-down), is, on this explanation, the sun

in the underworld, i.e. the sun after its setting. The presence of the sun-attributes is necessitated by the fact that without them the death-face would be indistinguishable from that of the death-god, whereas the head of the other god requires no special identification marks. There are a good many additional points which support this view, but I will mention two only. The magnificent carved lintel from Tikal, now at Basle, shows a figure with all the attributes of the death-god beneath a particularly elaborate example of the double-headed monster. The position of the monster here is unusual, since it is usually shown as a support rather than as a canopy, but I think that in this case it emphasizes the fact that the home of the death-god is below the earth. The other point is the following : in the relief at Palenque, known as the cross, the conventional tree (for such it is in reality), springs from the head with the combined death- and sun-symbols (Fig. 51). In this case the part is taken for the whole, the head represents the earth-monster, and the whole scene is an exact parallel to the Borgia codex, in which the trees of the world-directions are shown rooted in the body of the monstrous earth-goddess (Fig. 10 ; p. 79). The Vaticanus B codex is an even closer parallel, since the trees representing the quarters are there depicted as springing from a cipactli head, and it will be remembered that the Mexicans believed the earth to have been created from a monstrous cipactli (p. 59). It is true that the " foliated cross " is supported by a head of another type, but there is a particular reason for this ; the " foliated cross " is in reality a maize-plant, the head is that of a rain- or water-god (of whom parallels are found at Chichen Itza and other places), and the combination symbolizes the dependence of the maize-crop upon the water-supply. The finest example of the double-headed earth-monster is the remarkable monolith, designated P, at Quirigua (Pl. XXVI, 1 ; p.

338.) The illustration shows the principal head of the animal with widely-distended jaws enclosing the figure of a deity.

The earth-monster is not however the only two-headed animal in Maya art. Many of the stelæ, par-

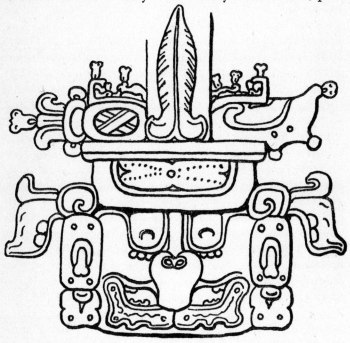

FIG. 51.—Rear head of the two-headed monster; Temple of the Cross, Palenque.

(*After Maudslay*)

ticularly those at Copan, Quirigua and Naranjo, show a figure bearing in its arms an object usually known as the " ceremonial bar " (see Pl. XXI; p. 236). In some cases the object appears simply as a two-headed snake, with drooping body, but in the majority of instances it resembles a beam with a snake-head at either end. In either case the heads are similar, and resemble the main head of the earth-monster; while

the open jaws enclose the head of a god, usually
God B, the rain-god, but sometimes the sun- or sky-
god. Where the body assumes the beam form, it
is divided into panels, enclosing glyphs which are
almost certainly symbols of certain planets, the sun,
moon, day and night. Now practically throughout
America the snake is the emblem of clouds, rain and
lightning, and I would suggest that this symbol represents the sky. From this point of view the association
of the planet symbols, and the gods of the sun and rain,
is explained, and one immediately recalls the myth according to which the creator placed the four Bacabs at
the cardinal points to support the heavens. It may be
that the figure which holds the " bar " may represent
one of these deities ; and this suggestion is to some extent supported by the following facts. Many, though
not all, of the stelæ bear dates recording even katun
quarters (a katun=7200 days, see p. 251), and it is
possible that these stelæ were erected to mark the lapse
of regular periods of time. The historical Maya were
in the habit, so Landa states, of setting up a "stone"
to commemorate the passing of a katun, and also of
holding certain ceremonies at one of the sacred piles
of stones outside the village in honour of the commencement of each solar year. These ceremonies were
in honour of the Bacab, who was supposed to preside
over the year in question (see p. 263). Now a large proportion of the figures portrayed upon stelæ at various
sites carry, instead of the "bar," an object hitherto
called the "mannikin sceptre." This is a short staff,
presumably of wood, carved to represent God B (or God
K, both rain- and wind-gods), and terminating below the
hand in a curved projection representing the head of a
snake (Fig. 52). Now the real nature of this object has
hitherto, most unaccountably, been misunderstood. It
is nothing more or less than a ceremonial axe, the stone
blade of which, bearing the marks which convention-

PLATE XXI

MAYA

STELA H.; COPAN, HONDURAS

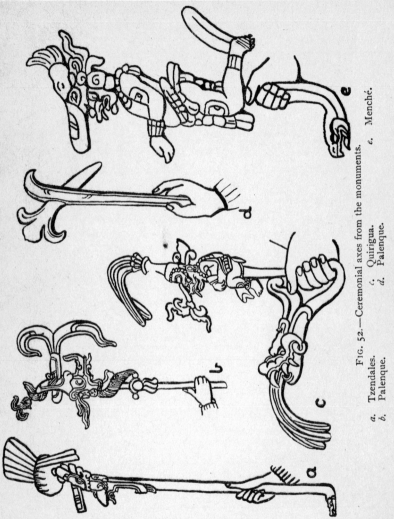

FIG. 52.—Ceremonial axes from the monuments.

a. Tzendales.   *c.* Quirigua.   *e.* Menché.
b. Palenque.   *d.* Palenque.

ally expressed a stone implement, can in nearly every case be clearly seen projecting from the forehead of the small figure. At Palenque this blade is replaced by a foliated ornament, which may represent an elaborate blade of copper, or, possibly, a bunch of feathers. Considering the ceremonial nature of the implement, the substitution in later times (for Palenque is perhaps the latest of the important sites) for the unornamental stone of a tuft of gorgeous plumage is easily understood and has many parallels in the history of ceremonial weapons. Now the haft is carved in the likeness of the rain-god, the snake is the emblem of rain, and the axe is *par excellence* the weapon of the rain-deity, emblematical of thunder (see p. 221). Thus again we arrive at the possibility that the bearer may be one of the Bacabs, who seem to be identical with the Chac, or rain-gods of Yucatan. Still, the identification of the main figures with the gods who support the sky is not one on which I would insist at present. The personages who bear the emblems of the sky and rain may be merely the priests of the all-important deities of fertility, or chieftains who are thus endowed with the symbols of divine power. I have given perhaps disproportionate space to the discussion of these three symbols, the earth-monster, the sky-snake and the ceremonial axe, because I wish to emphasize two points ; firstly that the accounts of the historical Yucatec do undoubtedly throw some light upon the monumental remains of earlier date ; and secondly that the root-ideas of Mexican and Mayan religion are closely akin and cannot with profit be studied separately. It is the full recognition of these two axioms, combined of course with his own remarkable intellectual gifts, which gives the investigations of Seler so signal and permanent a value.

Of other mythological animals, mention may be made of the *moan*-bird, a bird of the falcon variety, associated with the sky and clouds, and possessing rather sinister characteristics (Fig. 46, *a*). Also of the lightning-animal, sometimes pictured as a dog, sometimes as a hoofed creature with a snout resembling a pig's, and usually shown descending from the sky. When the horse first made its appearance among the Maya it was associ-

ated with this animal, and one of Cortés' sick horses
which he left among the natives was installed in a temple
and worshipped as such. Unfortunately the poor animal
did not long survive its deification, being unable to
adapt itself to a diet of chickens and flowers, the offerings made to it in all good faith by the natives.

Like the Aztec, the Maya and cognate tribes believed
that more than one creation had taken place, and we
find the tradition of a great deluge which put an end
to the age immediately preceding this. In the Quiché
legend, Hunahpu, Gukumatz and Hurakan are the
creating-gods; " Earth," said they, and immediately the
earth was formed. Then the animals were created, and
various functions were distributed among them, but
the gods were not satisfied, because the animals were
speechless and could not praise them. So man was made
from clay, but he was without intelligence and the gods
destroyed him. Then came the third creation ; after
consultation with Xpiyakok and Xmukane, the creators made men from wooden images, but these too were
without intelligence and paid no worship to the divine
powers ; so the majority were destroyed by a great
flood, while many perished at the hands of the animals
and domestic utensils which revolted against them, the
few survivors becoming monkeys. At this point the
Popol Vuh relates the story of the two heroes Hunahpu
(not the Hunahpu mentioned as the creator) and Xbalanque. They are first introduced as the slayers of a kind
of Titan, Vukub Kakix, and his two sons, Kabrakan and
Zipakna. It is said that the eyes of Vukub Kakix were
of silver, his body of precious metals, and his teeth inlaid with gems, and he became so haughty that he
usurped the power of the sun. The two heroes robbed
the tree, whence he was accustomed to obtain his food,
of its fruit, and when he ascended into the branches,
blew at him through a magical blow-gun, which dealt
destruction without ammunition, and he fell and broke

his jaw. The heroes however did not escape scot-free, for Vukub Kakix tore off Hunahpu's arm, which he hung up above his hearth in order to inflict torments upon its former possessor by sympathetic magic. Hunahpu enlisted the help of two magicians, probably Xpiyakok and Xmukane in disguise, who, under pretence of curing Vukub Kakix's jaw, extracted his teeth, so that his power departed from him and he died, and the arm was recovered. Zipakna and Kabrakan seem to have been earthquake deities; the former was the " creator of mountains," the latter the " destroyer of mountains," and they too incurred the enmity of Hunahpu and Xbalanque. Zipakna had been persuaded by certain four hundred young men to dig for them the hole in which to erect the main post of a house, and they intended to bury him alive while thus engaged; but he constructed a side-tunnel in which he hid, and cut off his hair and nails which he gave to the ants to carry to the surface so that the four hundred might believe him to be dead. Finally emerging from his hiding-place when the young men were making merry over his supposed decease, he pulled the house down over them and killed them all. In revenge for this he was destroyed by Hunahpu and Xbalanque by means of a stratagem, and his brother Zipakna perished in a similar manner. The next act of the two brothers was to avenge the death of their father and uncle at the hands of the inhabitants of Xibalba. Xpiyakok and Xmukane had two sons, Hun Hunahpu and Vukub Hunahpu, who one day while playing the ball-game tlaxtli attracted the notice of the lords of the underworld. " Who are these," they said, " who make so much noise and cause the earth to shake over our heads?" So they sent their messengers, the owls, to challenge them to a game. Hun Hunahpu and Vukub Hunahpu take up the challenge, and start off for Xibalba, passing down a steep descent, and across several rivers; one of

which is full of gourds, another of blood, and come to
four cross-roads, coloured yellow, red, white and black,
the colours associated with the four cardinal points.
They take the last and arrive at Xibalba, where they
are received by the rulers Hun Camé and Vukub Camé.
The court at Xibalba seems to have been conducted on
the principle of a secret society with a definite form of
initiation, for the new-comers are forthwith submitted
to various tests at all of which they fail, and they are
finally sacrificed by having their hearts torn out before
being allowed to engage in the game for which they had
come. Hun Hunahpu's head is suspended in a tree
which immediately becomes covered with calabashes so
that the head is indistinguishable from the fruit. The
head however retains its vital properties, since when
Xquik, daughter of one of the high officials of Xibalba,
is standing near the tree, it spits into her hand, causing
her to conceive. When her condition is discovered, she
is delivered over to the owl messengers to be killed, but
escapes to the upper world where she seeks out the
dwelling of Xmukané and gives birth to Hunahpu and
Xbalanque mentioned above. With Xmukané are
living Hun Batz and Hun Chuen, also sons of Hun
Hunahpu, who are accomplished musicians, dancers
and artisans. These two persecute their half-brothers,
who take their revenge as follows : The four start out
to hunt, and Hun Batz and Hun Chuen are persuaded
to climb into the trees to drive the birds. Hunahpu and
Xbalanque cause the trees to start growing, so that their
half-brothers cannot come down, and persuade them,
when they complain, to loosen their girdles so that their
movements may be the less restricted. The loosened
girdles immediately become tails, and Hun Batz and
Hun Chuen are transformed into monkeys. After a
series of events Hunahpu and Xbalanque, by the aid of
a rat, discover the existence of a set of implements and
ornaments, used in the ball-game, which had formerly

R

belonged to their father and uncle. They start to play, and again the noise of the game attracts the notice of the lords of Xibalba, who again send a challenge which is accepted. But this time affairs proceed on different lines. When they arrive at the cross-roads they send on a small insect, called *xan*, created from a hair of Hunahpu's leg, to act as a spy. The xan finds the lords of Xibalba sitting with their councillors among certain wooden figures, and by biting them one by one discovers their names, so that when Hunahpu and Xbalanque arrive they salute each one by his title, and do not, as their father and uncle, give greeting to the wooden figures ; they also avoid the hot stone which is offered them as a seat, and pass the later tests with success. One of these consisted in being shut up for the night in the " House of Gloom," with torches and cigars which must be kept burning all night and produced intact in the morning. This feat the heroes achieve by fixing red feathers to the torches and fireflies to the cigars. Eventually disaster falls upon them in the " House of the Bats," the Zotziha. The point of this test seems to be that the heroes must pass the night sleepless, erect and motionless, but Hunahpu moves his head just as the dawn is appearing, and is immediately decapitated by the Camazotz, the bat of the underworld, who leaps upon him from above. The head is suspended in the ball-court, but the tortoise affixes himself to Hunahpu's body in its place. Xbalanque then goes out alone to face the Xibalbans in the ball-game ; he hits the ball close to the ring, and the rabbit which is hidden near it leaps out and runs away. The Xibalbans give chase, thinking that the rabbit is the ball, and Xbalanque exchanges the tortoise for the head, and Hunahpu is revived. The heroes then immolate themselves, but return after five days in the disguise of travelling conjurers, performing many miracles, including the sacrifice and resurrection of a man. Hun

Camé and Vukub Camé desire to have this trick performed upon them, but the heroes after sacrificing them naturally do not revive them. Xibalba is thus conquered, and sentence is pronounced by the heroes upon its people, " Your blood shall endure for a little, but your ball shall not roll again in the ball-game," and the only occupations which they are allowed to retain are the making of pots and the keeping of bees. Following this, honours are paid to Hun Hunahpu and Vukub Hunahpu, who become the sun and moon respectively, while the four hundred slain by Zipakna are resuscitated and become stars. Certain similarities with Mexican mythology are apparent in this legend, notably the miraculous conception of Hunahpu and Xbalanque by a virgin, recalling the birth of Uitzilopochtli, and the transformation of the four hundred into stars, which is reminiscent of the legend of the Centzon Uitznaua (Four hundred Southerners) who also became stars. In this connection it is interesting to note that a legend is found in San Salvador, according to which four hundred youths disappeared into a certain lake and were transformed into fishes.

Such in brief is the myth of Hunahpu and Xbalanque as given in the Popol Vuh, but there are many extremely interesting details which lack of space compels me to omit, but which can be found in the translations, French or Spanish, or the English abridgment, of the original Quiché text.

The story of the fourth and final creation again shows a similarity with one of the Mexican legends given above. The creators decide to make man of maize, but the maize cannot be found. It is eventually discovered at Paxil, the Maya equivalent of Tonacatepetl, through the agency of the fox, coyote, parrot and crow. It is ground, and from the meal the body of man is formed, while Xpiyakok and Xmukané make from it nine different kinds of drink which give vigour to created man.

At this time the ancestors of the Quiché are created, and from this point the " historical " portion of the Popol Vuh begins. The Kakchiquel had a similar myth relative to the discovery of maize by the animals, and they believed that man, as finally created, was formed of maize and blood, the men of a former creation having been unable to speak or walk and feeding on wood and leaves. In Yucatan the first men were said to have been made of earth and straw, their bodies of the former and their hair of the latter.

CHAPTER X—THE MAYA : THE CALENDAR, CALENDRICAL FEASTS AND MINOR RELIGIOUS OBSERVANCES

BEFORE proceeding further with the account of Maya religion, it will be necessary to give a short description of the calendrical system. This was very similar to that of the Mexicans, but was more elaborate, and enabled the Maya to deal with longer periods of time. Throughout the Maya country a series of twenty day-signs was current, which, combined with the numerals one to thirteen, as described on p. 61, gave a period of 260 days, the Mexican tonalamatl, before the same day-sign recurred with the same numeral. The tonalamatl however did not occupy nearly so prominent a place in Maya ritual as in Mexican, though certain portions of the manuscripts seem to be devoted to it.

Some of the Maya day-signs show a close accordance with the corresponding Mexican signs, others seem at first sight quite different. But Seler has shown, by a careful comparison with the day-names current in the Zapotec country, that most of these differences can be reconciled. He calls attention to the fact that the Zapotec name is in most cases equivocal and can be translated to suit either the Mexican or the Maya sign. The Zapotec themselves used the Mexican signs, to judge from the remains in their country, but they carved them in Maya fashion, i.e. surrounded by a " cartouche " which does not appear in the glyphs of the Aztec period. The use of the cartouche, however, is found extending up through the Cuernavaca region to the Mexican valley, but only on pre-Aztec monuments, as I have stated on p. 174 (Figs. 15 and 33, *a*; pp. 106 and 176). It may be taken almost for certain therefore that the Zapotec acted as middlemen in the spread of the calendar in one direction or the other. But this is a subject to which I shall return later.

The Mayan day-signs are as follows (Fig. 53 and Appendix I) :—

Imix. This sign corresponds to the Mexican Cipactli, and the Zapotec word for it also has reference to the crocodile, while the Maya sign itself bears a close resemblance (not, I believe, hitherto noted) with the form of eye occasionally given to the double-headed earth-monster, as can be seen in Pl. XXVI.

Ik. This glyph contains the peculiar T-shaped eye found in the head which forms the name-glyph of God B (Fig. 46, *e*; p. 221). This I interpret as an eye from which tears are streaming, symbolical of rain, and it is noticeable that Eecatl, whose head constitutes the corresponding Mexican day-sign, is shown with a weeping eye (Fig. 4, *d*; p. 35).

Akbal. This is a conventional skull-face, and represents night or darkness, appearing frequently on the " sky-bar." The corresponding Zapotec word also implies night, and the Mexican calli (a house without windows) may well have the same connotation.

Kan. This probably represents a grain of " popped " corn, and the Zapotec word may be taken to refer either to corn or a frog. The Mexican sign is a lizard, and was associated with agricultural fertility.

Chicchan. This sign shows the peculiar cross-hatched spot so often seen applied as ornament to the bodies of serpents ; the Zapotec name appears to mean " omen-bearer," and the Mexican sign is a snake.

Cimi. The head of the death-god, as among the Mexicans.

Manik. A hand in the attitude of conveying food to

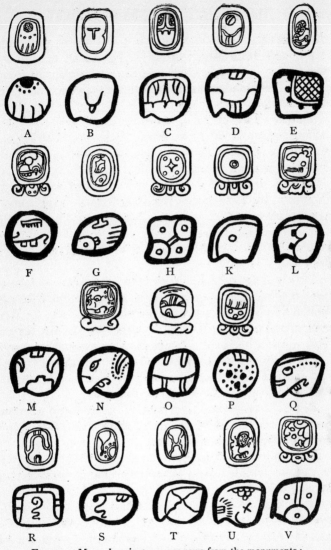

FIG. 53.—Maya day-signs; upper rows from the monuments;
lower rows from the MS.

A. imix.	F. cimi.	M. chuen.	R. cib.
B. ik.	G. manik.	N. eb.	S. caban.
C. akbal.	H. lamat.	O. ben.	T. eznab.
D. kan.	K. muluc.	P. ix.	U. cauac.
E. chicchan.	L. oc.	Q. men.	V. ahau.

the mouth. Seler suggests that the word may come from may-nik = cloven hoof. The Mexican sign is a deer's head or hoof, and the Zapotec word also means deer. The flesh of this animal was the principal animal food of the Maya.

Lamat. The Zapotec word means " divided," and this corresponds with the Maya sign ; but it is difficult to see how either can be brought into relation with the Mexican tochtli, a rabbit.

Muluc. Both the Zapotec and Mexican words mean " water," and probably the Maya sign, though much conventionalized, may have a similar significance.

Oc. The sign represents the head or ear of the dog as pictured in the MSS., and thus corresponds to the Mexican itzcuintli.

Chuen. Probably the conventionalized face of a monkey, in which case the sign corresponds to the Mexican ozomatli. The Kakchiquel word for this day is Batz and it will be remembered that in the Quiché legend Hun Chuen and Hun Batz were turned into monkeys.

Eb. The grotesque head with its prominent teeth and fringed " ear " corresponds to the jaw-bone and bunch of grass of the Mexican malinalli.

Ben. The Zapotec word means " reed," and so corresponds with the Mexican acatl, while the Maya glyph probably represents a reed mat.

Ix. The sign represents the spotted face of the ocelot, which also gives its name to the corresponding Mexican day.

Men. An aged face ; the Mexican sign is the eagle, closely connected with the aged goddess Tonantzin.

Cib. The sign seems to be connected in some way with honey-wine or mead, and frequently appears upon jars in the MSS. The Mexican sign is the vulture, a symbol of old age, and it will be remembered that in Mexico only the aged were allowed free use of intoxicants.

Caban. This seems to be the earthquake sign, used also to typify motion, as the Mexican olin.

Eznab. This sign appears on spearheads, and seems to indicate a flaked stone, thus corresponding with the Mexican tecpatl.

Cauac. This sign represents the thunder-clouds, while the small cross is emblematical of the wind which blows from all quarters ; it thus corresponds with the Mexican quiauitl, and the connection is emphasized by the fact that the Kakchiquel word for rain is *caok,* and the Tzental term for thunder is *chauk.*

Ahau. A face, sometimes, in the more elaborate of the sculptures, the head of a man of rank, which the word ahau implies. Xochitl, the flower, the last sign of the Mexican list, is, it will be remembered, the emblem of the god Xochipilli, the guardian of princes.

Like the Mexicans, the Maya observed the solar year of 365 days, divided into eighteen months of twenty days each, with five days over, called uayeb, and considered unlucky. The names of these months were as follows (Fig. 54 and Appendix II) :—

Pop, Uo, Zip, Zotz, Tzec, Xul, Yaxkin, Mol, Chen, Yax, Zac, Ceh, Mac, Kankin, Muan, Pax, Kayab, Cumhu, five Uayeb days.

Unlike the Mexican months, however, these were used in dating, and a given day was expressed with its month-sign, together with a numeral to show which day of the month it was. Thus 6. caban, 5. pop, means the day 6. caban, after 5 days of the month pop have passed. The numerals were not expressed on quite the same system as the Mexican. Dots were used for the numerals up to four, but a bar was used for five, two bars for ten, and so on, odd days over a multiple of five being expressed by the requisite number of dots. On the monuments, if the supernumerary dots were few, the space between or on either side of them was filled with small crescents, which are merely ornamental and must

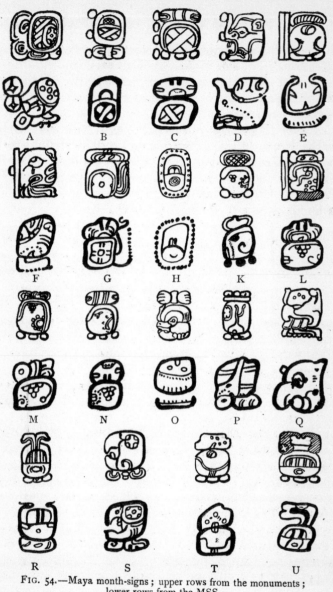

FIG. 54.—Maya month-signs; upper rows from the monuments; lower rows from the MSS.

A. pop.
B. uo.
C. zip.
D. zotz.
E. tzec.

F. xul.
G. yaxkin.
H. mol.
K. chen.
L. yax.

M. zac.
N. ceh.
O. mac.
P. kankin.
Q. muan.

R. pax.
S. kayab.
T. cumhu.
U. uayeb.

be carefully distinguished from the dots themselves. Occasionally in the more elaborate carvings the numbers from 0 to nineteen are expressed by faces. In the case of 0 the lower jaw is formed by a hand, and numbers over ten are expressed by the face assigned to the corresponding unit but with a fleshless jaw. Ten itself is the head of the death-god. Zero in the normal notation is expressed either by a hand or a figure shaped somewhat like a Maltese cross. The use of the zero is explained later. The Maya, like ourselves, were in the habit of expressing a high number by a succession of

FIG. 55.—Maya period-signs.   Upper row, face-signs; lower row, normal signs.

A. cycle.   B. katun.   C. tun.   D. uinal.   E. kin.

figures which combined to form a numeral, but they did not employ the decimal system. Their system, when applied to the computation of time, was on the whole, but not entirely, vigesimal, and was as follows. Twenty days, or *kin*, formed a *uinal*, and the uinal thus corresponded to one of their months ; but the next higher unit, the *tun*, consisted of eighteen uinal, and contained 360 days, being thus equivalent to a year *minus* the five uayeb days. Twenty tun made a katun (7200 days), and twenty katun went to another period of which the name is not known, but which is usually called a cycle (144,000 days). There are indications that a higher unit still was recognized, the so-called " great cycle," consisting of thirteen cycles (1,872,000 days). Each of these periods was expressed by an appropriate glyph, and these glyphs were in two styles, being either what is usually termed "normal" signs, or face-signs (Fig. 55). The latter exhibit considerable variation, especially that of the great cycle; but the cycle bird-face is recognizable by the jaw-bone in the shape of a hand (recalling the face-paint of the Mexican gods into whose name the numeral five enters as a component part), the katun by a similar bird-face with a normal jaw, the tun by the normal glyph which it bears on its head, or its fleshless jaw, the uinal by its frog-like appearance and the curl at the corner of its mouth, and the kin by the glyph on the forehead or the filed teeth. In many of the more elaborate carvings the significance of the sign is shown more by its position in the series than by anything else. Now a great number of the stelæ bear inscriptions which start with a high number expressed in this manner (Fig. 56); at the top is the great cycle glyph, which is an elaborate affair and really means little more than that a count of days is to follow, since there could hardly be any mistake regarding this period which represents over fifty-one centuries. Below, usually in two columns of glyphs, is a number of days, expressed in cycles, katuns, tuns, uinals and kins, and this is followed by a day-and-month date. In the transliteration of Mayan dates, the numerals alone are given as a rule; thus the date shown in Fig. 56, *b*, transliterated as 9.16.10.0.0. 1 *ahau*, 3 *zip*, means the day 1 ahau, after 3 days of the month *zip* have passed, being 9 cycles, 16 katuns, 10 tuns, 0 uinals, and 0 kins from the chronological starting-point of the present "Great Cycle." Now the astonishing fact is this, that throughout the whole of the Maya country, i.e. the area over which ruins in the Maya style are scattered, including Chiapas, Guatemala, Yucatan and northern Honduras, if the long count of days (expressed in cycles, katuns, etc.) be reckoned back from the final day-and-month date, the same day is always reached, viz. 4. ahau,

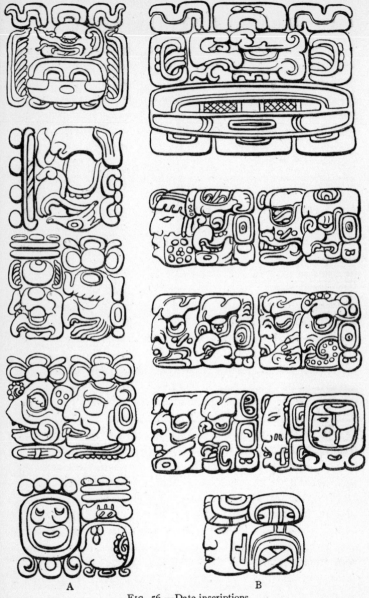

FIG. 56.—Date inscriptions.

A. Normal numerals, reading 9. 15. 0. 0. 0.* 4. *ahau*, 13 *yax*. (Copan, altar S).
B. Face-numerals, reading 9. 16. 10. 0. 0. 1. *ahau*, 3. *zip*. (Quirigua, stela F).

(*After Maudslay*)

* By an error the katun number has been drawn as two bars and three dots, instead of three bars.

8. cumhu. Thus all Maya reckoning dates from one definite day in the past, and this day must almost certainly be an artificial date in the sense that it must have been obtained by calculation at a far later time, since it is practically four thousand years from the earliest date which can in any sense be claimed as historical.[1] The starting date itself is found at Quirigua (on a stela which also bears a date in the ninth cycle), and here it is shown to be the concluding date of a cycle thirteen, which must be the last cycle of the preceding " grand cycle." Many, if not most, of the inscriptions seem to be devoted to the calculation of dates ; in the course of the glyphs, most as yet unreadable, one continually comes upon a " distance-number " expressed as above, and then the day-and-month sign to which this leads, reckoning from the date last given. In the longer inscriptions, notably that in the " temple of inscriptions " at Palenque, which contains over six hundred consecutive glyphs, these calculations extend over considerable periods of time. The great probability is that such calculations are not historical, but of a ritual nature. The Maya had no system of intercalary days by which the year of 365 days could be squared with true solar time, and it is probable that the feasts appropriate to certain seasons were shifted from month to month when the discrepancy became noticeable. Perhaps then these calculations had reference to the ritual calendar in accordance with which the various festivals were held. It must be remembered that the Maya in their count of days reckoned only elapsed time, expressing only a full tale of days. Thus each date is in one sense one day behind the date as we express it. This sounds complicated, but the difficulty disappears if we regard their method from the same point of view as our own

[1] The very early dates which occur at Palenque, a late site, must be themselves artificial or mythical, and so too, I believe, are the dates which occur on the celebrated Leiden plate and Tuxtla figure.

reading of the clock. Whereas we speak of the fifteenth of June while the day is yet incomplete, yet we refer to a point in the third hour after noon in terms of two o'clock, viz. 2.20, or 2.45. Thus for the first day of a month we find the symbol zero, and o. zotz means that the month zip is concluded, but that the first day of zotz is not yet complete. So it is that the katuns (and other periods) are known by the name of the last day of the previous katun, 5. ahau, 3. ahau, and so on, and are not named after the day imix which is the first of the series of twenty day-signs, and is actually the first day of the time-periods from cycle to tun. The Maya method of dating enabled them to fix the position of a definite day without risk of confusion over long periods of time. If the day-sign with its attendant number, and the position in a definite month, is given, that day is fixed for a period of 52 years. If the number of the tun in which it occurs is also stated, it is fixed for a period of 936 years (i.e. 936 years must elapse before a day with a similar series of signs and numbers can recur). If the number of the katun is also expressed, the position is determined for 18,720 years ; and if the number of the cycle as well, a period of 374,400 years.

Since the year contained 365 days, and the day-signs were 20 in number, it is obvious that the year began on one of four days. These days, later called " year-bearers," were, at the time of the monuments and the writing of the Dresden codex, ben, eznab, akbal and lamat, which correspond to the days which began the Mexican year, acatl, tecpatl, calli and tochtli. However, the year-bearers as given by Landa, and also as they appear in the Troano-Cortesianus codex, are kan, muluc, ix and cauac. This means that in the interval the commencement of the year had shifted $(5 \times x) + 1$ days, x being an unknown quantity. By this time too the long count in its most elaborate form seems to have been abandoned, and the katun became the highest

unit, known by the name of its "initial" day, e.g.
katun 6. ahau, or katun 4. ahau. It is this method of
reckoning which is employed in the books of Chilan
Balam. Most of the other races of Maya stock, as far as
is known, possessed calendars which included a series of
twenty day-signs (see Appendix I) combined with the
numerals one to thirteen, but the count of the Kakchiquel was different, being purely vigesimal. The periods
involved were one of 400 days (20 × 20), called *huna*,
and a larger of 8000 days (20 huna), called *may*. The
huna was known by its initial day *ah* (corresponding to
ben and acatl) together with the number which might

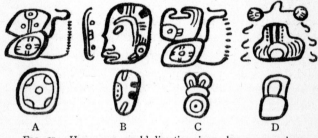

A   B   C   D

FIG. 57.—Upper row, world-direction signs ; lower row, colours.
A.   East and yellow.   B.   North and red.   C.   West and white.
D.   South and black.

be attached to it, and the time count dated from the
destruction of a rebellious sub-tribe, the Tukuchi,
which occurred in a huna 11. ah.

As among the Mexicans, the Maya years were related to the points of the compass. The later Yucatec
associated kan-years with the east, muluc-years with the
north, ix-years with the west and cauac-years with the
south, but the relation of the earlier year-bearers is not
clear, owing to the uncertainty which attaches to the
glyphs expressing the world-directions. On this point
the evidence is very conflicting, but I am inclined to
think that most probably they are as shown in Fig. 57.
The doubt lies between east and west on the one hand
and between north and south on the other. The world-

directions evidently possessed much ritual importance among the Maya, though not perhaps so much as among the Mexicans. In the creation myth in one of the books of Chilan Balam we read of the establishment of four trees at the four quarters, and one at the centre, a legend which recalls the five trees with their respective birds shown in the Mexican codex Borgia and allied manuscripts (Fig. 10; p.79). The "crosses" at Palenque, each of which is surmounted by a bird, probably also had reference to two of the world-directions, in any case their resemblance to the trees of the Borgia codex is striking. The four Bacabs who supported the heavens north, south, east and west, have already been mentioned, and also the four cross-roads on the way to Xibalba. Four colours are associated with the last, and these are the colours which the later Yucatec associated with the points of the compass, viz. yellow (kan) with the east, red (chac) with the north, white (zac) with the west, and black (ek) with the south (Fig. 57). The manuscripts however do not always show the colours in association with the same direction-signs. The colour assigned to the year appears in one of the series of names assigned to the Bacab which was supposed to be its regent. Thus Hobnil, regent of the kan-years, is called Kanal Bacab, Kanzicnal of the muluc-years, Chacal Bacab, Zaczini of the ix-years, Zacal Bacab, and Hozanek of the cauac-years, Ekel Bacab.

The Maya did not limit their calculations to the computation only of the solar calendar, but also reckoned the synodical revolutions of the planet Venus (584 days). Certain pages of the Dresden codex are devoted to this purpose, and the glyph representing the planet is thus known. Some investigators have tried to prove that the reappearances of other planets, Mars, Mercury, Jupiter and Saturn, were also computed, but the evidence is unsatisfactory, and even in many cases adverse to the supposition.

s

Our knowledge of the meaning of the Maya glyphs is practically limited to the day-, month- and period-signs and the names of the gods. The latter have been gleaned from the manuscripts. Here the figures of the various divinities are accompanied by a series of four or more glyphs, and after a careful comparison of the glyphs which are attached to one particular figure, it is found that one glyph is constant. It is a fair assumption that the latter expresses the name of the god, though we cannot say how it should be transliterated. As we have seen, the Mexican script is purely ideographic, that is to say the pictures are symbolical, or, in the case of names, constitute a rebus. It seems likely that the Maya writing had evolved a little further, and that many of the signs were of a syllabic nature. For instance, in the names of the months we find indications that definite signs were employed to express the syllables *yax* and *kin*; but as we cannot say for certain what was the dialect spoken by the builders of the monuments, and as many of the signs are so highly conventionalized that their origin is difficult to trace, the interpretation is beset with many difficulties. Lizana, writing in 1626, speaks of certain old men, sons of priests, who were able to read the manuscripts, and it is probable that the builders of the monuments spoke a tongue closely akin to the historical Maya. In any case a good knowledge of this language will be necessary for future students of the glyphs. As remarked before, it seems unlikely that much information of a historical nature will be extracted from the inscriptions if they are ever read; they probably consist for the most part of calculations for fixing the periodical feasts, and for bringing the year of 365 days into line with true time. It is practically certain, as remarked above, that the Maya did not intercalate days for this purpose, but it is equally certain that a people who were agriculturists and who computed the synodical revolutions of Venus,

could not have failed to notice that the months gradually gained upon the seasons. At the time of the discovery the month pop began the year, but it is worth
mentioning that the name of the month xul seems to
mean " termination," and it is possible that yaxkin was
at some period the first month. The displacement of
the commencement of a year by a month would not
affect the year-bearer, since each month began with the
same day-sign, and it is not unlikely that the feasts were
shifted from month to month when they became in-
appropriate to the seasons. If this is so, no doubt many
of the longer inscriptions consist of calculations relative
to the proper ordering of the festivals. It is not of
course absolutely certain that the initial dates of monuments refer to their erection, but even if such dates
have a historical value (and I am inclined to believe that
most of them have) it is not yet possible to correlate
them with our own system of dating, at any rate with
any degree of certainty, for the reason that the position
of their starting-point, 4. ahau, 8. cumhu, is not fixed.
But this is a subject to which I shall return later (p. 360.)

As in Mexico, so among the Maya, the importance of
the calendar from the religious point of view, and the
close connection between religion and agriculture, gave
the priesthood enormous influence throughout the
country. According to Landa, a high-priest of the
Yucatec was called Ahkin Mai, or Ahaukan Mai ; his
office was hereditary, and he was succeeded in it by a
son or near relation. A less exalted rank was held by the
Chilan, or oracular priests, who declared the will of the
gods, and performed the functions of diviners and
doctors. As might be expected, these functionaries enjoyed great respect, and rarely went abroad except in
a litter. The Nacon were officials whose duties were
partly sacerdotal and partly military. In their first
capacity, as the sacrificing priests, they held office perpetually, but there was also a military aspect to this

office, since the commander of the fighting forces was
elected from among the Nacon, and held the position
for three years. Other priests, who performed definite
functions as assistants in certain ceremonies, were
called Chac, and seem to have been to some extent the
representatives of the Bacabs, since four officiated at
once. Priests generally were called Ahkin, and the local
clergy were nominated by the high-priest after examination in ritual and " science," i.e. divination, writing and
calendrical interpretation. The priesthood at large educated candidates for admission to their order, including
also the younger sons of chiefs, who often "entered the
church." They lived in buildings close to the temples,
and there were similar religious houses for the accom-
modation of celibate " nuns " who were under the protection of a " mother superior." Any lapse from
chastity on their part was punished with death, but any
of the inmates might leave the establishment by permission and marry, just as in Mexico. It is probable
that the buildings other than temples which survive in
the ruined cities are either the residences of princes or
religious establishments of this nature.

It seems likely that in the earlier times the priestly
rule was paramount, and that the rulers were high-
priests or *vice versa*. Even in Yucatan the traditions
seem to point to a later transference of political power
from sacred to secular rulers. Among the Quiché too,
the first rulers, under whose guidance the principal
migrations were made, held authority as the interpreters of the will of the gods assigned to the various
divisions of the tribe, and the later chiefs claimed descent from them. Among the Kakchiquel there were
two high-priests who held office for life, and were
elected by the king and council. One of these seems to
have supervised the ritual, while the other was the
guardian of the sacred books and presided over the
calendar. There were also certain old men who lived

in the temple-buildings and were consulted as diviners on ordinary occasions. These were distinguished by their hair, which they wore in plaits.

In Campeche, Diaz mentions priests who wore their hair long and matted with blood, in Mexican style, and he further states that the people of Chiapas brought with them into battle a " priestess or goddess " with an incense-burner and stone idols. This priestess wore body-paint with white down stuck upon it, another Mexican custom. Many of the reliefs of the older Maya culture show priests engaged in various functions, and the elaborate dresses in which these are often clad have given rise to the supposition that many religious offices were performed by priestesses. Figures in flowing robes are particularly noticeable at Menché (Pl. XXII; p. 294), but, especially in later Yucatan, women as a general rule were excluded from the more important ceremonies, and I think that these figures merely represent men in priestly *insignia*, which would naturally be of a more elaborate nature than the ordinary dress. Sacrifice was common throughout the Maya region, but the question how far human offerings were made in early times is difficult to settle. There is only one scene upon the monuments which may be interpreted as a human sacrifice,[1] and this occurs at Piedras Negras, but the negative evidence afforded by the other reliefs throughout the Maya region would seem to suggest that the practice was, at most, exceptional. Even the Dresden codex furnishes no definite proof that the rite existed when it was written, though there are scenes which may possibly be interpreted as suggesting the custom. For instance, Fig. 63 (p. 301) shows a head lying on an altar; but as it

[1] There is a wall-painting at Chichen Itza which seems to picture a human sacrifice, but this is on a building which undoubtedly belongs to a later period, when the Maya had already come in contact with Mexican influences, as will be seen later.

is clearly the head of the maize-god, the scene may be interpreted as representing merely an offering of grain. In the Quiché myths, the introduction of human sacrifice is associated with the " Yaqui," a name afterwards used of the Mexicans, and it is the god Tohil, whom this people received from Tulan, who, by a trick, obtains the right to the hearts of the other tribes in return for the gift of fire. But the open and extensive practice of the rite belongs to a later stage of Quiché history, as the Popol Vuh also demonstrates. It is possible that the practice was, to speak generally, foreign to the original Maya, but was introduced in later times from Mexico. It seems to have been found among the Kakchiquel, accompanied on certain occasions by cannibalism, and we learn that at a certain festival children were killed with arrows, a ceremony recalling the Mexican festival of Tlacaxipeualiztli. An even closer correspondence with the ritual observed at this festival was found in Yucatan, where the victim was on certain occasions flayed and the priest assumed the skin. Here too the shooting sacrifice was practised ; the victim was tied to a tree, with a white mark painted over his heart ; the worshippers passed rapidly in front and each discharged arrows at the mark. Cogolludo speaks of many bloody arrows being found in a shrine at Campeche, which had probably been used in this rite. At Chichen Itza human sacrifice was made to the sacred *cenote* (natural well), which was supposed to be a place of great sanctity. The victim was cast into the water with other offerings and was believed to emerge alive after three days had elapsed. The usual method of sacrifice however in Yucatan was the tearing out of the victim's heart by the Nacon, who anointed the image with the blood. Here the custom had become very prevalent at the discovery, as the fate of Valdivia's crew in 1511 shows. Prisoners of war, slaves and even children constituted the usual victims, and the last were carefully guarded and paraded from village to village until the fatal day arrived. But even at this date human sacrifices were not made on the same scale as in Mexico, and the principal offerings consisted of incense, animals, and the worshippers' own blood. To obtain the latter, the tongue, ears or limbs were pierced, and a cord was frequently passed through the wound. Scenes showing the practice of this penitential rite are not uncommon on the early monuments, as can be seen from the slab from Menché (Pl. XXII; p. 294), where the worshipper is passing through his tongue a cord furnished with thorns, while a basket containing the implements for piercing lies on the ground beside him. But the ritual of the later Maya will appear best from a short description of the ceremonies observed at the commencement of the year and during the various months.

The new-year ceremonies were especially important, since the fortune to be experienced during the year depended to a very large extent upon their proper performance. They commenced in the Uayeb days of the dying year, that is to say in the second week of July, according to Landa. In preparation for a year beginning on the day-sign kan, an image of the Bacab Hobnil was taken to the pile of stones at the southern entrance to the town (the south being the point associated with the dying year), and a figure of Ah Bolon Tzacab was carried in procession and set up opposite it. Various offerings were made, including the worshippers' own blood, and Hobnil was then carried to the east entrance (the point associated with the commencing year) and left there to watch over the town, while Ah Bolon Tzacab was taken to the temple. Good luck and fertility were expected during the kan years, and if misfortune supervened, a special image of Itzamna-canil was made and sacrifices, including a man, were offered to it. At the end of this year, and in preparation for the

FIG. 58.—The ceremonies at the commencement and end of an *akbal*-year.
(*Dresden MS.*)

next, a muluc-year, the ceremonies commenced at the pile of stones where Hobnil had been left, and a figure of Kanzicnal was substituted for it. The figure of Ah Bolon Tzacab was replaced by one of Kinich Ahau, which was confronted with the new Bacab and then borne to the temple, Kanzicnal being taken to the north entrance, the quarter associated with muluc-years. This year was again supposed to be good, and in the event of misfortune special ceremonies were performed to Yaxkokahmut, another name of Itzamna, including a dance on stilts and the sacrifice of dogs bearing offerings of bread. It may be remarked in passing that both the Dresden and Troano-Cortesianus codices illustrate these ceremonies (Figs. 58 and 59), though there is reason to believe that the lower portion of two pages of the former manuscript have been transposed by the carelessness of the scribe. In this MS. (Fig. 58) the upper scene shows the emblem of the presiding god being carried in by a priest in an animal mask, the central picture shows him installed and receiving offerings, the lower (when properly arranged) illustrates the god of the next year confronted with a pillar representing the Bacab on the Uayeb days at the end of

FIG. 59.—The new-year ceremonies at the commencement of a *muluc*-year.
(*Troano-Cortesianus MS.*)
(*After Seler*)

the year.   Arranged in a column down one side of the page are the signs of the last day of the old year and the first of the new. As stated above the Dresden codex gives the days commencing the year as ben, eznab, akbal and lamat, as do the monuments. The ben-years here seem to correspond to the kan-years of later times, and so on. The Tro.-Cor. (Fig. 59) seems to picture, in the upper register, the ceremonies (including the dance on stilts in the muluc-year) which were corrective of ill-luck, while the lower register shows the year-god and the maize-god, the latter either flourishing, or the prey of birds and beasts, according to the fortune predicted for the year. For the ix-years the Bacab was Zaczini, and the presiding god Itzamna ; the ceremonies began at the north entrance and concluded at the west. Maladies of the eyes, plagues of locusts, wars and changes of dynasties were feared, and the year was considered bad for the food-crop but good for cotton. Ceremonies were performed to Kinich Ahau Itzamna to avert these evils. Cauac-years were the most unpropitious of all, for the presiding deity was Uacmitun Ahau, the death-god. The Bacab was Hozanek, and the ceremonies began in the west and terminated in the south. Many deaths were expected, together with plagues of birds and ants, to avert which four idols were made, Chichac-chob, Ek-balam-chac, Ahkan-uolcab and Ahbuluk-balam, and the ceremonies in their honour included a dance round a large fire, across which, when reduced to glowing ashes, the worshippers ran with bare feet.

The principal ceremonies connected with the months were as follows (for the signs, see Fig. 54, p. 250) :—

Pop. The year began, according to Landa, on July 16th. The priests and men of rank fasted for at least thirteen days in preparation, and the commoners employed themselves in cleaning their houses and renewing and repainting all utensils. Chacs or assistant priests were elected for the ceremonies, and the temple court was purified with incense, the Chacs holding cords to form a square, a proceeding which, ceremonially, was supposed to exclude all evil. Finally new fire was made by the Chacs and fresh incense was offered ; the proceedings terminated with a feast.

Uo. No special ceremonies attached to this month, but the priests commenced to fast in preparation for the next.

Zip. A festival in honour of Kinich-ahau Itzamna was held, at which the priests exhibited their religious books of bark-paper, and uttered the prognostications, regarding the fortunes of the year, which their calculations had revealed. Next day their bags of charms were exposed to view, including all images of the goddess Ixchel and the divining-stones, and the gods of medicine were invoked. The hunters and fishers also held a private festival during this month. The former performed a dance holding arrows and the heads of deer, while the latter painted their fishing-implements blue, a sacred colour. These ceremonies took place on different days, and in honour of special gods whose names are given by Landa. When the fishing-festival was finished in the towns, the lords repaired to the coast, where it was repeated.

Zotz. Bee-keepers prepared for their festival in the next month.

Tzec. The bee-keepers' festival, to Hobnil and the other Bacabs, during which much honey-wine was offered and consumed.

Xul. The great festival to Kukulkan, held at Mani after the destruction of Mayapan. The other provinces sent deputations with great feather banners, which were placed in the temple ; new fire was made, idols exhibited, and five nights were spent in singing and dancing, during which professional singers went from house to house of the lords. The offerings consisted mainly of food and drink, and the deputations departed taking with them the banners which they had brought.

Yaxkin. Preparations were made for a festival to be held in the next month to all the gods (corresponding in some degree to the Mexican Teotleco). The implements of all professions and domestic implements were painted blue, and nine blue dots were marked on the hands of children, to make them useful.

Mol. Besides the feast just mentioned, the bee-keepers held another, in order that the gods might send a full supply of flowers for the bees. In this month also began the preparations for the manufacture of wooden idols, which was a very serious matter. The wooden idols, which were more highly esteemed than those of stone or clay, were made by professional artists, and it was believed that certain penalties attached to the trade, viz. that the carving of an idol entailed the death of one of the artists, or at least the contraction of some heart-complaint. Certain priests, the Chacs and the artists themselves, observed a rigorous fast, while those who desired idols procured cedar-wood. A special hut was built, and the priests, Chacs and workers were closely secluded in it while the work proceeded, the images in course of construction being sprinkled with blood and censed with copal.

Chen. The new idols, now made, were taken to the temple, and there purified and blessed by the officiating priest, after which they were handed over to the new owners, wrapped in cloth and placed in a basket. The stipulated price was paid in game and the local currency.

Yax. In this or the preceding month the temple in honour of the Chac agricultural gods was renovated, and their pottery, idols and braziers were repainted or renewed.

Zac. The hunters held a festival in order to appease the gods for shedding blood, since bloodshed, except in the cause of religion, was considered displeasing to the supernatural powers, probably because blood was *par excellence* the divine offering.

Ceh. No festival is recorded.

Mac. A ceremony was held by those more advanced in life to the Chac, fertility gods, associated with Itzamna. A large fire was lit in the temple court, into which were cast the hearts of various animal sacrifices, lions, tigers and crocodiles. If animals of this size could not be obtained, imitation hearts, formed of copal, were offered instead. The Chac priests then quenched the fire with water, a ceremony which, by imitative magic, was supposed to ensure a good rainfall.

Kankin. No festival mentioned.

Muan. The proprietors of cacao plantations held a festival to their patrons, the Chac, Hobnil and Ekchuah, sacrificing a dog with a cacao-coloured patch and making other offerings, including feathers. At the ensuing feast not more than three cups of wine might be drunk by the participators.

Pax. During this month a ceremony took place which was supposed to bring good luck in warfare. The priests and lords of the provincial towns assembled at the capital and passed five nights in prayer in the temple of the god Cit-chac-coh, together with the Nacon who was carried thither in divine state amidst clouds of incense. After this the populace at large joined in the proceedings, a fire-sacrifice, similar to that in Mac, was made, and the Nacon was carried round the temple. A dog was then sacrified by the Chac, and its heart was offered between two plates, and after each of these officials had broken a vessel containing wine, a feast took place at which only the Nacon remained sober.

After this month no great festival was held until the new-year ceremonies, but various minor local feasts were celebrated, and a great deal of time was spent in eating and drinking.

The later Yucatec, we are told, were in the habit of setting up a " stone " to commemorate the commencement (or the end) of a katun (period of 7200 days, or 100 days less than 20 years). It is possible that this was a custom inherited from the earlier Maya, and if so it seems likely that the latter performed the ceremony every katun quarter. Certainly a large number of the stelæ, especially at Quirigua, bear initial dates of katun quarters, but there are also many to which this supposition cannot apply, and which must have served to mark some other occasion. It is certain that these stelæ were objects of worship, since in nearly every case an altar is found in front of each on which, presumably, offerings were made. Apart from the calendrical feasts, the Yucatec practised two interesting ceremonies, one of which was performed over children of about three years of age, and was known by a name signifying " to be reborn." A lucky day was selected, and four Chac were chosen to assist the priest. The ceremony took place in a house which was purified for the occasion ; the Chacs sat at each corner, holding cords enclosing the children and their fathers, the latter having fasted for three days ; and the priest sat in the centre with a brazier and incense mixed with maize-meal. The boys wore a white head-ornament, and the girls a shell suspended from a girdle ; each advanced in turn and offered meal and incense, receiving it from the priest. The cord, brazier and a vessel of wine were then given to a man to carry outside the village, and it was supposed that in this way evil was expelled from the house. The priest then assumed a tunic of feathers, chiefly red, with cotton streamers, and a feather head-dress (possibly similar to the costume shown on Fig. 82; p. 344), and held in his hand a brush made of serpent-tails. The heads of the children were covered with cotton cloths, and a bone was passed nine times over the forehead of each and dipped in a vessel of water with which their brows, faces and the interstices of their fingers and toes were anointed. This water had been procured from hollow tree-stumps or mountain pools, and contained certain flowers and cacao. This part of the ceremony evidently possessed a purificatory significance, while the next act seems to signify, as far as the boys were concerned, the entry into boyhood. Their head-ornaments were removed by the priest with a stone knife, and an assistant followed with a handful of flowers and a pipe, handing them to each of the candidates in turn, the bouquet to smell and the pipe to smoke, making at the same time nine passes with them before the face of each. The mothers removed the shell ornament from the girls, who from this time were considered eligible for betrothal; and after several minor ceremonies, including the distribution of gifts among the chief actors, the function was over. The other ceremony, to which allusion is made above, consisted in the confession of sins, similar to, but less elaborate than, that practised by the Mexicans. It was believed that absolution could be given only once, and for this reason it was usually deferred until the penitent was seriously ill. The confession was made to a priest, if the services of one could be obtained, or else to a near relation, husband, wife, father or mother.

Of Kakchiquel ritual little is known; they, and also the Tzental, observed eighteen months of twenty days, and brought the year up to 365 by the addition of five extra days, just as the Maya and Mexicans. Some, at any rate, of their ceremonies appear to have been connected with the tonalamatl count, since we are told that in early times offerings of fresh incense, green branches and bark were made on each seventh and thirteenth day, and a " cat, the image of night," was burned before the god. We are also informed that this was before the " worship of the idol of the great Chay Abah was begun." However, various rites in connection with agriculture were practised, such as fasting before sowing, and the offering of incense at each of the corners of the fields.

In later Yucatan, pilgrimages were made from all
parts of the country to important shrines, and we are
told that the temple at Cozumel was one of the most
celebrated at the conquest. Pilgrims were wont to
stop to offer incense at deserted temples, and Cogolludo mentions the fact that he found recent offerings of copal in a temple at Uxmal. The present-day
Lacandons also offer incense at the ruins, in the belief
that they are haunted by the ghosts of their forefathers. Divination formed an important part of a
priest's duties, and it was principally for this purpose
that the tonalamatl was employed in Yucatan. Thus at
the birth of a child its horoscope was cast to determine
its future profession. The Kakchiquel too practised
divination, not only by means of the tonalamatl, but
also with maize-grains, as the Mexicans. They also
used blocks of polished obsidian for scrying, one of
which was enshrined in a particularly celebrated temple,
whither state messengers were sent to consult it on important occasions. Obsidian was supposed to have been
produced in Xibalba at the creation, to be the " sus-
tainer " of mankind, probably as the source from which
the will of heaven could be ascertained. Maize was also
employed for divination in Yucatan, and omens were
taken from dreams and the voices of birds. Various
minor superstitions were found, of which a few have
been recorded. Thus if a man on a journey stumbled
over a stone, many of which were placed at the commencement of a road, he made an offering of a green
branch to it, and rubbed his knees with a pebble to
prevent fatigue. If a traveller feared he might be late
in arriving at his destination, he placed a stone in a
tree to stay the course of the sun, or plucked out hairs
from his eyebrows and blew them towards the heavens.
In eclipses, dogs were pinched to make them howl, and
a noise was made by striking the doors or furniture of
the huts. An eclipse of the moon was supposed to be-

token that the luminary was dying, or was being bitten by ants. The offering of eyebrows, and the pinching of the dogs during an eclipse, were also practised in Peru.

Many of the rites of the present-day Lacandons are survivals of the original worship. It has already been said that they are in the habit of making pilgrimages to ruined sites for the purpose of offering incense ; the censers are rude clay bowls, with a mask-like face attached, and each is reserved for a particular god whose image is usually kept within it. The images are of stone and are kept hidden, and inherited from father to son. The censers are renewed at the harvest, the old ones are considered " dead " and left in the ruins. For the manufacture of the new censers, as for the preparation of fresh idols among the early Yucatec, a special hut is built, new fire is made at which incense is kindled in them for the first time, and blood, drawn from the ears of the worshippers with a stone knife, is smeared upon the images of the gods. They also observe a " baptismal " rite, at which a priest singes the hair of the candidates with six miniature torches of pitchpine and confers a name upon them. The torches are then smeared with blood and burnt, together with incense, in the idol house. Confession is made to the cacique, or local chief, if a member of the community is seriously ill, and the penitent believes that some sin of his commission may be the cause. A lightning-god is still worshipped, and in the Uloa valley Gordon came upon the tradition of a golden dragon, believed to inhabit a particular pool, to which offerings were made in former times, but which has withdrawn itself from human view since the Spanish conquest, though it still controls the clouds and rain. It is highly probable that many other interesting and important survivals might be discovered among the present population, but owing to their extreme reticence on such subjects the task is by no means easy.

T

However, the district offers a good field to a student of folklore who is inclined to devote considerable time to the collection of these relics of a former religion, though he must certainly be gifted with an unusual degree of perseverance and patience.

CHAPTER XI—THE MAYA : BURIAL, SOCIAL SYSTEM, TRADE AND WAR

AS regards the disposal of the dead, we find the same two methods current among the historical Maya as were practised by the Aztec, viz. inhumation and cremation. The first was that most commonly observed among the generality of the inhabitants. Death was supposed to be due to some evil spirit, and the friends and relations of the deceased mourned for several days, by day in silence, at night with lamentations, and the bereaved husband or wife observed a fast. The corpse was enveloped in wrappings, the mouth filled with maize-meal and currency-stones for use in the future life, and burial took place in or behind the house. The house was usually abandoned, through fear of the dead, unless a number of individuals were living there together and consequently felt less nervous of the departed spirit. The personal idols of a man were buried with him, and, in the case of a priest, certain of his religious books also. Upon the latter fact rests the hope that more of the precious manuscripts may yet be discovered. Individuals of high rank were burned, and their ashes deposited in large urns or in cavities in the heads of wooden figures carved for the purpose. In the latter case only a portion of the ashes were so preserved, the rest being buried. It is said that it was customary to remove the heads of princes of the house of Cocom, and to attach the facial portion of the skull, made up with artificial features, to a statue which was kept in a private oratory, while the ashes of high-priests were preserved in figures of pottery. Thus it is evident that simple inhumation was characteristic of the lower orders, cremation of the superior ; and it is possible that the two methods may represent two separate cultural elements, since there is reason to believe that the ruling class belonged to a later immigration and were the introducers of certain Mexican practices and beliefs into the country. It seems possible that some form of cremation was practised also by the Kakchiquel, since we are told that the " ashes " of great men were mixed with the clay from which household idols were made ; but among this people also cremation may have been reserved for the ruling class, since Fuentes states that at death the body lay in state for two days and was then buried in a jar, omitting any reference to cremation. It is possible that the term " ashes " may refer only to certain portions of the body, and need not be taken to imply the practice of burning the corpse ; at any rate Gagavitz, the first Kakchiquel ruler, is said to have been simply buried. Leon states that a high-priest was buried in his house, seated upon his chair. The excavatory evidence, though at present very deficient, seems to point to the conclusion that cremation was a late practice among the Maya peoples. At Copan a number of burials have been discovered, in which the position of the bones implies that the body was arranged in a contracted position, recumbent or sitting. Stone-lined cists have been found as depositories for the dead sporadically from Quen Santo, through Alta Vera Paz to Copan and Benque Viejo ; but beyond, in the Uloa valley, large burial sites have been discovered in which the bodies have been simply laid in the earth. In Sacchana both extended and contracted burials have been found, and in the Quiché country bones have been discovered in such a position as to imply that the body was arranged in a seated position on a pottery dish. British Honduras shows several styles of burial, and our information is due almost solely to the excavations made by Dr. Gann. About eighty miles from the coast on the Old River, he found cist-burials, as mentioned above, urn-burials, in which the bones were partly cremated, and burials both in a recumbent and in a seated position. From the remains associated with the bones it is evident that the cist-burials, both here and elsewhere in British Honduras, contained the bodies of men of higher rank. At all the sites mentioned above burials were found marked by mounds, but the presence of the latter is not invariable, and it may be that as excavation proceeds many cemeteries will be found of which no indications exist upon the surface. At a site on the Rio Hondo, Dr. Gann was able to distinguish between three distinct types of burial. The poorest graves were found associated in some numbers in large flat mounds, sometimes half an acre in extent; the bodies were contracted, and the grave objects included hammer-stones, beads of clay and shell, rude weapons and unburnished pottery. A better class of interment occurred singly, in separate conical mounds of limestone blocks and dust, about 18 feet high, with finer pottery and beads of stone; in these the bodies were also contracted, and sometimes arranged head downwards. The finest graves were cist-burials, each in a separate mound from twenty to fifty feet high; in these the body lay at full length, and the associated objects included fine painted vases, beads of jadeite, pearl-shell and obsidian, and finely flaked stone implements. In Yucatan, burials have occasionally been found in the so-called " chultunes," or stone-lined cisterns used by the former inhabitants; and human remains, some suggesting cremation, have been discovered in the caves. The evidence respecting the latter, however, seems to suggest that these caves were not inhabited at an early period, and that the human occupation did not last for any length of time; it is probable that they were used only as places of refuge.

On the whole such information as we possess concerning the methods of disposal of the dead seems to imply
that burial was practised by the early Maya, and that
cremation was introduced by certain of those peoples
who are definitely known to be immigrants into the
country at a date, as I hope to show shortly, posterior
to the building of the monuments (with the exception
of the later constructions at Chichen Itza).

At the discovery, the rule in Yucatan was divided
among a number of princely houses who constituted a
sort of feudal nobility. A chief was succeeded by his
son, though his brothers ranked high and possessed much
influence. The rulers governed their territory through
sub-chiefs appointed in the outlying villages, who consulted them on all important matters, such interviews
usually taking place at night. They maintained considerable state, being accompanied by a retinue when
they left their residences, and etiquette enjoined that
all visitors should bring some ceremonial present when
they approached their overlord. This apart from the
ordinary tribute of cotton tunics, game, cacao and personal service (such as house-building) which constituted
the princely revenue. The scene on the vase shown in
Pl. XXIV ; p. 310, appears to represent an interview
between a chief and a subject ; the former is seated
on a daïs, while the latter presents to him an object
which is probably a pouch containing copal. Similar
pouches are seen on the reliefs and in the manuscripts.
Inheritance among petty chiefs followed Mexican lines,
that is to say a petty chief was succeeded by his
brothers in order of age, and his sons only came to
power after the death of their paternal uncles. At
an earlier period the various chieftains had been subjects of an overlord at Mayapan, to whom all paid
tribute. The city was founded, according to tradition, by the descendants of the Tutul Xiu, now called
the Itza, whose protecting deity was Kukulkan (in his

later and degraded manifestation). The family of the
Cocomes, however, seem to have gained the supreme
power, but in any case the government was for a time
centralized. The tributary lords possessed residences at
the capital which were under the charge of intendants
appointed by them, and were supported by their respective provinces ; the inhabitants of the actual district of Mayapan were exempt from tribute, but the
members of the aristocracy served in the temples, assisting in the festivals by day and night. Eventually, however, the centrifugal tendency so characteristic of Mexican and Central American politics reasserted itself, and
the " league " split up into a number of independent,
and often hostile, princelings. It is probable that each
important group of ruins marks the site of some former
centre of power, and the buildings not definitely associated with religion may have been in part the residences
of feudal lords.

But though the formation of the Mayapan " league "
seems to indicate the paramountcy of the secular power,
the priestly caste, as in Mexico, must always have possessed enormous influence, and the early traditions seem
to imply that they were the actual directors of tribal
policy. Kukulkan and Itzamna are both mentioned as
leaders of migrations, and from this it is fair to infer
that the latter were directed by the priests of the gods.
Little indication as to the *insignia* of the early chiefs
can be gleaned from the monuments, though the later
reliefs of Chichen Itza show many figures bearing a
diadem of Mexican pattern. It is, in fact, almost impossible to distinguish between priests and rulers, and this
very difficulty may perhaps be taken to imply that the
rule had a religious basis. Possibly some of the armed
figures may be taken to represent secular chieftains, but
the arms themselves seem to be rather of a ceremonial
nature, and at some sites, notably Copan, armed figures
do not occur at all, while at Quirigua and Palenque the

only weapon is the axe, which seems to be purely a religious emblem. The presence of subsidiary figures interpreted as prisoners may be thought perhaps to indicate secular might, but these only occur in any numbers at Naranjo. On the whole it seems reasonable to conclude that the early Maya lived under the sway of rulers in whom the priestly aspect predominated, and that the election of chiefs whose power rested on a secular basis was a later development.

In the Popol Vuh even clearer indications of this are given, and it is evident that the authority of Balam-Quitzé, Balam-Agab, Mahucutah and Iqi-Balam rested on the fact that they were the guardians and high-priests of the gods given to them at Tulan. The association between priest and god in this case seems to have been personal and not transferable, for their sons do not immediately succeed to their positions. In fact, the legend seems to indicate the substitution of a more secular form of authority, since the titles and *insignia* of power are sought and obtained from a people living to the east, though these titles and *insignia*, not unnaturally, are conferred upon the elder sons of the deceased leaders. The titles include that of Ahpop, afterwards held by supreme chiefs, and the *insignia* consist of canopy, throne, musical instruments, pigments, perfumes, animal head-dresses, heron-plumes and shell and other ornaments, many of which appear in the livery worn by the figures sculptured on the early Maya monuments. The power of the rulers grew, centres of authority, similar to Mayapan, but probably on a smaller scale, were formed, and tribute of gems, gold, feathers and honey was imposed upon the conquered tribes. In particular we are told that the ruling people grew rich upon the bride-prices paid by the suitors of their women, and it may be concluded that alliances with a princely house were as much sought in Guatemala as in Mexico, and that the belief, that rank could only be

conferred by an individual in whose blood it was inherent, was equally prevalent. The Popol Vuh gives a
list of the principal officers of the Quiché state, and
those of the Cavek division are quoted below. Nothing
is known concerning them save the probable translation
of the titles, but they will serve to indicate the nature
of the Quiché constitution, which may well have been
founded on some system prevailing among the earlier
Maya. The translations are those of Brinton.

Ahau-Ahpop, the ruler.

Ahau-Ahpop-Camha, possibly the sub-chief of the
Tziquinaha.

Ah-Tohil, the high-priest of Tohil.

Ah-Gukumatz, the high-priest of Gukumatz.

Nim-Chokoh-Cavek, the heir of the first.

Popol-Vinak-Chituy, the high councillor of Chituy.

Lolmet-Quehney, the overseer of tribute.

Popol-Vinak-Pa-Hom-Tzalatz, the councillor of the
ball-game.

Uchuch-Camha, the high steward.

In a later passage a functionary called Tepeu-Yaqui,
who may have been the chief sacrificer, is substituted
for the last. All these officials are described as "lords
of great houses." The other divisions of the Quiché
were organized on similar principles.

In the same way the Kakchiquel appear to have commenced their migration under priestly guidance ; at
any rate the election of the first ruler comes at a late
period in their "annals." The *insignia* of power seem
to have been the same; the electors say, "Thou shalt
be the first man among the Ahpo-Xahil and among the
Ahpo-Zotzil. . . . We will give to thee the canopy, the
royal seat, the mat, the throne, with power over men."
The enthronement of a later ruler is described as follows : "They seated him on the seat . . . washed him
in the bath, the painted vessel . . . clothed him with the
robe and the green ornaments; he received the colours,

the yellow stone, the pigment, the red earth." Later the Kakchiquel were ruled by a dual chieftainship, representing the two chief tribes, the Zotzil and Xahil. The Zotzil chief was called Ahpo-Zotzil, the Xahil chief Ahpo-Xahil, and the senior in office was regarded as paramount. Their heirs held respectively the title of Ahpop-Qamahay and Galel-Xahil, and they were supported by an hereditary aristocracy and a number of officials like those of the Quiché. Besides the mat, the canopy was an important *insigne* of rank, that of the rulers being triple, of the heirs double, and of the highest officials single. The populace was divided into warriors, freemen, tributaries and slaves, and there was also a clan system, similar to that of the Mexican calpulli, though based on relationship rather than on locality. The clans were called chinamitl, and were represented by officials called Ahtzalam, a word translated by Brinton as " Keeper of the tablets " ; besides allusions to the clans, there are frequent references to seven cities and to thirteen divisions or provinces. The Kakchiquel were never a large or very important people, and their position among other tribes seems to have varied a good deal at different periods of their history. At times they seem to have paid tribute to the Quiché, though at the conquest they were independent, while at other times they appear to have been able to extract tribute from some of the surrounding nations. Such tribute consisted of gold and silver, worked or unworked, engraved stones, feathers and cacao.

Of the land system among the Maya we know very little. No doubt, owing to the comparative sparseness of the population and the fertility of the climate, the land question had not attained the same importance as in Mexico. In Yucatan at any rate land was common property, and sufficient for the needs of each family was assigned to its representative by the chiefs. The salt deposits on the coast were also common, but were

worked by the inhabitants of the locality who paid
their tribute in salt.

Little, too, is known of the judicial arrangements;
official advocates and a kind of police existed, and important cases in provincial villages were referred to the
overlords, whose power was absolute. In the case of
minor offences, the local chief had jurisdiction, and if
the parties belonged to different villages, the chief of
the offender's village would send satisfaction to the
other, or else strife resulted. For many offences, even
homicide if accidental, compensation was possible, and
the relations of the guilty person would assist him in
paying the fine, though the right of retaliation in cases
of manslaughter lay with the relations of the deceased.
If the injury were obviously malicious, the question
was rarely settled without the parties coming to blows.
For theft the culprit was compelled to restore the plunder, and if he could not he was enslaved; thus the number of slaves in the community was considerably increased in times of famine, for nearly all cases of
stealing were connected with food. Captives of lower
rank also became slaves, but any slave might redeem
himself, though children born in slavery remained
slaves until compensation was paid to their owners.
Slaves could be sold, but if one died or escaped soon
after his purchase, part of the price paid for him could
be reclaimed. The robbing of a minor was considered
a particularly disgraceful offence. In ordinary cases a
man's property was divided among his sons, those who
had contributed most towards its increase receiving a
larger share. Daughters had no right to any of the
inheritance, though they were usually given a portion.
If there were no sons, the property went to the nearest
male relations, but if the sons were still young, guardians were appointed to provide the mother with the
necessaries for their education. The arrangements were
made in the presence of the local chief and the prin-

cipal men of the place, and any dishonesty on the part of the guardians involved them in infamy ; however, we are told that the system was the cause of frequent quarrels. Matrimonial cases were not infrequent, but the punishment was severe ; the male culprit was tied to a post in the chief's quarter and handed over to the injured husband, who might accept compensation, or take his revenge by smashing the head of his supplanter with a stone. The woman incurred perpetual obloquy, no light punishment, and was usually divorced by her husband. Among the Kakchiquel we read of an execution by fastening a prisoner to a tree and shooting at him with arrows, while among the Tzutuhil of Atitlan hanging and quartering were practised. At the latter locality the chief would send a relation to enquire into offences committed in outlying villages ; his decision was without appeal, and in cases involving a fine he received one-half as payment for his services. It is probable that similar systems prevailed generally among the Quiché and Kakchiquel.

There was no special education for the young as in Mexico, at least as far as our knowledge goes, apart from the training given to candidates for the priesthood. Children were taught to have great respect for their elders, and the young and unmarried associated little with the latter. The distinction between bachelors and married men was emphasized by the existence of a communal house where the former congregated for amusement and where, as a rule, they slept.

The Maya preserved their genealogies, and great pride was taken in descent from one of the Mayapan houses. Men bore, in addition to a personal name, the names also of their father and mother. In this way a system of surnames grew up, and community of name was taken to imply community of blood ; so much so, in fact, that all over the country a traveller on reaching a strange village would mention his name and immedi-

ately be welcomed and entertained as a relation by anyone who happened to bear the same name. As a general
rule travellers were well treated, and many of the village chiefs kept open house, a custom which lasted on
well into the days of the Spanish *régime*, as many poor
white voyagers found to their advantage. The priests
were the guardians of family tradition and genealogies.
Similar surnames existed among the Kakchiquel, and
each person bore, besides his personal name, the name of
his clan or chinamitl.

As regards marriage, Landa states that the Maya in
former times regarded twenty as a suitable age, but
that the tendency in his time was to marry much
younger. According to most authorities, the Maya were
monogamous, but one states that polygyny was permitted. Probably a plurality of wives was exceptional
and limited to chiefs. As in Mexico, a man never sought
a wife for himself, but his father employed the services
of a go-between. Marriage was not allowed with a deceased wife's sister or husband's brother, and no unions
might be contracted between persons bearing the same
name, since community of name implied blood-rela-
tionship. Further, a man might not marry his maternal
aunt. The occasion of the marriage, which was performed by a priest, was celebrated by a banquet in the
house of the bride's father, and the husband remained
and worked for his wife's family for five or six years.
Marriage was by purchase, that is to say the man's parents handed over certain property to the father-in-law,
but the presents were not of great value, the real price
being the personal service contributed by the bridegroom. We are told that divorce was both easy and
frequent.

A somewhat similar system prevails to-day among
the Lacandons, though the young man demands his
wife in person. If her parents agree, the couple live as
man and wife in the house of her father for a year on trial.

At the end of the year, the couple, their relations and friends, paint themselves and assume their best ornaments ; the bride presents her husband with a stool and five cacao grains, and receives from him a skirt and five cacao grains. Their hands are then joined by the cacique, and a feast follows. The Lacandons are monogamous, and divorce, probably owing to the system of trial-marriage, is rare.

Among the Quiché also marriage was by purchase, but the bride-price was a serious matter, and apparently often amounted to a considerable sum. We are told that the princes grew rich on the gifts which they received in return for their daughters, but the system brought abuses with it, and quarrels arose which became so frequent and serious that the tribe split up into nine " families " and twenty-four " great houses." The tendency to matriarchy seen among the Maya is even more evident among the Kakchiquel, since if the couple belonged to different clans (chinamitl), the man regarded all the male members of his wife's clan as either brothers- or sons-in-law, according to age. This would seem to imply that the man passed into his wife's clan rather than she into his.

Commerce flourished among the later Maya, and there was a good deal of travelling to and fro in the country. The pilgrimages to celebrated shrines along recognized routes have already been mentioned, and also the fact that there was a particular god of travel, Ekchuah. The Yucatec traded salt, textiles and slaves to Uloa and Tabasco, in exchange for cacao and stone money ; red shells were imported, and also copper from New Spain. Diaz mentions that the Spaniards found, in a village in Chiapas, a number of prisoners secured by wooden collars who had been captured on the road, and he states that some of these were travellers from Tehuantepec and Soconusco. On the border of Yucatan and in the hilly region of Alta Vera Paz there were well-

defined trade-routes, and Cortés after crossing the Usumacinta came to a district, which he calls Acalan, where
the inhabitants maintained trade-intercourse, mainly
by boat, with Tabasco, and had trade-outposts on the
Golfo Dulce and the Honduras border. In the earliest
times there must have been much extended intercourse
among the tribes, at any rate pendants of seashells constitute one of the most frequent ornaments seen on the
monuments, and the Quiché seem to have sent an expedition on a long journey to obtain royal *insignia*, as
mentioned above. Much of the trade was performed by
direct exchange, but there were certain forms of currency. Cacao formed the " small change," and Herrera
states that 200 of the nuts went to a *real*. Red shells and
stone counters are also mentioned as money, as well
as copper bells, the value of which depended on their
size. Both Cogolludo and Torquemada speak of copper
currency axe-blades, very thin and in the form of an
inverted T, which were imported from Mexico. The
latter author states that four of these, if new, were
equivalent to five *reales*, but that damaged specimens
were only valuable for melting down and went at ten
to the *real*. Feathers were also employed as currency,
and in some places cloth, as in Mexico. The system of
enumeration employed in commerce was in the main
vigesimal. The count proceeded by fives to twenty, by
twenties to one hundred, and by hundreds to four hundred ; from this point the higher numbers were reckoned in multiples of twenty.

    The question of war and weapons is particularly inter-
esting from archæological and ethnological points of view.
Taken as a whole the monuments show few traces of military activity, and at some sites, notably Copan, Quirigua
and Palenque, armed figures are not seen at all, for the
axe which appears at the two latter sites is obviously a
purely ceremonial object. To omit Yucatan for the
moment, it is worthy of notice that reliefs suggesting

the figures of warriors are practically only found in the northern portion of the region over which the earlier remains extend, viz. at Piedras Negras, Menché, Naranjo and Tikal. The suggestion is conveyed by the presence of one or more bound figures subsidiary to the main personage represented upon the sculpture, or by the fact that the latter stands upon a crouching figure of distinctly different, and far lower, type of physiognomy. Tikal may almost be omitted from the above list, since only one such relief occurs, and it resembles rather the sculptures of Menché than the archaic stelæ which appear to be more characteristic of the site. It is not absolutely certain, moreover, that the crouching figures which serve as supporters represent actual prisoners, since in some cases the main figure is shown with attributes which are of a purely ceremonial nature; still the arrangement is suggestive, and it is worthy of notice that by far the largest number of such stelæ is found at Naranjo. Where the main figure is shown with a weapon, that weapon is almost invariably a spear with a head of flaked stone. Such spears are always rather elaborate and ornamental in form, and in some cases it is difficult to distinguish them from a ceremonial staff. As stated above, I do not think that the ceremonial axe can fairly be considered a weapon, but one "axe" is shown in the hands of a figure at Menché (stela II), which seems to answer to the description of the "swords" seen by Columbus in Ruatan. The latter consisted of an edging of stone flakes set in a groove in a wooden haft, and secured by lashing of fish intestines. Shields are shown at most sites, and conform in the main to two types, square and round (or four-sided with gently rounded corners). Square shields are seen at Piedras Negras, the other pattern at Menché, Copan, Quirigua, and Naranjo, though at the last-named site one rectangular shield occurs. At Piedras Negras and Menché figures are found carrying objects which I take to be long shields

of some pliable material, and these are paralleled in the
reliefs on the ball-court at Chichen Itza (Fig. 60). It is

FIG. 60.—Detail from the relief in the great tlaxtli-court at Chichen Itza.

(*After Seler*)

worthy of note that both Diaz and Diego de Godoi mention long shields, covering most of the body, which could
be folded or rolled up and carried under the arm when

U

not required, as in use among the tribes of Chiapas. The shields of the rounded type nearly always bear on the field a highly ornamental sun-face (Fig. 82; p. 344). It should be observed that neither bows, arrows, spear-throwers nor, apparently, slings are figured on the monuments of the central region. On the whole it seems fair to conclude that the early Maya were men of peace, and that wars, when they occurred, were with the border tribes rather than among themselves; it should be mentioned that one representation of bound prisoners is found at Ixkun. When we come to consider Yucatan, we find that reliefs showing figures are practically absent except at Chichen Itza, and there they occur only on buildings ornamented in a distinctly later style, and accompanied by glyphs of a non-Maya character. In the famous relief on the ball-court (Fig. 60) is a long series of figures carrying a variety of weapons, chiefly spears of the type mentioned above, wooden lances with a single or double row of barbs, apparently cut from the solid, sheaves of light throwing-spears with stone heads and, seemingly, feathered butts, and spear-throwers of wood ornamented with feathers. Light bucklers of a circular pattern, and long pliable shields of the type mentioned before, both occur, but bows are absent. Other forms of defensive armour seem to be lacking on the whole, but there is one figure shown with a turtle-shell worn as a corslet. This may have some mythological significance, but it is worth recording in this connection that Diaz mentions turtle-carapaces used as shields at Ayagualulco, to the west of the river Tabasco. Many of the figures wear a flat circular object fastened to the girdle at the hip; this may possibly be the leather pad worn in the ball-game, as described on p. 166, but more likely it corresponds to the circular ornament which formed part of the military uniform of the Huaxtec warriors. Now spear-throwers and darts appear on the Dresden codex, but the absence, on the earlier

monuments, of anything remotely resembling either a
spear-thrower or a spear which could be hurled, seems
to suggest that their builders were ignorant of missile
weapons. Chichen Itza, of which the late buildings are,
to anticipate, in Toltec style, was intimately associated
with the Tutul Xiu, and we are told that the spear-
thrower was their principal weapon. Further, Landa
makes the statement that bows and arrows, which were
universal in Yucatan at the conquest, were introduced
there by the Mexicans, and that the Yucatec before
they came into contact with the latter were ignorant of
these weapons. It may be conjectured that their introduction was due to the Mexican mercenaries employed
by the later rulers of Mayapan. To turn for the moment to the Quiché and Kakchiquel, we find that
" arrows " were employed by the former in their wars
with the surrounding tribes shortly after the death of
the original leaders, but it is possible that these may
in reality have been throwing-spears. With regard to
the Kakchiquel the case is different ; this people are
always, in the Annals of Xahila, insisting upon their
status as a warrior tribe, and it is stated definitely that
the only riches which their fighting-men bore with
them from Tulan were their bows, their bucklers and
their rounded shields. Now both the Tutul Xiu and the
Quiché traced their origin from Tulan also, and if this
be taken to indicate some early contact with the Mexican valley, it follows that the Tutul Xiu migration
started before the introduction of the bow into the
valley by the Chichimec, while that of the Quiché
and Kakchiquel occurred subsequently. However, as
stated above, the Tulan of the Tutul Xiu tradition
is not necessarily that of the Quiché and Kakchiquel
legends (see pp. 214–216).

According to Landa the bows of the historical Yucatec were solid and straight, a little less than a man's
height, while the arrows, carried in a quiver, had shafts

of reed, foreshafts of wood and obsidian heads; the Yucatec also carried stone-headed spears, copper-bladed axes, the edges of which were hardened by hammering, and basket-work shields covered with deer-hide. The spear remained the weapon of the upper class, while the bow, as the arm of the mercenary, was used by the commoners. Corslets, quilted with cotton and salt, are mentioned as defensive armour, and Diaz speaks of slings and " swords " (probably corresponding to the Mexican macquauitl) at Cape Cotoche and Champoton respectively. The Maya forces were under the command of two generals, one elected for three years and called Nacon (see p. 259), the other hereditary. The generals maintained a force of regular soldiers, whose food in times of peace was provided by the commune. Palisades were practically the only defensive works known, and in fact very few of the buildings throughout the Maya country, with the exception of a few in western Guatemala, where traces of fortifications are seen on the summits of mountains, seem adapted for defensive purposes. The Yucatec carried off the jaw-bones of slain foes to be worn as armlets, a custom also found in New Guinea. Axes and clubs were used by the Quiché and Kakchiquel, and the latter also employed slings and blow-guns. In later Guatemala mention is made by Alvarado of long wadded corslets of cotton, three fingers thick and so cumbrous that, when the wearers fell in attempting to escape from the Spanish attack, they could not rise without assistance. A peculiar weapon mentioned in the Popol Vuh, as used by the Quiché in the defence of a fortress, consisted of a kind of bomb, formed of a gourd filled with live hornets; it is stated that by means of this ingenious weapon they succeeded in repelling an attack upon a fortified settlement. A good description of a fight between the Quiché and the Kakchiquel is given in the " Annals." " When the dawn appeared, the Quiché descended from the hills, the cries and the shouts of war broke forth, the banners were displayed. Then were heard the drums, the trumpets and the conches of the combatants. Truly this descent of the Quiché was terrible. They advanced rapidly in rank, and one might see afar off their bands following one another descending the mountain. They soon reached the bank of the river, the houses by the water. They were followed by the chiefs Tepepul and Iztayul, accompanying the god. Then it was that the battalions met. Truly the encounter was terrible. The cries and the shouts, the noise of the drums, the trumpets and the conches resounded, mingled with the enchantments of the heroes. The Quiché were routed in all directions, not one resisted, they were put to flight and delivered over to death and no one could count their slain. A great number of them were taken prisoner, together with the kings Tepepul and Iztayul, who delivered up their god." The capture of a god was evidently a feat much to be desired, as we have seen when treating of the Mexicans (p. 56), and there are passages in the Popol Vuh which relate the attempts made by other tribes to capture the deities of the Quiché. Both the Quiché and Kakchiquel seem to have been in the habit of executing prisoners by the arrow-sacrifice, and the Yucatec also offered up captives of rank, reducing those of lower status to slavery. Apart from the attempts at capturing the enemy's god, war did not have nearly so close a connection with religion as in Mexico, at least as far as can be ascertained. Most of the wars concerning which traditions have been preserved either were dynastic or resulted from the refusal on the part of a subject tribe to pay tribute.

CHAPTER XII—THE MAYA : DRESS, DAILY LIFE AND CRAFTS

THE historical Maya were of fair height and sturdy, qualities which appear also upon the monuments. A peculiar appearance was given to the head by the practice of cranial deformation which prevailed from the earliest times. Boards were applied to the heads of infants so that the forehead and occiput were flattened, and the crown assumed in profile a "sugar-loaf" aspect. Individuals exhibiting this form of distortion in a marked degree are shown in Figs. 49, 61, 82, and Pls. XXII and XXIV, pp. 294 and 310. Cranial deformation is relatively common in America, and the practice extended northwards along the west coast, and southwards into Peru, but the Maya were peculiar in considering a squint a mark of beauty. Landa states that the Yucatec mothers were accustomed to suspend some small object from the forelock of a child in order to produce the desired result. We have seen that tooth-chipping was characteristic of the Huaxtec, Totonac and Mixtec in Mexico, and that the Huaxtec and Mixtec were also accustomed to ornament the teeth further by means of inlay. Both these practices were widespread among the Maya. Allusion has already been made to the chipped teeth which appear as attributes of the sun-god (see Fig. 72 ; p. 316, and the cover-design), and it may now be mentioned that teeth mutilated in exactly the same fashion have been found in burials at Copan, in the Uloa valley, and in caves at Loltun. Teeth inlaid with small circular plugs of jadeite have also been found at the first of these sites. Tooth-filing

PLATE XXII

British Museum

MAYA
STONE LINTEL FROM MENCHÉ, CHIAPAS
(Scale: 1/8th)

was also practised by the later Yucatec, by rubbing with a stone dipped in water. The ears and nose were pierced and ornaments worn in the apertures. Plugs with long pendants were carried in the ears, and the monuments and manuscripts show figures with the lobes considerably lengthened by the weight of the ornaments inserted in them (e.g. Pl. XXII ; p. 294). In the nose a bar was worn, of the same pattern as is occasionally seen in Totonac pottery (Pl. XVIII, 5 ; p. 194). Sometimes the bar terminated each end in a long tuft of feathers, as among the Huaxtec, and ornaments of this description are common on the stelæ at Menché. The peculiar curved nose-ornament associated with the sun-god has already been mentioned. As a rule the ears of the men were much scarified from ceremonial blood-letting.

Paint was much used as a body-decoration by the historical Yucatec, red being the favourite colour for women and married men ; bachelors usually painted themselves black. Pottery stamps are among the remains commonly found throughout the Maya region, and no doubt some of these were used to impress designs upon the body as in Mexico. Tatu was also practised, and Landa states that the more ornamented a man was in this way, the more respect he won from his associates. The decoration was usually applied at marriage, the design being first painted on and then pricked in. Women also covered the body with tatu from the waist upwards, with the exception of the breasts. Probably the custom was of long standing, since ornament simulating tatu is often seen on the faces of the figures on the monuments. The Yucatec were fond of perfumes, and the women were in the habit of rubbing the body with a pottery brick impregnated with a sweet-smelling gum

The men of Yucatan at any rate wore no hair on their faces in Spanish times, and it is said that mothers scorched the faces of their children with hot cloths in the belief that its growth was thereby prevented. However, pottery fragments from Alta Vera Paz occasionally show faces with a heavy moustache, and certain of the gods appear on the manuscripts with beards. Bearded figures also occur on vases and among the sculptures, notably at Quirigua. The hair was usually worn long, and the priests in Guatemala had great difficulty in persuading their converts to cut it. In Yucatan a patch was burnt short on the top of the head, the rest of the hair being plaited and wound round the head with the exception of a small tail behind. The women wore it in two long plaits down the back. Head-ornaments existed in great variety and were extremely elaborate among the men; brilliant feathers were used in great profusion, and masks of animals or gods were frequently added, if we may accept the evidence of the sculptures. Clothing itself was made from textiles, and was usually assumed about the age of five or six, children under that age going nude. The principal garment worn by men was a girdle of about a hand's breath, the ends falling down before and behind (e.g. Figs. 61 and 82; pp. 297 and 344). These ends were ornamented by the women with embroidery or featherwork, and in the monuments they are shown furnished with the most elaborate designs, of which the most frequent is a grotesque face, often highly conventionalized, with long nose-ornaments, probably representing a water-deity. Wide, square shoulder-mantles were also worn, as well as sandals of plaited hemp or hide. The sandal-strings, again, were often highly decorative, and in the monuments the sandal itself is of so elaborate a nature that it may almost be said to be a shoe (Pl. XXII, and Fig. 61). The manuscripts seem to show some sort of a leg-covering also (e.g. Fig. 46, e). Women wore a skirt, and often covered the upper portion of the body with a cloth or a tunic open at the sides; the breast-cloth was

worn at Cam-
peche and Bal-
calar and tunics
elsewhere in
Yucatan at the
time of the con-
quest. It is pos-
sible that the
ceremonial
dress of the men
in early times
included a skirt,
for it hardly
seems probable
that all the
skirted figures
in the monu-
ments repre-
sent women.
Ornaments
were worn in
great variety,
beads of jadeite
and other hard
stone were
strung as neck-
laces; masks,
also of stone,
were worn as
breast orna-
ments, and
shells appeared
as fringes to the
edges of gar-
ments. But the
details of dress
and ornaments

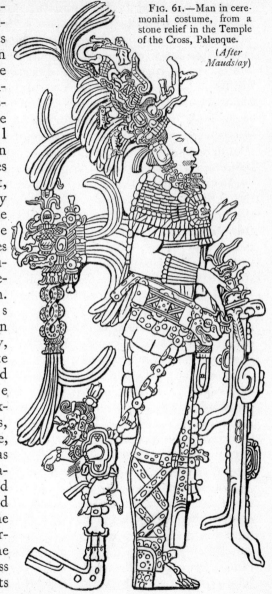

FIG. 61.—Man in cere-
monial costume, from a
stone relief in the Temple
of the Cross, Palenque.
(*After
Maudslay*)

can be understood better from the illustrations than from any lengthy description.

Agriculture was very important among the Maya, as may be judged from the study of their religion. Maize and cacao constituted the most important of the crops, but beans, yams and other food-plants were also grown. Co-operative labour was employed in the preparation of the fields, for weeding and for sowing, and the burnt weeds were the only manure. Sowing took place at the commencement of the rainy season ; the sowers were furnished with a bag containing the grain and a pointed stick with which they made holes in the ground for the reception of the seed. The right-hand figure in the upper portion of Fig. 59 is probably engaged in this occupation. The crop was stored in specially constructed granaries. Maize was set to steep over night in water mixed with lime, and was then pounded on stones and made up into cakes, which lasted a long time and were soaked in water before a meal when they became hard. Various kinds of bread were made, most of which were eaten hot, as they were indigestible when cold. Maize-meal was mixed with water to make a beverage, for water was not usually drunk plain; a drink was also prepared from the roast grain pounded and mixed with cacao and pepper. Much chocolate, prepared as described on p. 155, was consumed, and mead was prepared from honey to which an infusion of a certain root was added. For grinding maize a flat stone, called in Mexico metatl, was used together with an elongated stone rubber, circular or square in section, and often with a marked flattening on the side which was most constantly in use. At the present day the rubbers used in Mexico and in northern Guatemala are heavy, and the ends project beyond the edges of the metatl, so that they can be grasped by the user ; in Peten, Alta Vera Paz and south-eastern Guatemala, they are lighter, and shorter than the breadth of the

metatl. Rubbers of the first type, however, dating from
an early period, have been found in ruins in Alta Vera
Paz. Flesh food was not much eaten on ordinary occasions, but was reserved for feasts. The Maya were good
hunters, and organized communal drives besides manu-
facturing various forms of traps, principally springes
and deadfalls (Fig. 62). The deer was the principal

Fig. 62.—A. Turkey in a trap.   B. Hunter with deer.
            C. The black god making fire.
    D. Deer in a trap.   E. Alligator in a deadfall.
            (*Troano-Cortesianus MS.*)

quarry, but various animals were domesticated, including turkeys, geese and bees, and fish was considered a great delicacy. For fishing, canoes were employed, of the dug-out variety, and the inhabitants of
the lower Usumacinta led a semi-aquatic life. Between
Yucatan and Tabasco is a large lagoon, with many
small islands, teeming with fish and bird-life ; here the
navigation is very confusing, but the natives made their
way from point to point by the aid of signs which they

placed in the trees. Large canoes were constructed for use on the sea, propelled by oars and sails, and one is mentioned as being seen in the neighbourhood of Cape Cotoche large enough for a crew of forty men. In hunting and fishing, when practised in common, a portion of the catch was reserved for the lord and the rest was divided. One principal meal was taken during the day, about an hour before sunset, and the hands and mouth were washed afterwards; the women ate apart from the men. Most ceremonial occasions were marked by a feast, and the Maya were rather given to debauchery. The nobles frequently gave banquets, and the invited guests were supposed to be under the obligation of returning the compliment on some future occasion. Indeed, the debt was considered so binding, that it became transferred to their heirs in the case of their death. On such occasions the wine was handed by women, who turned their backs while the guest drank, and at the end of the festivities each of those present received a mantle as a gift, together with the cup from which he had drunk. Invitations to a wedding-feast, or to a banquet held in commemoration of some ancestor, involved no return invitation. Tobacco-smoking seems to have been practised, since pipes have been found in Guatemala, though only one is known to have been discovered in Honduras. It would seem as if some form of dramatic performance was occasionally given on festive occasions, since Landa speaks of " comedians who gave representations with much grace," but the principal form of amusement was the dance, of which there were many varieties. A number of musical instruments are shown in the manuscripts (Fig. 63) and mentioned in the early accounts. These include hollow gongs of wood, sounded with rubber-headed beaters, which could be heard over a distance of two leagues, drums of two types, gongs formed of tortoise-carapaces, beaten with the hand, and rattles and rattle-staves similar to the

Mexican chicauaztli. Wind-instruments comprised conches, several forms of trumpet, often with bell-mouths formed of calabashes, bone and reed flutes and whistles. Small bells or rattles of the "hawk-bell" pattern were often worn as ornaments.

As regards games, beans were thrown as dice, but the most interesting amusement was the ball-game, called tlaxtli by the Mexicans, and played in the same manner. In the Popol Vuh the outfit of the ball-player, which the rat discovers for Hunahpu and Xbalanque, is said

FIG. 63.—Priests with musical instruments.

(*Dresden MS.*)   (*After Seler*)

to consist of "hip-shields, rings, gauntlets, crowns and helmets." By far the finest example of a tlaxtli-court known is at Chichen Itza, and the semi-religious nature of the game is illustrated by the fact that a temple is attached to it. Before a court could be used it was formally consecrated; at midnight, on a lucky day, two idols, one of the game, the other of the ball, were set up on the lower walls of the court, and certain ceremonies took place, including the blessing of the court itself. Finally the ball was thrown four times as in the game, and the court was then considered consecrated and could be used by the players. The game was played for stakes, such as a bundle of cotton cloths, gold ornaments, or feathers, and a peculiar rule existed in accordance with which the player who was fortunate enough to send the ball through the ring, a feat which was but rarely performed, could claim all the cloaks of the spectators. Now it is an interesting fact that remains of tlaxtli-courts are not found elsewhere in the Maya country except at Chacula and Alta Vera Paz in the west of Guatemala, where they are exactly similar to those in the Zapotec region at Quiengola. Moreover, the ball-court at Chichen Itza belongs to the later buildings, since the temples attached to it are ornamented in Toltec style, the figures do not exhibit head-deformation, and the reliefs include glyphs of a non-Maya character. I think it is fair to assume that the game was not played by the builders of the earlier monuments, but was introduced in later times from Mexico. I believe that the Popol Vuh gives a hint of its introduction. It will be remembered that the heroes Hun Hunahpu and Vukub Hunahpu give offence to the people of Xibalba by playing the game. "Their game is an insult to us," are the words used, and they are forthwith challenged to a contest. But before they are allowed to engage in competition, they are submitted to a number of tests, a fact which seems to indicate that they were called upon to prove their acquaintance with certain mysteries peculiar to the tribe. Failing in these, they are put to death without being permitted to engage in the game. The idea that certain games are the property of certain tribes is not unfamiliar to students of ethnography, especially in the case of games which possess the ceremonial significance which is so noticeable a feature of tlaxtli. The tests therefore which the lords of Xibalba impose upon the heroes have the object of discovering whether the latter possess the right to play the game which they claim, and it will be remembered that the victory of Hunahpu and Xbalanque is in a sense regarded as the capture of the tlaxtli-game, since they pro-

PLATE XXIII

MAYA
STELA 24; NARANJO, GUATEMALA

nounce sentence upon the defeated Xibalbans in the words " Your ball shall not roll again in the ball-game." Now Xibalba is evidently regarded as an underworld, but the author of the Popol Vuh goes out of his way to explain that the inhabitants are not gods. That being so, one's thoughts are immediately directed to the Mixtec or Zapotec country as the site of Xibalba, since in this region alone certain localities were definitely pointed out as the openings of the underworld. On the whole I think the evidence suggests that the game found its way into the Maya region after the abandon-ment of the earlier Maya cities, and as a result of the migrations which the fall of Tulan set on foot. Further, that it reached the Maya by two channels (and perhaps at different times), i.e. Yucatan *via* Vera Cruz and Tabasco, and north-west Guatemala by way of Oaxaca. The presence of ruins strongly resembling tlaxtli-courts in the Huaxtec territory is, I believe, due to later in-fluence emanating from the Mexican valley. Besides the presence of the court at Chichen Itza, further evi-dence of the presence of the game in the east is found in the Kakchiquel legends, where a related people living far to the east, and almost certainly to be identified with the Olmec, are called the " Ball-play and fish people."

As regards habitations, no doubt the early inhabi-tants of the Maya country lived, for the most part, in huts constructed of perishable materials, and reserved the more permanent buildings for the service of the gods and the use of the tribal chiefs. So close a simi-larity does the present-day native house of Yucatan bear to the typical form of Maya room as exemplified in the ruins, that it seems probable that the early habi-tations did not differ essentially from those of later times. The Yucatec house is a rectangular structure of wood and leaves, with a gabled roof supported by a ridge-pole ; it is usually constructed on a raised foundation, which renders it considerably cooler than if built upon the ground level, and the floor is mortared. Like the early structures, it contains no windows. Landa describes the houses of Yucatan in much the same terms, stating that the building was divided by a longitudinal wall, pierced with doorways giving access to small rooms used as sleeping apartments. The front was open, and constituted the living and reception room, and in the houses of chiefs, the walls, which were plastered, were ornamented with frescoes. A certain amount of building in stone was carried on right up to the conquest, though the buildings erected do not seem to have been either as important or as ornamental as those of earlier date. Diaz mentions stone-built habitations in Yucatan, and waxes enthusiastic over the towns of Chiapas, which were of no great importance, a fact which goes far to prove that the great sites such as Palenque were never visited by the conquerors, and must have been even then deserted. The Quiché and Kakchiquel were good builders in stone and lime, and an early and somewhat high-flown description exists of their chief towns, Utatlan and Iximché, though the ruins in that locality show clearly that the chronicler's imagination has completely run away with him. But on the whole it may be concluded that the Maya, like the Mexicans, dedicated their architectural master-pieces to the purposes of religion, and lived for the most part in dwellings of a more temporary nature. The population seems to have moved about a great deal, probably around the religious centres distinguished by the more extensive ruins, and the construction of elaborate dwellings would have been rather a waste of time.

Like the Mexicans, the Maya were living at the discovery practically in an age of stone. Copper and gold they knew, but the former was rare, and gold ornaments have not been found in great numbers in the country.

The elaborate monuments, such as are described in the
next chapter, must have been worked almost entirely
with stone implements, though copper chisels, hardened
at the edge by hammering, may have been used to a
limited extent; indeed blocks of stone have been found
bearing marks which could hardly have been made
except by a metal tool. Stone, including jadeite, and
obsidian must have furnished by far the larger propor-

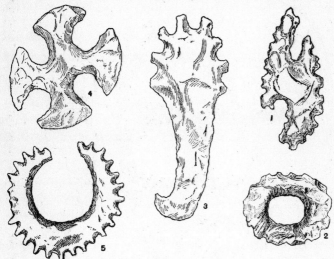

Fig. 64.—Objects of flaked stone; British Honduras.
(British Museum)

tion of the implements used by masons and carvers, and
the latter was imported into Yucatan from the volcanic
districts. Examples of stone-flaking are not very common in the Maya area, but little excavation has been
carried out. It must have been widely practised, since
the glyph representing a knife, and the spear-heads as
shown on the reliefs, both exhibit marks indicating
flaking. Objects of flaked stone, of a very interesting
class, are found in some numbers in British Honduras;
these include obsidian arrow-heads of extremely graceful design, and a large number of what may be orna-

x

ments or ceremonial objects made from a kind of chert and exhibiting great variety of type. A few of these are shown in Fig. 64, but it should be mentioned that human and animal forms are also found. Objects of exactly similar type have been found at Naranjo in Guatemala. Maya stone-carving is considerably more elaborate than Mexican, and their art stands on a higher plane. It is

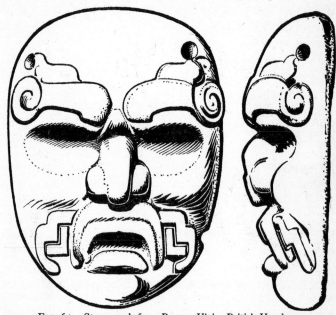

FIG. 65.— Stone mask from Benque Viejo, British Honduras.

true that much of it is in fairly soft material, but the remains of certain sites, notably Quirigua, prove that the Maya mason could handle large masses of hard stone with almost equal facility. Still many of the large Mexican carvings are in much harder material than any in the Maya area. Smaller works of stone art consist for the most part of jadeite beads and pendants, carved in relief (Pl. XI, 1 and 2; p. 140), and stone masks, furnished with holes for suspension and probably worn

as breast-ornaments, as shown in Pl. XXII; p. 294).
A fine stone mask discovered in a cist near Benque
Viejo, in British Honduras, is illustrated in Fig. 65, and
is interesting as showing the connection which this
region evinces with the Totonac country, a specimen
almost identical having been discovered in Vera Cruz.
Unfortunately no early author has left an account of
Maya arts and crafts as Sahagun has of Mexican, but it
may safely be conjectured that the methods of the two
peoples were similar.

Maya carving is seen at its best when applied to wood,
but owing to the perishable nature of the material

few examples
have survived.
Nearly all of
these are from
Tikal, and con-
sist of lintels on
which designs
are sculptured
in low and beau-
tifully model-

FIG. 66.—Women weaving.
(*Troano-Cortesianus MS.*)

led relief (Fig. 48; p. 225). The fact that practically no
idols have been discovered seems to indicate that they
were carved in wood and so have failed to survive, and
indeed Landa states that amongst the historical Yucatec
the most venerated idols were wooden. The relation
which the reliefs, especially those of the northern Maya
region, as at Palenque, bear to wood-carvings is evident,
and no doubt proficiency in wood-carving antedated
skill in sculpture.

Of weaving and embroidery nothing is known, save
that the historical Yucatec were experts in the art.
However, the dresses of the figures sculptured on the
monuments prove that the early Maya had attained
great proficiency in the textile arts. Garments heavy
with embroidery, and with elaborate inwoven designs,

are sculptured with great care, and a fine example is shown on Pl. XXII; p. 294. The loom used must have been of the same type as that found throughout Mexico and Central America in historical times (Fig. 66; compare Fig. 27, *b*; p. 148).

The subject of Maya pottery, though extremely interesting, has not yet been studied sufficiently to yield any very important results, as far as indicating the direction in which the culture spread. It is complicated moreover by the fact that there was evidently a considerable trade in pottery in early times, and the ware of a good factory spread far and wide over a large area. Besides this the available material has not yet been fully classified, and much more excavation must be performed before really representative collections, illustrative of the various districts, can be brought together. Seler has attempted to trace to some extent the wanderings of pottery from certain centres of manufacture; he calls attention to the finding in Guatemala of ware of Tarascan type; and concludes that the ware of Huehuetenango and Chiquimula spread over the whole of south-western Guatemala and south-eastern Chiapas, while that of Jilotepec in the Guatemalan province of Jalapa was carried to south-eastern Guatemala and western San Salvador. The Maya had carried the fictile art to a high degree of development, though they never obtained such a mastery over their material as the coastal tribes of Peru. Naturally the quality of the ware varies considerably according to the use for which the vessel was intended, but the paste in the best specimens is hard, well mixed and fired, and varies in colour from a bright terra-cotta to pale cream, though the majority of fragments are of a reddish tinge; black pottery is rare. Some of the Guatemalan vases are moulded from a clay containing a large percentage of mica, and these are usually softer than the better-class ware; while certain vessels from the Peten district are composed of a very coarse grey clay containing small pebbles. The latter have not been fired at a high temperature and are very soft. Another form of coarse, soft and brittle ware is found in British Honduras, chiefly in the form of small figurines probably made for funerary purposes (Pl. IX, 7–11 ; p. 82).

The shapes in which the pots were moulded exhibit great variety, and most of the types characteristic of Sacrificios are found scattered over the whole area, though they are more common in Guatemala than in Yucatan and Honduras. In particular a very close connection appears to exist between Sacrificios pottery and the ware of the Alta Vera Paz region. The similarity is not confined to shape, but relates also to the peculiar slate-coloured earth-glaze (see p. 194), which is found on many of the vases of this district, and extends westward into the neighbourhood of Quen Santo in western Guatemala close to the Chiapas border. Another interesting similarity exists between the spouted vases of the Huaxtec country and certain pots discovered in British Honduras, and further south in Honduras. The resemblance which certain forms of the Uloa valley bear to the regular Huaxtec " teapot " (Fig. 42 ; p. 196) with its vertical spout is very striking, but the bodies are not ornamented with painted designs, being either plain or decorated with faint gadroons.

The shape which is perhaps of widest distribution is the tripod bowl, the feet of which terminate in grotesque animal heads, like those of Sacrificios (Pl. XIX ; p. 198), or are moulded in cascabel form and contain a rattle (as Fig. 36, 9; p. 185). The former type appears rather to be limited to Vera Paz, while the latter has a wider range. The beaker-form with expanding foot, so common at Sacrificios (e.g. Pl. XVIII, 10; p. 194), extends through Vera Paz to the Chacula district, while bowls, invariably with a flat base, and bottle-forms, appear to be found in greatest numbers in the Uloa valley. The pottery of the latter district is distinguished by the frequency of loop-handles attached to the bodies of vases, usually two in number, but sometimes four, and always disposed symmetrically. Bowls with the peculiar flat feet characteristic of the Mexican valley (Fig. 36, 3 ; p. 185), and the dishes with a single expanding foot (Fig. 36, 8), so common at Sacrificios, have not yet been found in this area. Characteristic of the Quiché area are vases of coarse ware in " slipper " form, a type which is also common in Nicaragua, where it is often used as a funerary urn.

Vases painted in the early Maya style are unhappily very rare, though two magnificent vases have been discovered, one at Chama and the other at Nebaj. The design on the latter I am enabled to figure (Pl. XXIV ; p. 310) through the kindness of Mr. C. Fleischmann, the possessor. It is cylindrical in shape, of the best quality red ware, hard, light and well-fired, and covered with a highly burnished yellow-brown slip on which the designs are painted in red and yellow with black outlines. The scene represents a visit paid to a chief by an inferior ; the former is seated on a dais, and wears a head-dress terminating in a flower from which hangs a fish, a form of ornament also observed on reliefs at Naranjo, Palenque and Chichen Itza. His visitor is offering a pouch containing copal, and the rest of the field is filled with the figures of three attendants, one of which is engaged, apparently, in pouring some liquid from a vessel over two egg-like objects on a small table. The treatment of the figures and accompanying glyphs is particularly free and bold, and the whole scene is an excellent example of Maya draughtsmanship at its best. Fragments of vases painted in similar style, though not quite so good, have been found in the same region, and also in the Uloa valley, though the specimens from the latter locality exhibit certain peculiarities of drawing which prevent them from being considered typically

Maya (Fig. 67). The use of a slip-covering to pottery is found throughout the whole area, though it is by no means constant ; the colour is most commonly red or yellow, though white and brown are also found. Painted decoration is also in slip, of similar colours, and where figures are represented they are usually outlined in black (e.g. Pl. XXIV). The funerary pottery of British Honduras shows a greater variety of hue ; in many cases the slip (white) is so thick as almost to amount to a kind of stucco, and on this the details are painted in brilliant colours, including a bright red and a turquoise-blue (Pl. IX, 7–11 ; p. 82).

FIG. 67.—Bat-design from a vase ; Uloa valley.

(*After Gordon*)

Designs are frequently found engraved in slip, and the most interesting of such vessels come from the Vera Paz district. Beakers with expanding foot, exactly similar to the specimens from Sacrificios, are found here, with incised patterns from which, in some cases, the background has been cut away. Such vases have been found also in the neighbourhood of Chacula, but the engraved pots most characteristic of Guatemala belong to the type of which a fine specimen is shown in Fig. 68. Here the design is cut in a thick white slip, and represents the sky-god emerging from a shell, probably symbolizing his connection with the moon. A vase of interesting type and ornamented in somewhat similar fashion,

FIG. 68.—Pottery vase from Chama,
Guatemala.
(*After Seler*)

FIG. 69.—Pottery vase from Ococingo,
Chiapas. (*After Seler*)

is illustrated in Fig. 69. This specimen was found at Ococingo in Chiapas, and is furnished with a cover. Vases found with covers are rare, but no doubt the covers of many have been lost; three vessels however with covering plates of black ware have been discovered at La Cueva near Coban, and with them were found certain vases of a type unique in this region, representing a human figure of which the head could be removed and constituted a lid. Pots somewhat similar in design are known from the lower Amazon in South America. A certain proportion of the pottery is mould-made, and this method appears to have been most extensively employed in the Alta Vera Paz area, where moulds for the manufacture of whole pots have been found. Some of the mould-made vases are of good quality and shape, and the design often includes a row of glyphs. Vases of this type have been discovered also at Copan and in the Uloa valley. From Vera Paz also come plaques with excellent designs, including figures holding the "ceremonial bar," together with the moulds in which they were made. These are in hard terra-cotta coloured clay, and are not furnished with a slip. Many details to serve

FIG. 70.—Pottery vase from Coban, Guatemala.
(*After Seler.*)

as applied ornament to vases and censers were also made in moulds (e.g. the sun-face which forms the cover-design), while a great proportion of the figurines and whistles throughout the Maya region were similarly constructed.

Relief ornament moulded by hand is common throughout the Maya area, and in the Vera Paz region vases are frequently found in the shape of birds and beasts, sometimes with a human face enclosed in the jaws (similar to Pl. XVIII, 5). The combination of human and animal forms is characteristic of Yucatan, but interesting specimens of this type have been found in the Vera Paz region, as well as the plain bird and beast forms (Fig. 70), though here both types bear a striking similarity to the Sacrificios vases. An extremely interesting vase, with a human head moulded in relief, has been found near Coban. This is exactly similar to

FIG. 71.—Pottery censer from Nebaj, Guatemala.
(*Fleischmann Collection*)

certain Zapotec pots, and the head and head-dress are in true Zapotec style; but the paste is different, and the vase is coated with the slate-coloured earth-glaze, mentioned above, which has never been found in the Zapotec area. All indications seem to prove that it was made locally, and if this is so, it affords a striking instance of the borrowing of forms and illustrates the danger of basing arguments as to tribal migration on pottery types alone, though it provides a valuable hint of cultural contact. It is worthy of remark that the animal forms seem borrowed from the fauna of the Tierra caliente, a fact which goes far to indicate that the potters of Alta Vera Paz borrowed from the Totonac and people of Tabasco and not *vice versa*.

The most elaborate relief decoration, not made in moulds, seems to have been applied to censers, and the large specimens in cylindrical form which have been found from the Chacula district to that of Coban, are particularly bold and vigorous in treatment (Fig. 71). In the case of vessels of this type much of the ornament appears to have been applied, but fragments of censers of another pattern, with handles, and conforming more closely to the type shown in Pl. IX; p. 82, have been discovered, perhaps more frequently in Vera Paz. These exhibit considerable artistic and technical skill in their construction; the handles are hollow, and usually terminate in a grotesque face, the eyes and mouth of which form apertures connected with the cavity in the handle. The numerous fragments of figurines of rather coarse unburnished clay found throughout British Honduras seem in most cases to have formed part of large vessels, which probably served as censers (Pl. X, 3; p. 108). Free use was made of applied details in this district, as can be seen from the illustration on Pl. X, 3; p. 108. From the Pokomam region come peculiar circular dishes, with broad flat rims, the vertical walls of which are studded with conical projections; it is possible that these vessels also, which appear to be characteristic of the district, were censers. In the Uloa valley fragments of vases of a peculiar type have been found, distinguished by lugs in the form of animal heads. Pots of this description are usually further decorated with painted designs of good quality in yellow, orange, brown and black (as Fig. 67; p. 311). Pottery figurines, serving as whistles, with one or more finger-holes, are not uncommon, especially in the Uloa valley. As said before, the majority appear to have been made in moulds, but the funerary figurines of British Honduras (Pl. IX, 7–11 ; p. 82), also mentioned above, seem to have been modelled by hand. Large solid hand-modelled heads have also been found in Vera Paz, and were probably the heads of idols, since Landa states that the lat-ter were fre-quently made of clay among the Maya. A fine specimen, which, to judge from the peculiar-ly cut teeth, may be iden-tified with the sun-god, is shown in Fig. 72. Smaller solid figurines, but mould-made, have been found at Copan, Tikal and

FIG. 72.—Pottery head of the sun-god ; Nebaj, Guatemala.
(*Fleischmann Collection*)

other ruined sites ; many of these show traces of paint, including a turquoise-blue, and the details, though less bold, belong to a higher type of art and correspond very closely with those of the stelæ.

An interesting peculiarity of the Vera Paz repre-sentations in pottery of the human face lies in the fact that beards and even moustaches are not infrequently shown. The former class of adornment can be paralleled in the ancient stone carvings, but the moustaches on the latter are rather problematical, and in any case are not nearly so full as those of the pottery faces of Vera Paz. Another find in the same district, highly interesting from the point of view of technique, consists in a number of spherical pottery beads, overlaid with gold-foil of extreme thinness. The process by which the gold was applied to the clay constitutes a problem of some difficulty, though the specimens themselves recall the wooden beads, similarly overlaid, discovered in the Totonac region (p. 144).

A certain amount of pottery has been discovered in the caves, both in Yucatan and in the neighbourhood of Copan, which show traces of human occupation. This pottery is peculiar in the fact that it appears in no case to bear any definite relation to the other pottery of the district. The Copan cave-pottery is for the most part in bottle form, with faint gadroon mouldings or impressed key-patterns ; while fragments from a cave at Loltun, in Yucatan (immediately south of Uxmal), seem to be in the main of bowls, sometimes with small ring-handles, and usually with fine incised linear designs. The ware of the latter is black and thin, and fragments of figurines occur, the technique of which recalls that of British Honduras.

As stated before, the material is not sufficient to furnish support to important theories, but the close connection of the Vera Paz pottery with that of Sacrificios appears obvious, a connection which extends through to the Chacula region. But too much stress must not be laid upon this, because many forms and details of ornament connect the Vera Paz area with the Copan district, notably the engraved, mould-made and painted pots which bear glyphs. The practice of cutting away the background extends from the Totonac country, through Vera Paz and the Chacula district up into Oaxaca, but no trace is found of the champ-levé work discovered at Sacrificios, Teotihuacan and in the Tarascan country. The turquoise-blue colour occurring on pots in the last style is rare in the Maya area, and is limited to the pottery of British Honduras and certain figurines which seem to bear a close relation to the early culture to which the ruins belong. The ware of the Uloa valley, which has been investigated with some care by Gordon, displays technical qualities which are identical with that of Copan, but is distinguished by a number of features, principally relating to ornament, which give it a character of its own. Many features suggestive of Totonac influence appear in the pottery of British Honduras, and though the ware is, to speak technically, of inferior quality, considerable artistic skill is shown in the modelling of the human face (e.g. Pl. X, 3 ; p. 108). The attribution of forms, as given above, to different districts can however only be regarded as tentative, and will probably have to be modified in the light of subsequent discoveries. The most pressing need is an accurate classification of Maya pottery, together with a careful investigation of the various qualities of paste employed in different districts. The latter is particularly important, since it would afford far more valuable evidence regarding centres of pottery manufacture than a mere study of the forms. Community of form after all only implies connection, and often merely trade-connection which may be second, third, or fourth hand ; but a careful investigation of the material will often reveal the actual locality of manufacture, and when this has been fixed for a number of centres, the main lines of trade and the artistic influence exerted by one locality upon another can be estimated with some degree of accuracy.

CHAPTER XIII—THE MAYA: ARCHITECTURAL REMAINS

THE architectural remains exemplifying the early Maya culture are scattered over a wide region, roughly between 87 and 94 degrees of west longitude, and between 14 and 22 degrees of north latitude. The western portion of the area consists of the high plateau, intersected with river-valleys, and distinguished by much relatively open country. Over this ground various tribal migrations have passed, but the ruins do not show a culture of so high a type as those of the country further east. Between the plateau and Yucatan, buildings of the highest type are found, in low-lying alluvial country, densely forested, in which stone is, practically speaking, only procurable where the hills approach the rivers. In Yucatan, material for architectural construction was ready to hand in the soft limestone of which the peninsula is formed, and the action of the underground streams in causing the land-surface to collapse in places, had broken up the limestone into slabs of all sizes, almost as if to suit the convenience of the builder. But the Yucatec buildings belong on the whole to a later date than those of the central region, and though technically they may equal the latter, yet signs of artistic decadence make their appearance in over-luxuriant conventionalization, and indications of foreign influence are seen at certain sites, notably at Chichen Itza.

In a book intended mainly as an introduction to the study of Mayan archæology a full description of the many ruined sites is out of the question, and this chap-

ter will be limited to a consideration of the main points
of Mayan architecture, with illustrations taken from the
chief groups of remains. Those who desire fuller details may be referred to the magnificent plates of
Maudslay, and the extremely valuable and illuminating
descriptions of Palenque, Chichen Itza, Uxmal and
Mitla (besides Monte Alban and Teotihuacan) of
Holmes. Spinden's monograph on Maya art should
also be studied, as well as Seler's book on the ruins at
and around Chacula.

The sites to which especial reference will be made are
the following : In the Usumacinta valley, Palenque,
Piedras Negras and Menché ; in the level country near
the British Honduras border, Tikal, Naranjo and Seibal ; on either side of the Guatemala-Honduras frontier, Quirigua and Copan ; and in Yucatan Chichen
Itza, Uxmal, Sayil and Tulum. Some allusion will also
be made to remains in British Honduras, notably at
Santa Rita, and to the district of Huehuetenango in
western Guatemala.

One of the principal features of Mayan architecture,
as also Mexican, is the fact that all buildings of importance are constructed on raised foundations, varying in
form from low platform mounds, often of irregular
shape, to lofty pyramidal structures (Fig. 73). The two
are not infrequently found combined, and a platform-
mound sometimes supports a group of pyramids on which
temples were erected. The sides of the platform-mound
are sometimes given a steep slope, or are sometimes
built vertical or nearly so, the latter form being characteristic rather of Yucatan. The pyramids are usually
of the stepped variety, and the risers of the steps are
frequently sloped ; they are provided with a main
stairway on one face, and sometimes with supple-
mental stairways on the other faces, as in the case of the
so-called " Castillo " at Chichen Itza, which can be seen
to the left of Pl. XXVIII ; p. 348. In this building, and

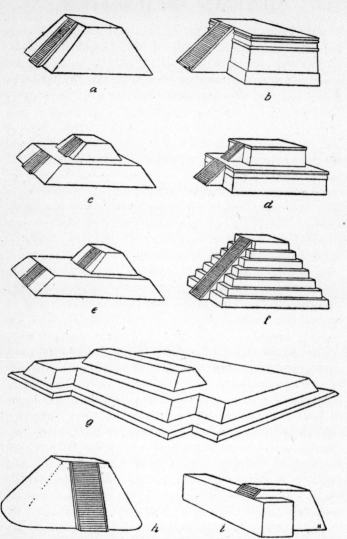

FIG. 73.—Examples of Maya terraces and pyramids (buildings omitted).

a-e.   Most common forms.
f.   "El Castillo" at Chichen Itza.
g.   "Governor's Palace," Uxmal.
h.   "Temple of the Magician," Uxmal.
i.   Ball-court temple, Chichen Itza.

(After Holmes)

Y

also at Copan, the stairway is furnished with ornamental balustrades, those at Chichen being carved in the form of two monstrous snakes of which the heads are extended on the ground at the foot of the pyramid. Practically all pyramid-mounds served as the support for buildings, though a certain number, without stairways, have been found which are simply burial-mounds. An exception occurs at Tikal (according to Tozzer), and perhaps in other places, where high pyramids with stairways appear to have had no crowning structures, and were possibly used as sites for offerings made in the open air. The material of which such structures are built is earth and rubble, and they have usually been faced with stone dressed with more or less accuracy, any imperfections being concealed with stucco. In some cases, notably at Copan, excavation has revealed the presence of a cement layer at some depth beneath the surface. This is probably an indication that the pyramid at some period has been enlarged, and it may be said that similar evidence of the practice of adding to existing structures is found elsewhere in the Maya area. The buildings which crown the foundation-mounds vary in type from simple, single-chambered edifices to elaborate complexes such as are found at Palenque and Menché, but as a matter of fact the construction is essentially the same throughout. The form of the typical Maya building was to a great extent conditioned by the fact that the primitive architect was ignorant of the principle of the true arch. It is possible that some buildings may have been furnished with flat roofs by means of wooden beams, but if so the beams have decayed and the buildings have fallen in ; such structures as have survived were built as follows (Figs. 74 and 77; pp. 323 and 329) : The walls, built very thick, were carried vertically up to the desired height, and then the mason commenced to build inwards at a very wide angle, allowing successive courses to overlap, until those on opposite walls approached near enough for the space to be bridged by single slabs. Meanwhile the outer faces of the walls were carried up vertically or at a slope, and the exterior

Fig. 74.—Transverse section of a typical Yucatec building.

- *a.* Lower wall with doorway.
- *b.* Doorway.
- *c.* Wooden lintels.
- *d.* Communication doorway.
- *e.* Inner face of arch.
- *f.* Capstones of arch.
- *g.* Lower string-course.
- *h.* Decorated entablature.
- *i.* Upper string-course.
- *j.* Flying façade with ornament (sometimes added).
- *k.* Cornice of last.
- *l.* Roof-crest with ornament (sometimes substituted for *j*).

(*After Holmes*)

of the roof was finished off flat or with a very slight gable respectively. The distance between the spring of the vault and the apex was considerable, and this gave to the exterior face of Maya buildings a very deep entablature (Fig. 74, *h*) which afforded a magnificent space for ornament. The entablature is separated from the wall proper, which is usually unornamented, by a projecting cornice or " string-course " (Fig. 74, *g*), the design of which varies according to locality, and in some of the Chichen buildings the lower portion of the wall is battered. The form of vault limited the width of the chamber to ten feet or so, but placed no restrictions upon its length, and at Palenque we find long corridor-like chambers, with frequent doorways, built upon this principle. In Yucatan the entablature is nearly always perpendicular (Fig. 74, *h*), at Tikal and Menché it slopes slightly backward, and at Palenque the slope is considerable (Fig. 77 ; p. 329) ; but these are inessential details, and it may be said that the typical Maya building is a solid, box-like structure containing a narrow chamber vaulted as described above. Even the more complex edifices are nothing more than an agglomeration of such chambers, and the type holds good for the whole of the Maya region. The nature of the Maya vault embodies the principle, in the words of Spinden, of " the downward thrust of a load on over-stepping stones," and this thrust was often increased by the addition of a superstructure, usually known as a " roof-comb " (Figs. 74, *l*, and 75, *e*). This addition reached its greatest dimensions at Tikal, where it usually resembles a very high-pitched stepped mound, sometimes solid, sometimes enclosing one or more very narrow blind chambers (Fig. 76, 9, *a*, and 11). The roof-comb was present also at Menché and probably at Naranjo and Piedras Negras (though not at Copan or Quirigua), but attains its greatest artistic development at Palenque (see Pl. XXVII ; p 342), where it is a light

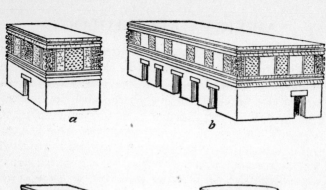

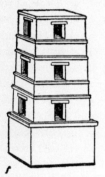

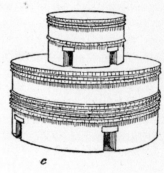

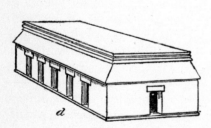

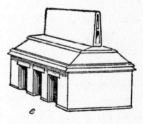

FIG. 75.—Examples of Maya buildings.

  a. Single-chambered building.
  b. Multiple-chambered building.
  c. The round tower at Chichen Itza (restored).
  d. Building at Chichen Itza with sloping entablature
     of Palenque type.
  e. Palenque type of temple.
  f. The square tower at Palenque (restored).

(After Holmes)

and airy structure, pierced with openwork, and elaborately ornamented with stucco reliefs. In Yucatan the
roof-comb, where found, differs from those of the
central Maya area in consisting, not of two inclined
walls, but of a single vertical wall (Fig. 74, *l*), and
it is often replaced by an elaborate false front,
(Fig. 74, *j*), rising above the vertical entablature, the
ornament of which it carries up to a greater height.
But though the roof-comb may by its weight have
assisted in giving stability to the Maya building, it was
by no means essential, the thick walls and solid roof were
constructed of stones freely mixed with mortar, and
the result was a structure which was practically a monolith ; in fact, the Maya built caves, the exterior surfaces of which they faced with a veneer of dressed
slabs, often, especially in Yucatan, carved and arranged
to form elaborate mosaic decoration. Their method of
building was extremely wasteful of space, and Holmes
says of the so-called " Governor's Palace " at Uxmal,
figured on Pl. XXX ; p. 358, " We find by a rough computation that the structure occupies some 325,000
cubic feet of space, upwards of 200,000 of which
is solid masonry, while only about 110,000 feet is
chamber-space. If the substructure be taken into
account, the mass of masonry is to the chamber-space
approximately as 40 to 1." In the case of the buildings
at Tikal, the proportion of chamber-space is considerably less (see Fig. 76, 11). In some cases at any rate the
connection of the superimposed building with the foundation-mound on which it rested is emphasized by the
fact that the walls of the former continue downwards
into the heart of the latter (according to Holmes),
possibly even to the ground-level. The doorways by
which these buildings were entered are for the most
part simple. In the more massive structures, such as
Tikal and Copan, a single doorway seems to have been
the rule ; but at the sites which display greater archi-

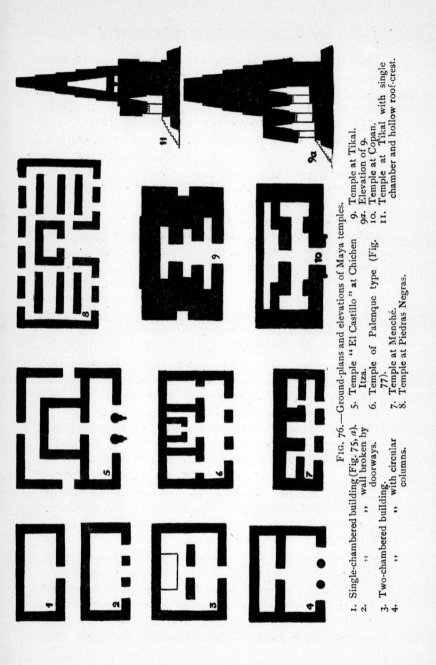

Fig. 76.—Ground-plans and elevations of Maya temples.

1. Single-chambered building (Fig. 75, a).
2. „ „ wall broken by doorways.
3. Two-chambered building.
4. „ „ with circular columns.
5. Temple "El Castillo" at Chichen Itza.
6. Temple of Palenque type (Fig. 77).
7. Temple at Menché.
8. Temple at Piedras Negras.
9. Temple at Tikal.
9a. Elevation of 9.
10. Temple at Copan.
11. Temple at Tikal with single chamber and hollow roof-crest.

tectural advancement, such as Palenque, the front is often broken by a series of doorways so close together that the wall becomes little more than a series of square pillars (Fig. 75, *d*). Round columns are found only in Yucatan, especially at Chichen Itza, associated with those buildings which are attributed to a later date (Pl. XXIX). It is interesting to note that, while in the Old World the column is based for the most part on vegetal forms, in this country the animal world has been laid under contribution. The Chichen columns are carved to represent feathered serpents, with their heads upon the ground and their tails elevated in the air, exactly similar to the columns which have been found at Tulan in Mexico. Stone was employed for lintels, especially at Menché, where they are elaborately carved, but wood was used almost more frequently. The carved lintels of Tikal (see Fig. 48; p. 225), of the durable zapote wood, are among the finest examples of Maya art, and have survived owing to the solidity of the buildings and their single doorways. At Palenque and in Yucatan the wooden lintels, being less well protected, have vanished, and their decay has often contributed to the downfall of the structure; at the same time the fact that many of the buildings have not suffered to any extent from the removal of the lintels emphasizes the monolithic character of the Maya building. Windows are practically non-existent, though openings in the walls between chambers are common, especially at Palenque (Fig. 77; p. 329). As stated above, the typical Maya building is a simple rectangular chamber, as shown in the plan, Fig. 76, 1. But it was capable of considerable elaboration, and the succeeding plans show some of the variations produced by the addition of subsidiary chambers and the breaking of the wall by means of doorways. The highest degree of complexity is seen at Palenque, where the main building contains a specially-built cell, furnished with a separate roof, to enshrine the mural tablet which probably served as an object of worship (Fig. 77).

The methods of the Maya builder, and in particular

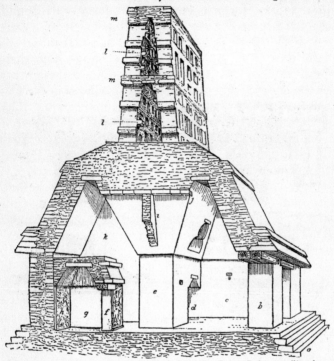

FIG. 77.—Section through the Temple of the Cross, Palenque (lintels restored) : see Fig. 76, 6.

a. Stairway.	*h.* Original position of mural tablet.
b. Pillar (restored).	*i.* Masonry arch-brace.
c. Vestibule.	*j.* Capstones of doorway arch.
d. Doorway to inner side chamber.	*k.* Partition-wall.
e. Large doorway to inner main chamber.	*l.* Steps for ascending roof-crest through middle floor.
f. Doorway to shrine.	*m.* Middle floor and roof of roof-crest.
g. Shrine.	

(*After Holmes*)

his ignorance of the true arch, rendered the construction of an edifice of more than one storey (apart from the roof-comb) a matter of considerable difficulty. Nevertheless buildings of two, and even three tiers of chambers are known, though the plan on which they were erected was extremely wasteful of material and space. Usually the higher or highest tier was supported on a solid construction, around which the chambers of the lower tier or tiers were grouped (Fig. 78). The whole edifice thus resembled in the main a huge stepped mound, with rooms built in each of the steps. Sometimes the outer chambers of a superior tier would overlap those of an inferior to some extent, but in such cases the floor

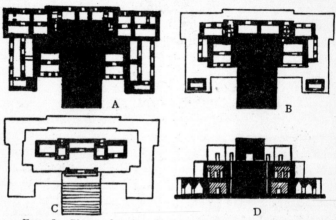

FIG. 78.—Plans and section of building at Santa Rosa Xlabpak.

A. Plan, ground floor.   C. Plan, second floor.
B.   ,,   first floor.   D. Section.

(*After Spinden*)

of an upper chamber was almost always supported on the dividing wall of two of the lower. The cave-like structure of Maya buildings is particularly evident in such architectural monstrosities. However, many of the sites do not include buildings of more than one floor (apart from the roof-comb). In some cases, as at Tikal, the upper tiers must have been reached by ladders, as no stairway leads to them, and it is interesting to note in this connection that more than one stela at Piedras Negras represents a god seated in a niche to which a ladder gives access from below (Pl. XX; p. 224).

The finest example of a three-tiered building is found
at Santa Rosa Xlabpak (Fig. 78), but in this case a
broad stairway leads from the ground to the highest
tier. Two remarkable buildings of more than one
storey call for mention, if only as exceptions to the
general rule. These are the square tower at Palenque, and the circular edifice known as the "Caracol"
at Chichen Itza. The first (Fig. 75, f) had originally at
least three floors, as well as two intermediate blind
storeys, the chambers of which are grouped around
a square core of masonry in which is built a staircase.
The second (Fig. 75, e), which has two storeys, is constructed round a circular core, in which is a very small
spiral stairway. The essentials of construction are the
same, the chief differences lying in the facts, firstly,
that whereas the chambers of the Caracol are all
vaulted, those of the Palenque tower are in some cases
furnished with flat ceilings of beams, and secondly, that
while the upper storey of the Caracol is considerably
less in diameter than the lower, the square tower retains the same diameter throughout. Architecturally
the latter is considerably superior to the former, but
the shape of the Caracol is interesting since it is the only
circular construction now existing in the Maya country,
though Landa states that a circular temple to Kukulkan
was built at Mayapan, and further remarks that this
shape of building was particularly related to this god.
It will be remembered that circular temples, according
to tradition, were erected to Quetzalcoatl, his counterpart, in Mexico.

The Maya architects did not attempt to handle large
masses of stone in the construction of their buildings ;
no blocks comparable in size with the great lintels of
Mitla enter into the composition of Maya temples and in
the art of masonry the Maya were far behind the megali-
thic builders of the Peruvian and Bolivian highlands. The
only attempt at stone building, where regularly squared

blocks are laid in rows with due attention to the breaking of courses and the bonding of corners, is found at
Copan, and that too in only a very small proportion of
the ruins of that site. Elsewhere no regard is paid to
these two important architectural points, and this fact
has contributed in some degree to the downfall of many
of the buildings. However, the fault is the less serious
owing to the extreme solidity of the stone-and-mortar
hearting. As stated above, Maya buildings were faced
with a veneer of blocks dressed on the exterior surface ;
these were usually cut away to some extent behind, so
that the mortar in which they were set extended in
tongues nearly to the outer face of the wall, just as at
Mitla ; but in many cases the tenon-like backs of the
surface-blocks were not sufficiently prominent, and in
consequence they have fallen away from the core of
stone and mortar, leaving the latter exposed. This
method of facing enabled the builders to ornament their
temples with the most elaborate mosaic designs, which
are seen in their greatest complexity in Yucatan (Pls.
XXIX, 2, and XXX; pp. 350 and 358). The designs here
fall roughly into two classes, geometrical patterns, which
often appear to be based upon textile art, and grotesque
representations of the human face (e.g. Fig. 86, g; p.
356). The latter is particularly characteristic of the
region, and represents probably the face of the god B,
the counterpart of the Mexican Tlaloc, whose nose
is frequently prolonged into a regular trunk (see Pl.
XXIX, 2). Some of the geometrical patterns are produced by the regular repetition of a small element,
and these naturally were easier of construction since
they are composed of similarly carved blocks; but
many of the designs are formed of blocks each of which
has been carved to fit the particular place which it
occupies in the whole scheme of ornament, and this
fact not only bears witness to a vast amount of patient
labour, but implies also that the architect was work-

PLATE XXV

Photo. Col. F. H. Ward

1

Photo. Dr. A. P. Maudslay

2

MAYA

1. BUILDING AT SAYIL, YUCATAN
2. TEMPLE AT TIKAL, GUATEMALA

ing in accordance with a definite plan prepared before-hand. In Chichen Itza grotesque masks are found in some of the buildings, composed of details which do not fit into the scheme, a fact which proves that the Maya mason was not above utilizing material gleaned from the ruins of former buildings, besides affording evidence that such structures are of later date. It has already been mentioned that circular columns are peculiar to Yucatan, and it may be added that a variety of ornament derived from them was also applied to the outer surface of buildings, in the form of series of pilasters, such as are found at Sayil, and Labna and elsewhere (Pl. XXV, 1 ; p. 332).

Mortar, obtained by burning the local limestone, besides being used in great quantities for the hearting of buildings, was also employed for flooring, and, as stucco, for making up defects in wall-surfaces and designs. Besides this it was extensively used for moulded decoration at certain sites, notably Palenque. Here the limestone is of a very hard variety, and difficult to work with such tools as the Maya possessed ; as a result, the art of modelling in relief attained a great development, and some of the finest works of Central American art are those produced by the stucco-workers of Palenque. Where the relief is low, the stucco has been employed alone, but where bold effects were desired, as on the roof-combs, a regular skeleton of the design has first been prepared, of limestone blocks, over which the stucco has been applied and moulded to the requisite form.

Colour formed an important aid to Maya ornament, and was frequently applied to stone carvings. It seems to us rather barbarous to cover fine stone reliefs with a coat of coloured stucco, but the Maya artist had no scruples on this score, and reliefs have been found at Palenque to which several layers of the above have been applied at different times. Many of the stelæ, especially at Piedras Negras, still show evident traces of colour, and it must be remembered that when the details were picked out in different tints the designs appeared far less complicated than in monochrome. But apart from the colouring of reliefs, fresco designs in a variety of hues were commonly applied to the interior walls of buildings, and their graceful and flowing lines prove that the Maya was no mean artist with the brush. This form of ornament has been observed at Menché, where a design of scrolls, leaves, flowers and figures of men and animals is painted on the walls of one of the chambers, in two reds, two blues, yellow and dark brown. At Chichen Itza the art of fresco was highly developed ; not only were the columns, doorposts and interior reliefs painted in colours, but many chambers were elaborately ornamented with coloured designs. According to Miss Breton, who has made a careful study of these frescoes, two different hands may be traced in the method of execution. One artist employed outlines but sparingly, and carried out the greater part of his work in dry colour, sometimes superimposing one tint on another to obtain the desired effect. The other drew all his figures in outline and added the principal colour masses while the plaster was still damp, putting in the details subsequently in dry colour. The hues include two reds, two blues, four greens, yellow, white, black and purple. The practice of ornamenting wall-surfaces with painted designs extends into British Honduras, where a building with very important frescoes has been discovered under peculiar circumstances. This is at Santa Rita, and the building in question was found buried in a large mound, which had been heaped over it, apparently with intention. The frescoes are painted on the walls below the cornice, and had been shielded from the earth by protecting walls built about an inch from them to meet the cornice. The colours include red, pink, blue, yellow, grey and black, and the design represents a number of human or divine figures accompanied by date-glyphs in the Maya style. Among the figures the Maya gods B and K of the manuscripts may be easily recognized, while one with bird and serpent attributes may well be Kukulkan (Fig. 79). At the same time one figure is shown with black paint around the eye, exactly as worn by the Aztec Mixcoatl and other stellar gods, while other details peculiar to Mexican art appear, such as a frieze of

FIG. 79.—Detail of fresco at Santa Rita, British Honduras.
(*After Gann*)

star-eyes, very similar to that of Mitla (compare Fig. 80), and sun-discs in Mexican style. Many of the figures are represented with bound hands, and in one place a sacrificial scene is depicted. It is possible that the fresco commemorates some victory, but the occasion, as well as the reason of the burial of the building, remains a mystery.

Apart from the buildings reserved for ceremonial or residential purposes, tlaxtli-courts are found in the Huehuetenango district, at Rabinal, and again in northern Yucatan, though not in the central area. These courts have the floor and walls carefully plastered, and the stone rings which project, one from each wall, are usually well carved. The court at Chichen is the largest known, and is associated with a special temple with serpent columns in the style of Tulan (Pls. XXVIII and XXIX, 1; pp. 348 and 350). The western courts resemble very closely those of the Zapotec area. The question of the introduction of the game into the Maya area has already been discussed on p. 302.

A
B

FIG. 80.—Details from frescoes.

A. Santa Rita, British Honduras.
B. Mitla, Oaxaca.

Living as they did in a climate with an abundant rainfall, the Maya were not under the necessity of constructing elaborate irrigation works as were the ancient inhabitants of Peru. One watercourse alone is known, and that appears to be rather in the nature of a drain to carry off superfluous water than an aqueduct. This is at Palenque, and consists of a stone-lined subterranean channel, roofed with the typical Maya vault.

As regards the arrangement of buildings it is impossible to discuss in detail the ground-plans of the various sites, but attention may be called to the prevailing tendency to group the most important structures round square or rectangular courts. Beyond this, little community of plan is observed, and indeed in the central area the builders were often obliged to suit their arrangement to the exigencies of the site. Thus Palenque and Copan, being built in river-valleys, exhibit less regularity of arrangement than such sites as Tikal, where the country is more or less of a plain. There is evidence too that many of the cities grew by accretion beyond the limits intended by the first builders, and this fact will explain much of the irregularity observable in plan. But throughout, the assemblage of buildings round a court is a prominent feature, and the court would seem to have been the unit of growth (see Pl. XXVI, 2 ; p. 338). It is a noticeable fact that none of the sites in the east and centre of the Maya area exhibit any defensive qualities. The courts are open at the corners, and the sites selected for building are evidently not chosen with any strategic insight. In the west, however, the case is somewhat different, and we find settlements, such as Iximché and Utatlan, built as it were on peninsulas almost surrounded by inaccessible barrancas and connected with the " mainland " only by a narrow neck which could be easily defended by a mere handful of men. This fact goes far towards indicating that the ruins in the centre were centres of religious and ceremonial life rather than cities in the modern sense of the word.

The question as to how far Maya buildings were definitely oriented is rather complex. On the whole far fewer indications of the practice occur in the Maya region than in the Mexican. To speak generally the sites at Seibal and in southern Yucatan, as far as surveyed, are more carefully oriented than in northern Yucatan and elsewhere. The buildings at Copan are not oriented, but here and at such sites as Palenque, the surrounding hills and forests obscure the true horizon, and the arrangement of courts may yet be found to square with the apparent point of rising of certain heavenly bodies. An accurate survey of Tikal would throw a good deal of light upon the problem, since the situation of the ruins in comparatively level country, combined with the great height of the pyramids, would have enabled the inhabitants to obtain a far truer horizon than at most sites.

z

Though the Maya did not for the most part use large masses of stone for building, yet they were able to handle monoliths of considerable size, as may be seen from the number of carved stelæ which constitute so important a feature of many of the ruined sites. These stelæ consist of monolithic pillars, approximately rectangular and decorated with relief carving, usually on all sides. The largest of these are found at Quirigua, but the art of the neighbouring site of Copan (Pl. XXI; p. 236) is the finer, since many of the stelæ here are carved in such bold relief as to approximate to sculpture in the round. At these two sites most of the stelæ present on their principal faces a human or divine figure, usually represented *en face*, and holding the sky-bar (occasionally replaced at Quirigua by the ceremonial axe). At Tikal, Naranjo (Pl. XXIII; p. 302), and Menché (Pl. XXII; p. 294) the relief is less bold, and the figures are usually therefore shown in profile, at any rate as far as the face is concerned. At Seibal and Piedras Negras profile figures predominate, but a few occur shown *en face* (Pl. XX; p. 224), among them the figures seated in niches already mentioned as characteristic of the latter locality. At Palenque only one stela has been found, but on the other hand comparatively little stone-carving occurs here, though the deficiency is amply supplied by the quality of the magnificent mural tablets in relief which constitute the chief feature of the site. The sky-bar does not appear on the stelæ of Piedras Negras, though the ceremonial axe is occasionally seen. Both emblems occur at Naranjo, Tikal, Seibal and Menché. A few stelæ have been found in Yucatan, e.g. at Sayil; but they are confined to the northern portion of the district and even here are rare and poorly carved. The exact purpose of the stelæ is problematical. In the large majority of cases they stand in definite relation to certain buildings, in fact all at Naranjo, Seibal, Menché and Piedras

PLATE XXVI

Photo. Col. F. H. Ward

I

After Maudslay

2

MAYA

1. Sculptured monolith P., Quirigua, Guatemala
2. Plan of ruins at Copan, Honduras

Negras are connected with temples. At Copan and Quirigua some appear to be independent. They are usually found situated in the courts, though at Piedras Negras a series exists arranged along the lower terrace of a foundation-mound. Many are furnished with altars in front of them (Fig. 81), and they appear to have been the objects of some cult. A most important point in connection with them lies in the fact that so many of them bear dates in the long count as described in chapter X, and this fact, combined with the statements of early authors that the historical Maya were wont to mark the

FIG. 81.—Stone altar (Q) at Copan.   (*After Maudslay*)

passage of a katun by setting up a " stone," lends colour to the opinion that the early Maya followed a similar practice. Many of the dates mark quarter katuns, but many again do not, and though we may conclude that they were in some way commemorative monuments, it is impossible at present to define their use more exactly. As stated before, many of the stelæ were painted in colours, and plain stelæ occur at Tikal and elsewhere, which probably once bore some painted design. The evident relation which Maya sculpture bears to wood-carving renders it probable that many wooden stelæ may once have existed, especially in the earliest times. It is worth noting that at Copan the stone foundations which support the stelæ enclose small cruciform vaults, reproducing in miniature the souterrains found in connection with some of the buildings at Mitla.

At present the attention of most archæologists has been confined to the ruins themselves, and little search has been made for the sources whence the building-material was obtained. Quarries however have been located in the neighbourhoods of Naranjo, Copan and Quirigua, and the presence at the last site of canal-like excavations suggests that the blocks were conveyed thither by water. A thorough investigation of such quarries as can be discovered would be most valuable in casting much light upon the process of working stone among the early Maya.

In the east of the central area the most important site is that of Tikal; the ruins are extensive, and suggest that the place was long an important centre. The dates attached to the monuments are of great interest (for the comparative dating of the monuments, see Appendix III), since they range from an early period, and the extreme solidity of the buildings as compared with those of other sites seems to hint that they were the work of more primitive architects than those of Palenque for instance. The pyramids are of interest, since they present a far steeper pitch than those of any other locality (Pl. XXV, 2; p. 332). Certain of the stelæ and inscriptions are of a rather rude and archaic character, but the wood-carvings (Fig. 48; p. 225) are of particular merit, and are very similar in style to the stone lintels in low relief of Menché. The fact that the wooden lintels have been preserved here while they have for the most part decayed at other sites, is no argument against the antiquity of Tikal, for they are situated well within the buildings, which are, as remarked above, of very solid construction, and furnished with small single doors, besides being raised far above the ground on lofty foundation-mounds. On the whole I think that the architectural and artistic evidence supports the early dates which appear on the stelæ, and I should place Tikal as perhaps the earliest Maya site of which we have definite knowledge, though it is evident that it was inhabited well on into later times when the Maya had become far more expert in stone-carving than when the first buildings were erected there. The neighbouring site of Naranjo bears certain similarities in plan to that of Tikal, and the reliefs are in very similar style. The dating of the monuments falls into two well-defined periods, the western court being earlier than the eastern; both however are considerably later than the earlier buildings of Tikal, of which Naranjo was probably an offshoot, outlasting the mother city by more than half a century. Seibal, where the ruins are far less extensive, is evidently a related site, though the reliefs are comparatively clumsy in style, and probably represent a decadent and " provincial " form of art. It is interesting to note that the earliest date at this site falls about the same time as the last of Tikal, the latest recording the same katun as the latest at Naranjo.

Menché, like Copan, is built upon the bank of a river, and the physical character of the site prevented anything like symmetrical arrangement. The courts do not correspond one with another in position, and careful investigation would be necessary before it could be stated that any of the pyramids were so placed as to provide for the observation of the rising of a planet over the surrounding hills. The dates would make Menché later than Tikal as far as its foundation is concerned, and the less massive nature of its architecture and the high quality of its relief-carving would imply the same. But it is noticeable that the most numerous reliefs consist of sculptured lintels, and though these are of stone, and not of wood as at Tikal, the technique is that of wood-carving, and the style is very similar to that of Tikal. The artistic quality of the Menché sculptures is relatively very high, and the lintels, one of which is figured on Pl. XXII, 2; p. 294, are some of the finest examples of low-relief carving found in the Maya area, ranking with the bolder sculptures of Copan, and not far behind the stucco work and still lower reliefs of Palenque. Further features of this site will be mentioned in connection with Palenque.

Copan (Pl. XXVI, 2; p. 338) and Quirigua evidently bear a close relation one to the other, and are differentiated from all other sites by the size and workmanship of the stelæ. Unfortunately but few traces of buildings remain, and it is impossible to determine their exact type. All that can be said is that the walls were thick, and that both in this respect and in the ground-plan (see Fig. 76; p. 327) the buildings probably represent a stage of development midway between Tikal and other sites. With this placing the dates on the Copan monuments agree, but Quirigua was a later site, almost certainly founded from Copan, though it flourished alongside of it until both records cease at the end of the ninth cycle. The monuments of Quirigua show a certain technical superiority over those of Copan, the stelæ are larger, and often ornamented with far greater wealth of detail. The broader treatment of the Copan carvings (Pl. XXI and Fig. 81; pp. 236 and 339), however, gives a nobler effect to the stelæ of that site, though Quirigua cannot in any sense be regarded as decadent, as witness the magnificent monster with a human figure in its jaws shown on Pl. XXVI, 1; p. 338.

Piedras Negras is a site of great interest. On the one hand the stelæ manifest a very great range of quality, on the other the dates commence early, though not so early as Tikal, and end in the same katun as those of that city. The rudest stelæ bear a rather interesting resemblance to the Huaxtec sculptures of the Panuco valley (Pl. X, 1; p. 108), while the best are of a type peculiar to this locality. The latter represent a figure *en face*, seated in a niche to which a ladder gives access,

PLATE XXVII

MAYA

RUINS AT PALENQUE, CHIAPAS

1. THE "TEMPLE OF THE SUN"
2. THE "PALACE"
3. THE "TEMPLE OF THE CROSS"

and before which a priest is sometimes represented standing (Pl. XX ; p. 224). It may be noted in passing that the board, or, more likely, cloth with the footsteps marked on it, laid upon the ladder, is paralleled in the Dresden MS. by the streamer with similar markings attached to the tree which represents the god (see Fig. 58; p. 264, lower register). The exact relations of Piedras Negras are difficult to determine. On the one hand certain points in connection with costume, notably the voluminous turban-like head-dresses seen on many of the figures, recall the art of Copan (e.g. Fig. 81) ; on the other hand many of the flatter reliefs bear a distinct resemblance to those of Naranjo, without attaining the perfection of those at Menché. An interesting fragment represents a figure seated in profile with a colossal jaguar towering behind him ; unfortunately only the feet and legs of the latter remain, but sufficient to show that the whole scene must have been almost a replica of one of the wooden lintels of Tikal. Jaguar figures, or men with jaguar masks and claws, or claws alone, also occur on stelæ at Seibal and Quirigua.

Palenque stands alone. Architecturally it is by far the most advanced of the cities of the central area, while the artistic qualities of the stucco reliefs, and the low-relief stone carvings (Figs. 49 and 52), the technique of which appears to be based on stucco-work, place them in a category by themselves. It was, in fact, only at Copan and Quirigua that the Maya showed anything like mastery over stone. The deficiency lay no doubt not so much in the artistic faculties of the mason, as in the lack of suitable tools, but it is a fact that only at the southern sites he displayed definite signs of modifying the technique borrowed from wood-carving to suit a less tractable material. Even the fine reliefs of Menché are wood-carvings translated into stone, and the same applies to the reliefs at other sites, except perhaps to the figures in niches at Piedras Negras, which in other re-

spects noted above display a certain similarity to the
Copan sculptures. When the Maya artist began to de-
velop the art of modelling in stucco he showed that the

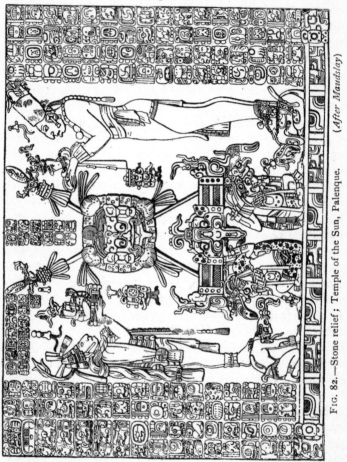

FIG. 82.—Stone relief ; Temple of the Sun, Palenque.   (*After Maudslay*)

quality of his work depended to a great extent upon the
plasticity of his material, while he had gained much in
technique from his experience in stone. A peculiar
feature of Palenque is the comparative restraint exhibited by the artist. That he still loved complexity of

detail is shown by such reliefs as Fig. 61 (p. 297), but he no longer feared the vacant space, and appreciated its value as a background. The dates on the monuments do not assist us in any way to determine the epoch which saw the rise of Palenque. The initial series in the temples give dates relating to the first cycle or even before, that is to say more than 3000 years B.C., and as such they must be regarded as purely legendary. It is impossible to believe that the site was of early foundation compared with the others. It would be against all experience to suggest that the people who built Palenque could at a subsequent period have adopted the clumsy and unnecessarily laborious architecture of Tikal. On the other hand, the site of Palenque bears a certain similarity to that of Menché, including the presence at both of buildings with underground passages and chambers, though the " palace " at Palenque is a far more elaborate construction than the analogous building at Menché, being in fact a complex of associated buildings. All the evidence seems to point to the conclusion that Palenque is the latest of the central Maya sites, and that it is most closely associated with Menché. In further proof of the latter supposition I might mention the so-called " crosses," surmounted by birds, held by the figures in more than one of the Menché reliefs, which have their counterparts in the " crosses " of Palenque alone. The significance of these I have already discussed on p. 257.

I think, then, that the various dates found on the monuments may be taken as a fair indication of the relative periods at which the various cities flourished, except of course those at Palenque. Arguments based upon the style of decoration alone are apt to be misleading, especially as far as the lesser sites are concerned, since it is only natural that at these the workmanship should be of an inferior and " provincial " character. Allowance too must be made for the varying capacity of local artists, and above all for the relative tractability of the local materials. The evidence of architecture is more valuable, and, to speak generally, supports the dates as given by the glyphs, though the possibility of greater conservatism at some sites, as compared with others, must not be overlooked. On the whole the best results must necessarily accrue from a careful consideration of all three, with due allowance for a natural tendency to quote dates relating to past and often mythical history.

With respect to certain similarities presented by the attributes of the figures depicted at certain sites, allusion has been made above to the hand appearing as part of the head-dress at Copan, Piedras Negras and Palenque (p. 227), to the jaguar-man at Tikal, Seibal, Piedras Negras and Quirigua (p. 343), and to the fish and flower, also shown as a head-dress, at Naranjo, Palenque, Chichen Itza and on the Nebaj vase (p. 310). Attention will be called later to a peculiar interlaced ornament, also borne on the head, by figures at Copan, Piedras Negras, Menché and Naranjo, and found again at Xochicalco, Teayo and in the Mexican valley (p. 355). One more may be mentioned, the head-dress representing a heron with a fish or frog in its beak, seen at Palenque (Fig. 61 ; p. 297) and twice at Seibal, an ornament which recalls the Quiché legend of how they sent eastward to a country, most probably to be identified with the Usumacinta valley, to obtain royal *insignia*, and received amongst other objects the plumes of the heron.

Of the Yucatec sites the most important is that of Chichen Itza. The remains here are considerable, though they conform to no definite plan save that the same arrangement of building round rectangular courts prevails. The buildings themselves are typically Maya, though structurally they exhibit a certain advance upon those of the central area, and Maya glyphs are found throughout, with certain important

exceptions. Of the peculiarities which distinguish the
architecture of Yucatan from that of the last region,
many have already been mentioned, including the
mosaic ornament with which the façades of buildings
are decorated. But another important feature remains
to be recorded. Throughout the whole of Yucatan only
two dates in the long count have been discovered, and
one of these is at Chichen Itza. The site is interesting
as providing evidence of more than one stage of construction. One of the finest buildings, the so-called
Monjas, shows plainly that a considerable addition was

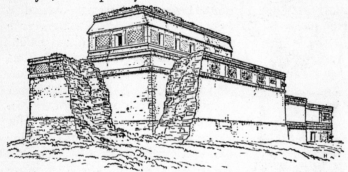

Fig. 83.—The " Monjas " at Chichen Itza, showing how the original
structure has been enlarged.
(*After Holmes*)

made to the foundation at a time later than the original
building (Fig. 83). At the same period an additional
storey was added, and one of the chambers in the earlier
structure was filled solid with masonry to support the
weight. Certain annexes were also built (Pl. XXIX, 2;
p. 350), in the decoration of which ornamental frag
ments from the façades of previous " palaces " were
included, but the inscriptions are in regular Maya characters, though no date in the long count is included.
Other buildings in the immediate neighbourhood are
in similar style and belong presumably to the same
epoch. But further north is a large group of structures
of an entirely different character of ornamentation.

These include the famous ball-court and attached temples (Pl. XXVIII; p. 348), the Castillo (also seen in Pl. XXVIII), a large structure of which only the numerous square sculptured columns remain, and the so-called " Temple of the Tables." On these buildings neither Maya glyphs nor mosaic masks are found, while the Castillo and upper ball-court temple are furnished with serpent-columns similar to those of Tulan. In the lower temple attached to the ball-court is an elaborate relief showing figures, exhibiting no signs of cranial

FIG. 84.—Caryatid figure, Chichen Itza.

deformation, armed with spears and spear-throwers, assisting, so it would seem, at the obsequies of some personage in the centre who is distinguished by a huge feathered snake which overshadows him. Many of the figures are accompanied by glyphs which are distinctly Nahua in type, while their ornaments and dress combine both Nahua and Maya characters; further, a sun-disc in Nahua style occurs at the top of the relief. In the Castillo are atlantean figures carved in relief in similar style, and in the Temple of the Tables were found a number of slabs supported by small caryatides (Fig. 84), carved in the round, exactly similar to some which have been found at Tlaxcala. Finally, several stone recumbent figures supporting vases, of the type shown on Pl. VIII, 2; p. 74, have been discovered buried in the neighbourhood.[1] The buildings themselves, as far as preserved, present, architecturally speaking, Maya characteristics, except the large site with the numerous square columns, which probably supported a flat roof laid on transverse beams. To the west and south of the buildings first described are many unexplored

[1] One of these was also found by Maudslay, near Quirigua.

PLATE XXVIII

Photo. C. B. Waite

MAYA

THE TEMPLE OF THE BALL-COURT (LEFT) AND THE "CASTILLO," AT CHICHEN ITZA, YUCATAN (See Plate XXIX, 1)

mounds, probably the remains of the earliest settlement of all, and it is in one of these that a slab
bearing a date in the long count, but later than
any in the central area, has been discovered. Thus we
appear to have three, or possibly four, periods represented at Chichen Itza, the first by the mounds where
the initial date was found, the second and possible
third by the Monjas group with its reconstructions in
typical Yucatec style, the last by the northern group
with its definite " Toltec " affinities. It is to be noted
that this corresponds in a most remarkable manner with
the Tutul Xiu tradition. The first settlement would be
that of which they heard when they were yet at Balcalar, the second and doubtful third periods would
represent their own occupation and reoccupation, while
the last would illustrate the result of the Nahua influx
which brought about the fall of the league of Mayapan.
The other date in the long count which has been found
in the Yucatec area is at Tulum. This is a very early
date, in the sixth katun of the ninth cycle, and may
possibly relate to some event in past history. At any
rate it supports the evidence furnished by Chichen Itza
that the Maya peoples who reckoned by the long count
and built the cities of the central area had penetrated
into Yucatan before the arrival of the Tutul Xiu.
Tulum has not yet been satisfactorily explored, but
the buildings there are neither imposing nor richly
decorated ; the site however presents one feature of
interest in so far as it is surrounded on three sides by a
wall, the fourth being protected by the sea.

Uxmal, which, according to the Tutul Xiu account,
was founded from Chichen Itza, shows, as regards the
majority of its buildings, a very close correspondence
with the Monjas group of the latter site. Most of the
buildings exhibit the true Yucatec character, including
the mosaic masks with projecting " trunks," and pilastered ornament is also found. A few however do not

show these characteristics to the same degree, and present abnormal varieties of cornice, while others display signs of alteration and modification which imply at least that the site was inhabited for a considerable period. The most striking buildings, perhaps the finest in the true Yucatec style which exist, are the so-called "House of the Governor" (Pl. XXX; p. 358), the "Temple of the Magician," peculiar in its oblong pyramid with rounded corners (Fig. 73, *h*; p. 321),[1] and the "House of the Doves," distinguished by a vandyked roof-comb ornamented with open-work tracery. Lack of space forbids allusion to the many other Yucatec sites, such as Labna, Sayil, Kabah, and so forth, but it may be said that they embody similar forms of decoration such as the grotesque mosaic mask, and geometrical and pilastered ornament (Pl. XXV, 1; p. 332), though the structures can hardly be said to compare with those of Chichen Itza and Uxmal.

As regards British Honduras, mention has already been made of the interesting building at Santa Rita, decorated with frescoes somewhat akin in style to those at Mitla, though rather nearer the true Maya in type. It is difficult not to see in this art an extension of the "Toltec" influence so evident at Chichen Itza, combined with a stronger element of the local Maya art. But buildings in this region are few, though the substructures of former edifices are common. On the Colombia branch of the Rio Grande is found an extensive two-tiered foundation-mound, supporting a number of stepped pyramids, which recall to some extent the site of Uxmal, in so far as the corners of most are rounded. Both mound and pyramids are faced with cut stone, and quantities of brick are also found which appear to have been used as hearting and paving material.

[1] The corners of the Castillo at Chichen Itza also appear to have been slightly rounded and not square, as shown in Fig. 73, *f*; p. 321.

PLATE XXIX

I

Photo. Dr. A. P. Maudslay

2

MAYA

1. RESTORATION OF THE BALL-COURT TEMPLE AT CHICHEN ITZA,
   YUCATAN; AFTER MAUDSLAY. *(See Plate XXVIII)*
2. BUILDINGS OF THE "MONJAS" GROUP, CHICHEN ITZA, YUCATAN

One of the most interesting ruins of British Honduras consists of a huge mound near Benque Viejo, sixty feet high and built of limestone, which supports a three-storeyed stone building. This is surrounded by three others of similar type, at the foot of each of which is a plain stone monolith, recalling the plain stelæ mentioned above, which doubtless were once ornamented with painted designs. The ruins of this site probably belong to the same series as Tikal, Naranjo, Seibal, etc., and though more excavation, combined with accurate surveying, is necessary before we can speak with confidence regarding the monuments of British Honduras as a whole, we may assume that they fall into two classes, viz. ruins connected with the early central Maya area, those to the north of British Honduras at Tulum being in part a " provincial " extension of the early culture,[1] and later edifices which owed their birth to Toltec influence filtered southward through Yucatan.

In the west of the Maya area, the remains, though plentiful, are inferior in quality, and have not attracted the attention of explorers to the extent which their importance, as indicating the spread of Maya culture, and its relation to that of Oaxaca, deserves. Sacchana and its neighbourhood is a site of great interest, since Seler has discovered there two stone slabs bearing initial dates in the Maya style, falling just each side of the date at Chichen Itza, which is otherwise the latest known. The style of these slabs is rude and decadent, but they are of the highest importance as indicating that the early method of reckoning time had spread as far west at least as the department of Huehuetenango. Otherwise the remains of this district are rude and coarsely built, of unsquared blocks usually without mortar ; but mortar is found in some cases, notably in the tlaxtli-courts, which, as well as the pyra-

---

[1] The qualification is necessary, since Tulum appears to have been inhabited at the conquest.

midal mounds, bear a very close resemblance to those of Quiengola in Oaxaca (p. 175). A feature of this district is constituted by the number of cave-temples, which again recall the last-named province of Mexico. It is perhaps worthy of mention that a tendency appears in this neighbourhood to arrange temple-mounds in groups of three, in a straight line from north to south, with the stairways facing west. The western position of pyramid stairways, which implies that the worshippers faced east, has already been observed in Oaxaca and Mexico. An account of certain ruins at Utatlan, Iximché and Rabinal is given in the works of Maudslay, but they cannot compare with those of the central Maya area, and seem rather to resemble those of the district of Huehuetenango.

The Maya appear to have resorted occasionally to caves as dwelling-places, and certain investigations have been made in caverns at Copan and Loltun (immediately south of Uxmal), in Yucatan. The remains however do not imply that their occupation was of early date, and it is probable that the caves served as places of temporary refuge in times of war. This chapter would be incomplete without some mention of the peculiar bottle-shaped subterranean structures found at certain sites in Yucatan. These are known as "chultunes," and, since they invariably occur at places remote from rivers, may almost certainly be regarded as cisterns for preserving a supply of water, though in some cases they have served the secondary purpose of burial chambers. They are lined with dressed stone or a coat of stucco, and the mouth is furnished with a stone ring which is closed by a slab. Careful exploration of the chultunes at Labna has been made by Thompson and reported in the "Memoirs" of the Peabody Museum.

It will be unnecessary to enter into a discussion of Maya art, since the subject has been fully treated by Spinden in a monograph which was published only a week or so before this chapter was written, and, more-over, much may be gathered from the preceding pages supplemented by the illustrations. The kinship of the stone reliefs with wood-carving, except at Copan and Quirigua, has already been indicated, and the symbolic nature of Maya ornament is too obvious to need especial mention. Attention may be called to the use of glyphs, extremely ornamental in themselves, to give balance to a design, and to the *horror vacui* which appears in all reliefs except those of Palenque. Though bound by convention, the result in a large measure of the symbolic nature of his designs, the Maya artist occupies a relatively high plane amongst barbarous peoples. In particular the quality of his line is excel-

FIG. 85.—Stone gargoyle, Copan.   (*After Gordon*)

lent, even in stone, and in certain respects, notably foreshortening (especially in the treatment of feathers, for which see Figs. 61 and 87; pp. 297 and 367), he was superior to the sculptor of Egypt or Assyria. One peculiarity of Maya art lies in the fact that the artist was obsessed by the motive of the serpent (rattle-snake) head. In nearly all its essentials this design appears in the remarkable gargoyle from Copan shown in Fig. 85. We have here the exaggerated upper jaw, the front fang, and the curl at the corner of the mouth. One detail is lacking, viz. the nose-ornaments which were usually added to the reptile. Maudslay has shown how derivatives of this design, often modified almost beyond identification, are constantly applied to every form of ornament, such as the edges of girdle-flaps and so forth, and the point has been elaborated by Spinden. Most interesting is the almost invariable occurrence of the serpent-motive on the wings of birds (e.g. Figs. 48 and 49; pp. 225 and 230), the combination no doubt expressing the high god Kukulkan, who, among the early Maya, seems to have been represented only in this indirect way (see p. 226). In the later art, especially that exhibiting Toltec affinities, we have a more direct delineation of the deity in the shape of a human figure whose face is surrounded by the jaws of a serpent, but who is provided with wings carved in the best Maya style (Fig. 87). The foreshortening of feathers has already been mentioned, but it may be added that perhaps no people has shown in its art such an appreciation of this form of ornament as the Maya, and for sheer beauty the feather-motive shares the honours with the plant-design (see Fig. 60; p. 289), often shown in combination with fishes and grotesque masks, which appears not only on the sculptures, but also in the frescoes.

CHAPTER XIV—CONCLUSIONS

IT is obvious that the two forms of culture described in the foregoing chapters, Mexican and Maya, were at least very closely related the one to the other ; but it is equally obvious that the connection was closer between the Maya and the pre-Aztec inhabitants of the Mexican valley than between the former and the Aztec. Religion in both areas ran on similar lines, and the pantheons included certain more or less otiose high gods, and a rain and thunder agricultural-deity whose worship was of primary importance. The importance of blood-offerings, combined with the late introduction of human sacrifice, the existence of a ritual and solar calendar, both similar in nature, and the habit of constructing buildings of ceremonial importance on lofty pyramidal mounds or terraces are features common to both. Besides this, as far as the later Maya are concerned, we find traditions of a historical nature which make mention of places, such as Tulan and the Seven Caves, which occur in Mexican legends, and at Chichen Itza, where at least one section of the population traced their origin to " Tulan," we have ruins corresponding exactly in style to those found at the pre-Aztec site Tulan in the Mexican valley. Other similarities relating to material culture are equally numerous, as well as similarities in art and symbolism. Many of these have already received attention, but, as a further illustration of the latter, mention may be made of a small detail which is of comparatively frequent appearance on sculptures throughout the Mexican and Mayan area. This consists of a trapezoidal

355

figure interlaced with a triangle or another trape-
zium, and occurs usually as a head-ornament. A series
of its manifestations is illustrated in Fig. 86. Here
the earlier monuments where it appears are represented by Copan (*a*), Menché (*c*), Piedras Negras (*b*)
(for Naranjo see Pl. XXIII; p. 302); in Yucatan
it occurs at Uxmal (*g*); on the fringe of the Mexican valley, at Tehuacan (*d*) and Xochicalco (*e*); in
the valley itself, at Tenango (*k*), Xico (*m*), and, to
the north, at Tulan (*h*); and in the Huaxtec country,
at Teayo (*f*). The sign moreover bears a close analogy to that by which the Aztec expressed the period
of a year (*l*), and the triangular portion of it is
exactly similar to a conventional sun-ray. It is perhaps worth noting that at Copan, Uxmal and Teayo
it is associated with the head of the rain-god. The
significance of this symbol is obscure, but its presence over so large an area can hardly be due to
coincidence.

I think it is obvious from what has gone before, that
the Aztec may be left out of account in any consideration of the source of such similarities as may be traced
in Mexican and Mayan culture. They were admittedly
late immigrants, from the north, into the Mexican
valley, and were, at the time of their arrival, in a very
low state of culture; moreover, as stated above, it is
the pre-Aztec remains which show the closest relation
to the Mayan. The question therefore resolves itself
into an enquiry which was the earlier, the culture exemplified in the ruins of the central Maya area, or that
which gave birth to the pre-Aztec remains at such early
valley sites as Tulan, Teotihuacan and Azcapotzalco?
Any solution of this question must also fix the relation
of Oaxaca to both, and account for the Huaxtec, a
Maya-speaking people whose sculptures bear no trace
of a hieroglyphic script. Included in this question is
that of the origin of the calendar. Let me say at once

FIG. 86.—Details from various monuments showing the interlaced
head-ornament.

a. Copan, stela 6.	g. Uxmal.
b. Piedras Negras.	h. Tulan.
c. Menché.	k. Tenango.
d. Tehuacan.	l. The Mexican year-sign.
e. Xochicalco.	(*Zouche MS.*)
f. Teayo.	m. Island of Xico.

that the evidence at our disposal is not sufficient to permit these questions to be answered with certainty. Much patient excavation, both in the Mexican valley and in the central Mayan region, is necessary before the origin of the pre-Spanish civilization can be traced with any degree of finality ; but I think it is possible to put forward a working theory, which must of necessity be modified in accordance with future researches, but which may at least be of service to critics as an invitation to concentrate their minds upon the subject. It is solely with this idea that I have ventured to draw up a scheme of dating (see Appendix III), and I will deal with this first, pointing out its weaknesses with as much impartiality as possible.

First of all I should like to say that the dates are not intended to be more than approximate ; even the records of Mexican history are not in absolute accordance, and contradictions become more frequent and serious in proportion with the remoteness of particular events from the date of the conquest. However, the history of the valley can be compiled with some degree of probability when the different accounts are studied from the point of view detailed on p. 19, though the dates of Toltec history, before the fall of the city, are in the highest degree problematical. The books of Chilan Balam give a chronology for the history of the Tutul Xiu which can be related to European time, though they do not agree exactly among themselves, and interpolations of a whole cycle appear to occur in places. The dating which I have adopted, which is in the main that of the book of Chilan Balam of Mani, is a conservative interpretation of these records, and may, I believe, be credited with reasonable probability. The dating of the monuments, the most important question of all, is unfortunately the most problematical, and the chain of evidence by which I seek to assign them a place in chronology has two weak links, one considerably weaker than the other. The first

PLATE XXX

Photo, Guerra

MAYA

The "House of the Governor," Uxmal, Yucatan

of these is the assumption that the initial dates on
stelæ refer to the erection of the monuments in question. In considering this question I would omit
Palenque, which is obviously, from the architectural
and artistic point of view, one of the latest ruins in the
central Mayan area. Further, the dates do not occur on
stelæ, but for the most part on mural tablets in temples, and may well be " mythical," and based upon calculations into past time made at a period when the art
of chronology, if such a phrase be permitted, had attained a great development in the hands of a specialist
priesthood. At other sites the fact that the dates form
more or less connected series, and correspond on the
whole to the development of architecture, lends a certain probability to the theory that they are " historical " and the theory receives some support, in a negative way, from the extreme difficulty of assigning them
any other reasonable function. The other link, which I
frankly admit is far weaker, consists in an attempt to
correlate them with the dating of the books of Chilan
Balam, and this I will now explain. I have tried to show
that the buildings at Chichen Itza may be divided into
three main classes, corresponding in a rather remarkable
manner to the principal epochs of Tutul Xiu tradition ;
and I have pointed out that what may be considered
the earliest group is distinguished by a date in the
" long count " characteristic of the central Mayan region. I have also explained that there is reason to
believe that Chichen was inhabited before the arrival
of the Tutul Xiu, and the presence of the early Maya
in Yucatan is supported by the " long count " date at
Tulum. It seems probable that the Tutul Xiu themselves did not use the long count, but reckoned time,
as in the books of Chilan Balam, by the " short count,"
i.e. by the initial day of the katun alone. It is an interesting fact that in more than one of the versions we find
a statement that, after their arrival at Chichen Itza,

" Pop was first counted in order," with the variant " Pop was set in order," and this is, I think, capable of explanation in one of two ways. In the first place, it may refer to some change in the calendar, necessitated by the fact that the absence of intercalary days had brought the commencement of the year noticeably out of tune with the seasons. In the second, it may indicate the actual adoption of the early Maya month-system, which they found prevailing at Chichen. We may assume, from what evidence exists, that the month-names were never expressed in dating in the Mexican valley, and we know that the Tutul Xiu placed their original home within the realm of " Tulan." It may be remarked in passing that, whichever explanation be adopted, this was probably the occasion when the change in the " year-bearers," from the early system to the later, was made, and it may further be noted that such a change would not necessarily affect the katun count. In any case the essential point on which I would lay stress is that the initial date at Chichen belongs to the period before the arrival of the Tutul Xiu. Now the katun expressed in this initial date would be termed in the short count " katun 3. ahau," and I think it reasonable to assume that this corresponds with the last " katun 3. ahau " of the Tutul Xiu chronology *before* they arrived at Chichen Itza. It may of course be earlier, but I think this extremely unlikely, having regard to the similarity between such buildings as the Monjas group and those of the central Mayan area. If this assumption be admitted, then the dates of the monuments can be brought into line with historical chronology as appears in the Appendix.

From this it follows that the inhabitants of the Mexican valley received the calendar from the Maya, but, before accepting such a proposition, it will be as well to examine the calendar itself for contributory evidence. We have seen that the Zapotec calendar forms a most

important link between the day-signs of the Mexican and
Maya respectively, and the suggestion has been made by
Seler that the Maya obtained these day-signs from the
west *via* Oaxaca, calling attention to the comparatively
simple nature of the Zapotec signs, which agree in this
respect with those of Mexico. The Mexican valley as
the place of origin of the day-signs may be, I think, dis-
regarded, if only for the reason that certain of the
animals serving as such do not occur in that region, and
the choice therefore would lie between Oaxaca on the
one hand and the central Mayan region on the other.
Now the difference in form between the Mexican and
Zapotec signs can be explained in many cases by the
fact that the Zapotec term is equivocal. That being so,
it seems to me obvious that the Zapotec must have
borrowed from the Maya and not *vice versa*. My argument is as follows : The Zapotec signs are simple and
obvious ; those of the Maya are often highly conventionalized. It would be remarkable, therefore, that the
Maya should have translated the Zapotec name in the
wrong sense, while it would be perfectly natural for the
Zapotec to have made a mistake and to have simplified
the sign in accordance with their idea of the meaning
of the term. If we add to this the fact that the only
two initial dates discovered in the western Maya area are,
together with the Chichen date, the latest known, the
conclusion seems to me inevitable that early Maya culture, enumeration, and calendar spread together from
Guatemala, through Oaxaca to the Tlalhuica country
(Xochicalco) and the Mexican valley, becoming attenuated in the process. The question of the development
of the calendar itself is interesting. The whole system
seems to show traces of several modifications and to ex-
emplify the efforts of a primitive people to adapt their
chronology to solar time. The presence of five nemontemi
or uayeb days over and above the period of 360 bears the
stamp of an afterthought, while the 360-day period, of

eighteen months, each of which comprises a full round
of the day-signs, is complete in itself and suggests that
this was the original " year." The number of the day-
signs, viz. twenty, is obviously based upon the vigesimal
system of counting current among these peoples, but
the selection of the thirteen numerals which accompany
them has not yet been satisfactorily explained. As remarked before, it is obvious that an agricultural population would soon observe that the seasons gradually became out of harmony with the year, and they must have
cast about to find some check by which the discrepancy
could be corrected. This check they found in the
synodical revolutions of the planet Venus. We know
that the Aztec and Maya both calculated the reappear-
ance of this planet (as seen in the codex Borgia and
analogous MSS., and the Dresden codex), and the
glyph which has been identified as that of the morning
star appears upon the early monuments. It is worth
noting that the early Maya method of calculating time,
by means of a long count of days rather than by years,
rendered the discrepancy of comparatively small account. The lack of harmony between the year and true
solar time would, it is true, affect the seasonal feasts, but
these could be transferred from month to month as
occasion demanded. As said before, I believe the greater
proportion of the inscriptions embody calculations
which had as their object the due allocation of the
feasts to the proper seasons. I have already made the
suggestion that the previous " suns " marking world-
periods may typify periodical rearrangements of the
calendar to square with solar time, and it is to be noted
that both in the Aztec and in the Quiché account the
tribes await the rising of the sun while observing the
morning star. The first rising of the sun, awaited with
such impatience by Aztec, Quiché and Kakchiquel alike,
means, I believe, the adoption of the solar calendar, or
rather the fixing of a date to form a starting-point for

a time-count modelled on solar time; and in the legends of the two first peoples, the morning star is the herald of the "dawn," which in the Aztec myth is called the "dawn for the administration of society." The Kakchiquel account seems to hint that the "dawn" was not the same for all the tribes of this people. The translation runs as follows : "Three of our tribes had seen the dawn appear, the Zotzil, the Kakchiquel and the Tukuchi. As for the Akahal they were but a little distance from the place when the dawn appeared to the three nations. At the spot called Tohohil the Quiché saw their dawn, and those of Rabinal saw it at Zamaneb; and the Tzutuhil sought to see their dawn at Tzala, but their labours had not been completed by this tribe when the sun arose. They had not yet finished drawing their lines in Tzala when it arose in the sky, precisely above the place Geletat." The last sentence at least suggests that some process analogous to observation of the solstice is implied. I think that the passages relative to the appearance of the "dawn" in the various tribal legends are worth careful study, especially in view of the fact that no entirely satisfactory translations of the annals of Xahila and the Popol Vuh exist. As for the books of Chilan Balam, no mention of a "dawn" is made, but it may be argued that the statement "Pop was first counted in order" has the same essential meaning.[1]

[1] The use of the rising of the morning star to commence a solar time-count would explain the peculiar fact that the commencement of the year never coincided with that of the tonalamatl. It has been stated (p. 77) that the initial days of the Venus-periods were cipactli, coatl, atl, acatl, and olin; cipactli being the initial day also of the tonalamatl. But the day acatl was not only one of the initial days of the 365-day year, but was the initial day also of the Mexican double cycle of 104 years, which was in addition the initial day of a complete cycle of Venus-periods. The conclusion is tempting, that after the invention of the tonalamatl, correlated with the observation of the planet Venus, a change was made to solar time as near as it could be observed. As a starting-point for the new system, the next heliacal rising of the

The reason for the decline of the early Maya civilization is rather obscure. A glance at the scheme of dating will show how closely the last dates at each of the ruined sites correspond one with another. It does not of course follow that the cessation of initial dates implies the abandonment of the "cities," for they may have been centres of religious life for years later; indeed Cichen was visited as a sacred place until Spanish times, and the Lacandons of to-day still make offerings in the deserted temples. But the abrupt termination of the dating system at least implies some important change, and it may be that about the beginning of the tenth cycle the " long count " was abandoned in favour of the " katun count " as exemplified in the books of Chilan Balam. In any case none of the buildings show evident signs of forcible destruction, and no traces of a military invasion of Maya territory appear. The instability of Central American political organizations is very marked; there was a strong tendency for a state, composed originally of independent self-contained pueblos, to split up into smaller elements under the slightest pressure applied from within or without. The Maya, to judge from the monuments, had enjoyed centuries of peace, and only in the north-east and north do we find reliefs which give any hint of war. But these may be significant, and no doubt the decline of the old culture was due to pressure exercised by their northern neighbours, a pressure which had its origin in the steady southerly drift of tribes from regions considerably further north, and which led to the occu-

planet was awaited, and this occurring on an acatl day fixed the " year-bearers " as acatl, tecpatl, calli, and tochtli. It will be remembered that the Mexicans believed that the historical sun rose on the day 13. acatl (p. 73). At any rate, the Venus-period seems to form a link between the tonalamatl and the year of 365 days. The fact that none of the gods of the hunting-tribes find a place among the deities presiding over the tonalamatl would seem sufficient proof that the Chichimec, Aztec, and Otomi had no hand in its invention.

pation of the Mexican valley by the Nahua-speaking Toltec.

A word may now be said concerning the " Toltec " culture of the Mexican valley. The fact that this is related to the early culture of the Maya is, as said before, obvious. Many points of similarity exist in religious symbolism, art (such as the interlaced trapezoidal sign described above), glyphs surrounded by a cartouche, and the bar-form of the numeral five. If my dating of the monuments be accepted provisionally, and also the suggestion that the calendar had its origin with the Maya, then it follows necessarily that the Toltec culture was due at least to Maya inspiration. The myth of the arrival of the god Quetzalcoatl, inventor of the calendar, symbolizes the spread of Maya culture northwards. There are so many instances of the god being taken as the representative of his people, and I have already shown how the high mysterious creator-god Kukulkan seems to have lost dignity when he became personified as a tribal leader. The myth of the immigrant Nahua tribes awaiting the " dawn for the administration of society " at Teotihuacan then represents their first contact with the culture derived from the Maya. So far the matter is simple, but a difficulty now arises. The last Maya date in the long count, at Chacula on the Chiapas border, falls about the middle of the fourth century A.D. The Annals of Quauhtitlan give the foundation of the Toltec state as 752 A.D. The migration-myth last mentioned states that the Toltec were with the other Nahua immigrants at Teotihuacan when the " dawn " appeared. These Toltec are definitely stated to have been Nahua-speakers, while the name of the first Toltec ruler, Mixcoamazatzin, is distinctly Nahua. Finally, the list of Toltec rulers, seven only in number, is far too short to account for the thick stratum of Toltec remains at Azcapotzalco. The only explanation possible surely must be the following : The early Maya culture had slowly crept up into the Mexican valley, through western Chiapas, Oaxaca and Teotitlan, becoming somewhat attenuated in the process. There it persisted for some centuries without striking development, and perhaps gradually deteriorating. Then began the southerly drift of the Nahua tribes, of whom the first to arrive, the Toltec, imposed themselves as a ruling caste upon the agricultural population, adopting their mode of life and culture, and developing the latter in accordance with their own particular genius, but imposing their own language upon the tribes whom they welded into an empire. But the pressure from the north continued, wave after wave of " Chichimec " migration broke upon the valley. The Toltec power fell, and the incursion of the wilder tribes gave rise to migrations, such as those of the Olmec, Quiché and Kakchiquel, which followed for the most part an easterly route, at any rate in their initial stages. In the valley, the history of the Toltec was reflected in the short-lived attempts of the Chichimec and Tepanec to establish empires, but was practically repeated by the Aztec, who also developed, and to some extent travestied, the remnants of the earlier culture of their predecessors. The fall of Tulan had an important effect upon Yucatan. At this period the League of Mayapan was in full flower, but within a century we hear of the introduction of " Mexican " mercenaries, and of political troubles at Chichen Itza, and at this very site we find a group of buildings in unmistakable Toltec style, with decoration in which a personified Kukulkan appears. This Toltec influence spread further still, to British Honduras, where it is exemplified in the frescoes of Santa Rita, and in certain pottery vases (Pl. IX, 10; p. 82) with relief ornament in the shape of a descending Quetzalcoatl-Kukulkan figure, similar to the Chichen Itza relief shown in Fig. 87. In the Mixtec country, too, traces of immigration occur in legends, almost certainly due to the same causes, and the Toltec influence is found in the frescoes at Mitla, which resemble those at Santa Rita, though, be it noted, they are by no means necessarily contemporary with the buildings on which they occur. Thus the Maya culture completed its circle, a branch passing, as I have indicated, from Guatemala to the Mexican valley, and then through Vera Cruz and Tabasco to Yucatan, where it came into contact with a more legitimate offshoot of the early Maya stock. In the west the wave of Toltec influence appears to have reached as far south as Santa Lucia Cozumalhuapa, and the presence of tlaxtli-courts in the Chacula and Alta Vera Paz regions are probably to be attributed to the same agency; for it will be remembered that a body of Toltec, after the fall of their city, are reported to have migrated to Soconusco (p. 11).

The position of the Huaxtec now arises. In them we have a Maya-speaking people, practising certain definitely

FIG. 87.—Stone relief at Chichen Itza, showing Kukulkan-Quetzalcoatl. (*After Maudslay*)

Maya customs such as tooth-filing and -inlay, and inhumation as opposed to cremation, yet apparently without a script. As far as their art is concerned, the sculptures of the Panuco valley bear a closer re-

semblance to those of the Maya, especially to certain
stelæ at Piedras Negras, than the Aztec. The isolation
of this definitely Maya branch would seem to imply
that the Maya in the earliest days of all must have
spread from Guatemala up the east coast of Mexico as
far as Tampico, penetrating into Chiapas, and possibly
Oaxaca, and colonizing the Mexican valley, where they
found a primitive people akin to the earliest population
of Michoacan. In times subsequent to what I may call
this proto-Maya movement there took place in the
southern fertile region a great cultural development,
culminating in the organization of a calendar, the invention of a script, and the construction of the ruined
" cities." The culture developed here spread, as I have
indicated on p. 361, but slowly, since the land was by
no means overpopulated, and life was easy. For some
reason it took a westerly course, *via* Oaxaca, and never
reached the Huaxtec, who remained confined to the
coast by the eastern cordillera and held little communication with their western neighbours. In later times,
at any rate, they were cut off from the southern Maya
by the stream of migration which passed from the
valley of Mexico and its neighbourhood eastward, and
they may well have been isolated at an earlier period
by some similar movement in this direction. At any
rate an early tendency towards migration on these lines
is seen in the legends of the Tutal Xiu, who left
Nonoual in the second century, probably under pressure
exercised by tribes to the west.

The chief objection to this theory of the origin and
development of the Maya culture, as far as I can see, is
that in Guatemala and Honduras no certain traces of a
proto-Maya culture have as yet been discovered, but
that the civilization springs, as it were, full-blown from
the earth. The answer would be that the finest ruins
have focussed all attention up to the present, and that
earlier manifestations of the culture have not been

sought, while the difficulties afforded by environment and climate place serious obstacles in the way of systematic excavation. Further, the art itself affords many indications that it is based upon wood-carving, and the conditions are not favourable to the survival of any remains save those constructed in stone.

The position which must be assigned to the Zapotec raises a question of considerable interest. Their indebtedness to Maya culture is obvious from the consideration of a large proportion of their architectural remains and their art, but certain peculiar features make their appearance. In the first place, no migration legends are recorded, while the fact that certain localities were held to be the entrance to the underworld rather emphasizes the " indigenous " nature of the population. Again, though cremation makes its appearance among the later Maya, the Zapotec, for religious reasons, held out against it, practising, in the main, secondary burial. Finally, certain forms of ornament applied to architecture (as at Mitla) and to pottery (as at Cuicatlan) are unique in this part of America. Of interest is the fact that the geometric ornament at Mitla finds an exact parallel in the stucco decoration of some of the early ruins of the Peruvian coast, while the designs of the Cuicatlan pottery reproduce with equal exactness a favourite textile ornament belonging to the same region. Certain of the Peruvian coast-dwellers preserved traditions of immigration by sea, and these combined facts might be taken as a vague indication of early coasting-voyages down the west coast of America. It would be rash to put this forward as a definite theory, but at any rate further investigations in this direction might prove of great interest. The Zapotec at one period seem to have extended considerably further north than in later times, and to have been driven south by the Mixtec who at least contained an immigrant element. The peculiar slab discovered at Placeres del Oro seems to

2 B

bear some affinity with Zapotec reliefs, but here again the " Peruvian " character of the decoration is paramount. Affinities with Peruvian archæology extend into Michoacan, where the practice of providing the mummy-pack of the dead with a false head prevailed, and similarities with Peruvian beliefs may be seen in the Mexican custom of providing the deceased with a dog to convey his soul to the underworld, and in ill-treating dogs during eclipses of the moon. Resemblances also exist between the Peruvian and Maya cultures; certain stone reliefs showing a figure seated in a niche have been found at Manabi in Ecuador (where again traditions of immigration by sea survive), which look very like travesties of some of the Piedras Negras stelæ; while the famous monolith discovered at Chavin de Huantar in the Andes bears a very distinct " Maya " stamp, though it is related also to the art of the Nasca valley. But great caution is necessary in dealing with similarities of this nature, which may arise from no more than a common psychology, and may bear witness only to the " American " basis shared by both cultures.

With the possible relations which Mexican and Maya culture may bear to those of the outer world I do not propose to deal at all. The past has shown the futility of speculating upon insufficient evidence, and it is sad to note how large a proportion of the literature dealing with American archæology serves only as a monument to wasted energy and misplaced zeal. It is impossible to deny a certain superficial similarity, often surprising, between the Maya ruins and those of south-east Asia, but these disappear for the most part upon closer analysis. Mere similarity of ornament means nothing when the ornament in question is found to symbolize beliefs of an entirely different character; from the constructional point of view the buildings differ essentially; while the absolute gulf which separates the American language, calendrical system and vegetable

means of sustenance from those of Asia provides difficulties which must be explained before any theory suggesting contact in any form can legitimately be put forward. The question of the ultimate origin of the
American population lies beyond the scope of this book,
but it is an evident fact that the Americans physically
stand in comparatively close relation to the Asiatics.
That being so a somewhat similar psychology is natural,
and this would lead, subject to modifications produced
by environment, to the evolution of a culture and art
in which certain analogies might be expected to appear.
But what I have elsewhere written of Peruvian culture
applies with equal force to that of the Mexicans and
Maya. The *onus probandi* must necessarily be upon
those who wish to prove that contact with the external
world existed, and the evidence which we possess points
rather to the undisturbed evolution of Mexican and
Mayan civilization on American soil, and that civilization may therefore be regarded as in every sense
American.

APPENDIX I

NAMES OF THE DAYS IN THE MEXICAN AND MAYA CALENDARS

MAYA			MEXICAN
Yucatan	Tzental (Chiapas)	Quiché and Kakchiquel	Aztec
Imix	Imox	Imox	Cipactli
Ik	Igh	Ig	Eecatl
Akbal	Votan	Akbal	Calli
Kan	Ghanan	Kat	Quetzpalin
Chicchan	Abah	Can	Coatl
Cimi	Tox	Camey	Miquiztli
Manik	Mozic	Quieh	Mazatl
Lamat	Lambat	Ganel	Tochtli
Muluc	Mulu	Toh	Atl
Oc	Elab	Tzii	Itzcuintli
Chuen	Batz	Batz	Ozomatli
Eb	Enob	Balam	Malinalli
Ben	Been	Ah	Acatl
Ix	Hix	Itz	Oceloti
Men	Tziquin	Tziquin	Quauhtli
Cib	Chabin	Ahmak	Cozcaquauhtli
Caban	Chic	Noh	Olin
Eznab	Chinax	Tihax	Tecpatl
Cauac	Cahogh	Caok	Quiauitl
Ahau	Aghual	Hunahpu	Xochitl

APPENDIX II

NAMES OF THE MONTHS IN THE MEXICAN AND MAYA CALENDARS

MAYA		MEXICAN
Yucatan	Kakchiquel	Aztec
Pop (July 16)	Tacaxepual (Feb. 1)	Atlcaualco (Feb. 2)
Uo	Nabey Tumuzuz	Tlacaxipeualiztli
Zip	Rucan Tumuzuz	Tozoztontli
Zotz	Zibix	Uei Tozoztli
Tzec	Uchum	Toxcatl
Xul	Nabey Mam	Etzalqualiztli
Yaxkin	Rucab Mam	Tecuiluitontli
Mol	Likinka	Uei Tecuiluitl
Chen	Nabey Tok	Tlaxochimaco
Yax	Rucab Tok	Xocouetzi
Zac	Nabey Pach	Ochpaniztli
Ceh	Rucab Pach	Teotleco
Mac	Tziquin Kih	Tepeiluitl
Kankin	Cakan	Quecholli
Muan	Ibota	Panquetzaliztli
Pax	Katik	Atemoztli
Kayab	Itzcal Kih	Tititl
Cumhu	Pariche	Izcalli
Uayeb	*Tzapi Kih*	*Nemontemi*

INDEX

375

PRINTED BY WILLIAM BRENDON AND SON, LTD., PLYMOUTH